The American Assembly, *Columbia University*
and
Council on Foreign Relations, Inc.

CANADA
AND
THE UNITED STATES:
ENDURING FRIENDSHIP,
PERSISTENT STRESS

Prentice-Hall, Inc., *Englewood Cliffs, New Jersey*
A SPECTRUM BOOK

Library of Congress Cataloging in Publication Data
Main entry under title:

CANADA AND THE UNITED STATES.

Background papers prepared for a meeting of the
American Assembly at Arden House in Harriman, N.Y.,
Nov. 15–18, 1984.
Edited by Charles F. Doran and John H. Sigler.
At head of title: The American Assembly, Columbia
University; and Council on Foreign Relations, Inc.
"A Spectrum Book."
Includes index.
1. United States—Foreign relations—Canada—
Congresses. 2. Canada—Foreign relations—United States—
Congresses. I. Doran, Charles F. II. Sigler, John H.,
(date). III. American Assembly. IV. Council on
Foreign Relations.
E183.8.C2C335 1985   327.71073   85-598
ISBN 0-13-113812-X
ISBN 0-13-113804-9 (pbk.)

This book is available at a special discount when ordered in bulk quantities. Contact Prentice-Hall, Inc., General Publishing Division, Special Sales, Englewood Cliffs, N.J. 07632.

Editorial/production supervision by Betty Neville and Eric Newman
Cover design © 1985 by Jeannette Jacobs
Manufacturing buyer: Anne Armeny
A SPECTRUM BOOK

10 9 8 7 6 5 4 3 2 1

ISBN 0-13-113812-X

ISBN 0-13-113804-9 {PBK.}

PRENTICE-HALL INTERNATIONAL (UK) LIMITED (*London*)
PRENTICE-HALL OF AUSTRALIA PTY. LIMITED (*Sydney*)
PRENTICE-HALL CANADA INC. (*Toronto*)
PRENTICE-HALL HISPANOAMERICANA, S.A. (*Mexico*)
PRENTICE-HALL OF INDIA PRIVATE LIMITED (*New Delhi*)
PRENTICE-HALL OF JAPAN, INC. (*Tokyo*)
PRENTICE-HALL OF SOUTHEAST ASIA PTE. LTD. (*Singapore*)
WHITEHALL BOOKS LIMITED (*Wellington, New Zealand*)
EDITORA PRENTICE-HALL DO BRASIL LTDA. (*Rio de Janeiro*)

Table of Contents

Preface

In 1964, the Twenty-fifth American Assembly, entitled *The United States and Canada,* produced a book with the same name, edited by John Sloan Dickey. For twenty years, this volume served as a significant reference work during a time when relations between the two North American neighbors went through a number of changes in emphasis and intensity.

In 1984, shortly after elections in both countries returned governments with substantial majorities and the apparent assurance of continuity over a number of years, the Assembly, together with the Council on Foreign Relations, revisited the subject. The techniques applied in this second examination were essentially the same as in the first, and the focus of interest was only slightly altered from the earlier effort.

Insofar as possible, the undertaking was binational. One codirector was Canadian, the other from the United States. They in turn selected authors to write background papers. Four of these were from Canada and two from the United States. Fifty-eight participants came to an Assembly at Arden House in Harriman, New York, from November 15 through 18, 1984, to discuss an agenda developed from the subject matter of the background papers. These participants were divided about equally between Canada and the United States.

The report emanating from that meeting, which is included as an appendix to this book, reviewed the major areas of mutual concern to the two nations and their societies, made recommendations for policies to satisfy those concerns, and, in general, attempted to suggest ways in which neighborly relations could be enhanced. In order for such efforts to be successful, responsible citizens on both sides of the border must have the best possible understanding of the issues involved. This volume is published in order to stimulate more informed views in both Canada and the United States.

Funding for this project was provided by The Ford Foundation, The Andrew W. Mellon Foundation, The Rockefeller Foundation, and The Donner Canadian Foundation. We are very grateful for this crucial support. The opinions expressed in this volume are those of the individual authors and not necessarily those of the sponors nor of the Council on Foreign Relations and The American Assembly, which do not take stands on the issues they present for public discussion.

Winston Lord	William H. Sullivan
President	*President*
Council on Foreign Relations	The American Assembly

The scattered excerpts in Chapter 3 from H. English, editor, "Canada–United States Relations," *Proceedings of the Academy of Political Science*, vol. 2, no. 2, 1976, are used by permission of the Academy.

The excerpt on page 104 from H. G. Johnson, *The Canadian Quandry,* is used by permission of McGraw-Hill Ryerson Limited, Scarborough, Ont.

Charles F. Doran and John H. Sigler

Introduction

The last volume in this American Assembly series on Canada and the United States appeared just over twenty years ago, and, despite the changes in events and personalities, much of its wisdom and insight on the relationship has endured the test of time. The writers had wide learning, often had lived on both sides of the border, frequently had some government service experience or were otherwise familiar with administration and politics, and had learned to admire the complexity and subtlety of relations between these two great democracies.

CHARLES F. DORAN *is a professor of international relations and the director of the Center of Canadian Studies at the School of Advanced International Studies, The Johns Hopkins University, Washington. Previously he was a professor at Rice University and the founder and director of its international management program. A noted television analyst, Dr. Doran has appeared on the national networks in both Canada and the United States. In addition to lecturing internationally, he serves as consultant to government organizations, private firms, and universities. The author of many articles for distinguished journals and several books, his most recent is* Forgotten Partnership: U.S.–Canada Relations Today.

JOHN H. SIGLER *is a professor in the Department of Political Science and International Affairs, Carleton University, Ottawa. Dr. Sigler is the recipient of several professional honors and has held a number of prestigious advisory positions, including one with the Canadian Delegation to the United Nations' General Assembly. He has written for prominent international journals and lectured in Canada, the United States, and the Middle East. Dr. Sigler has also written several books and is the coauthor of* Canadian–U.S. Relations: Policy Environments, Issues, and Prospects.

While the Canadian authors, James Eayrs, John Holmes, and Douglas Le Pan, wrote from a Canadian university base, Holmes and Le Pan had long experience in the Canadian diplomatic corps and had dealt extensively with the United States in both bilateral and multilateral settings. This was also the case with the editor, John Sloan Dickey, then president of Dartmouth College, who had developed particularly close ties with Canadian diplomats and leaders during World War II and its immediate aftermath when he served in senior positions in the U.S. Department of State. During his tenancy at Dartmouth, Canada–United States relations permeated life in Hanover and influenced a generation of Dartmouth students. American author Jacob Viner, a distinguished Princeton economist who had served in various capacities in the U.S. government, was himself born and educated in Canada and knew both countries in the intimate manner that only transnationals can. Mason Wade, who wrote the historical section, had served as cultural attaché in the U.S. embassy in Ottawa and had taught at Canadian universities where his scholarship on Canada, particularly Quebec, brought him widespread recognition that included the vice presidency of the Canadian Historical Association. Everett Hughes, also a specialist on Quebec, began his academic career in Canada and played a major role in building the sociology department at McGill University from 1927 to 1938. For these writers, the analysis of Canada–United States relations was as much avocation as it was vocation, and the light-hearted wisdom about the relationship that they expounded was testimony to the arms-length objectivity that they were able to give to their analysis.

In the intervening twenty years, the bulk of writing on Canada–United States relations has increased substantially. Canadian studies in the United States and, to a lesser extent, American studies in Canada have expanded in universities and professional journals of research. More than 1,000 members, for example, subscribe to the *American Review of Canadian Studies,* the official publication of the Association of Canadian Studies in the United States. An abundance of subspecializations has emerged, and specialized experts now dominate the field. At the same time, a diffusion of interests and assumptions about Canada–United States relations has occurred among these specialists, and value differences have begun to emerge in the writings of many of the analysts on both sides of the border, leading to some spirited debate about the overall purpose of Canadian studies in the United States. While the debate by no means has been settled—perhaps in part because it *remains* unsettled—the output of articles and manuscripts on the subject has increased dramatically.

Although the far greater interest in things Canadian on the American side is certainly welcome (it has become "un-chic" for major periodicals like the *New York Times,* the *Wall Street Journal,* and *Time* magazine to ignore Canada), one may well wonder whether or not greater knowledge on the part of some of the authors always has led to greater wisdom. This is not to argue that American ignorance can ever mean bliss for Canada—only that generalists can sometimes be more perspicacious than specialists. But as it becomes more specialized, the analysis frequently becomes more earnest. The positive result is that Canada is treated more and more as an important subject for discussion and research in the United States.

A whole new generation of scholars, journalists, policy makers, and executives in Canada and the United States is moving into leadership positions affected by the more professional and specialized treatment of Canada–United States relations. As a result, the degree of intimacy based on long experience and broad historical perspective has declined. The generalists have handed the baton to the specialists at a time when, concurrently, nationalism is on the rise in the global international system and when personal experience of the tumult of the first half of the twentieth century is not recorded in the minds of contemporary specialists. The closeness that arose from the experience of World War II and the shared responsibilities for building the international institutions in the immediate postwar world have passed. Now the differences accompanying the process of decay of those institutions take priority among those whose life experiences do not include that earlier golden age of diplomacy when Canadians worked closely with Americans nearer the center of the international arena. Thus, the fragility of Canada–United States relations is highlighted at a time when analysts and advocacy have been entrusted to a very different group of actors and observers. Canadians and Americans frequently have gone their separate ways in the intervening years, and the search for common, unifying themes has become more difficult. The language of "special relationship" and "partnership," current at the time of the Dickey volume, has disappeared from the political vocabulary as internal domestic problems in both countries and the pressures of adapting to a rapidly changing and more threatening international environment beyond North America have diverted the leaders and public away from the Canada–United States agenda, itself more complex and contentious than before. It is not surprising that the new notion of "managing complex interdependence" was coined to express some of these changes without fully accounting for the division of sovereignties and the fundamental notion of an equilibrium of power and interest.

These shifts of attention and the more contentious and complex agenda are reflected in the chapters of this update of Canadian-American relations in the 1980s. Gordon Robertson's chapter is devoted to a review of the crisis in Canada in federal-provincial relations, particularly the question of Quebec, already anticipated in the 1964 volume. The political compromise that led to the patriation of the Canadian Constitution in 1982 failed, however, to address many of the longstanding grievances by Quebecers; yet the country emerged somehow stronger and more confident of its identity and unity than it had been in the mid–1960s. Americans, who had paid all too little attention to the internal problems of the "peaceable kingdom" on its northern border, were shocked by the election in 1976 of a political party seeking Quebec's independence. Having paid too little attention before, many Americans then overreacted, underestimating the Canadian potential for conflict management and commitment to peaceful change. The concentration on violence in the media has dulled sensitivity to the greater importance of the political processes of "peace, order, and good government" that have long characterized the Canadian scene and have earned for Canada in international opinion a respect and admiration, which are undoubtedly more subtle than those measured by military and economic power, but still not without influence. The Canadian model of democracy—in terms of population size, linguistic and regional diversity, role in the international system, and political style—may be a great deal more relevant for many countries in the Third World than that of the United States.

In the closing paragraphs of chapter 1, Gordon Robertson picks up on a theme enunciated by Douglas Le Pan in the earlier volume and subsequently developed by John Sloan Dickey in his Council on Foreign Relations volume, *Canada and the American Presence* (1975). For Dickey, the preservation of a strong, independent Canada on its northern frontier should be a fundamental tenet of U.S. foreign policy. By this he meant not only the political stability that has preoccupied American foreign policy makers in other troubled areas of the globe, but also an independence in foreign policy that is "in the self-interest of a great power to be exposed to knowledgeable scrutiny from the outside which is free of both the hostility of an adversary and the acquiescence of a sycophant." If this vital role is to be played effectively, the leaders and public on both sides of the border will need to monitor very carefully the concerns and interests of the other.

Through a review of the postwar record Jack Granatstein, in chapter 2, demonstrates how this independent Canadian foreign policy frequently has led to strong reactions in Washington. While the relationship has retained its overall cooperative nature, it has been tempered by successive moods of caution, anxiety, mistrust, and suspicion. Much of this criticism on the Canadian side has stemmed not from bilateral problems as such, but from doubts over the direction and style of American leadership in international defense and security questions—precisely in the area where the Canadian contribution is the most modest and also in an area where Washington has had to contend with substantial criticism from Congress, the public, and its allies. Because of these sensitivities, Canadian reservations have been particularly unwelcome in Washington.

In chapter 3, in his discussion of economic issues, Richard Lipsey emphasizes that U.S. macroeconomic policy is largely determined by domestic considerations, while Canadian macroeconomic policy is heavily conditioned by U.S. policy. U.S. trade policy is conditioned by the broad international environment, while Canadian trade policy is again heavily directed toward the United States. While trade policy dominates Canadian foreign policy, U.S. trade policy is often used as an instrument to support broad political goals. Because trade policy in the United States is also subject to pressures of special interests on the U.S. Congress, Canada, like Japan and other principal U.S. trading partners, has been forced to involve itself more and more in U.S. congressional lobbying. Lipsey also takes a strong stand in favor of an internationalist position in the ongoing debate between economic nation-alists and internationalists on the proper direction of Canadian foreign economic policy. At the heart of this debate is the question of the relations between the goals of political autonomy and economic well-being. For many, these are seen as competing goals with difficult trade-offs among them. Lipsey argues that they are not necessarily closely linked, and the experience of the European Common Market provides evidence of the failure of closer political integration to follow economic integration even when it was intended by the founders of the European community. For many Canadians, the fear is that closer economic ties inevitably will bring closer political integration even where it is not intended or wanted.

The authors in both the earlier and present volumes concentrate on explaining Canadian attitudes, politics, and economics to Americans on the assumption that there is basic asymmetry in information that accompanies the differences in power and size. The result is the lack, as John Dickey complained in his introduction to the earlier volume, of any comparative, cross-cultural perspective on American and Canadian differences and similarities. He pointed to the pioneering work of Seymour Martin Lipset in beginning scholarly treatment of this longstanding issue in Canadian-American understanding. Lipset's work in the 1960s led to a rich intellectual controversy in Canada as sociology textbooks probed the Lipset thesis on the deep differences in political culture between the two countries. In recent years, social science research on political culture has waned as greater emphasis has been placed on the view that culture is subordinate to social structures, particularly in the stratification of societies and the structuring of the economy. Indeed, the widely held Canadian fear that greater economic integration will lead to greater political integration and more Americanization of Canadian values is based on this same thesis. Lipset, however, returns to the debate in chapter 4 with much new evidence, suggesting that Canadian and American cultural values and institutions have converged in some areas, such as education and law, but widened in others, such as trade-union membership and religious attitudes. Much of the Canadian criticism of Lipset's early work was based on challenging his proposition that the United States was the more democratic society, less deferential to authority than at least the English Canadians who retained much of their British political culture.

In his study, Lipset qualifies his earlier work and argues that the more elitist Canadian political culture has produced a more egalitarian society than the United States when measured by attitudes toward distribution and redistribution of rewards. There appears to be a wider measure of consensus in Canada on protecting the benefits of the welfare state than in the United States, although the political arguments on this point are likely to intensify in the coming years, particularly as long as deficits play such major havoc with overall economic policy in each country. The extensive research and interpretations reported in this chapter are likely to set off a new debate on the nature of the differences and similarities in the two countries.

In chapter 5, Albert Legault concentrates on how changing military technologies have altered the strategic significance of Canadian territory in continental defense where, since 1940, the United States has made clear its vital national interest in defending Canada as well as the United States. Geopolitical realities dominate this discussion and highlight the problems of Canada, with a population only 10 percent that of the United States, trying to defend a territory even larger than that of the United States. Relations between the Canadian and U.S. military establishments have been very close within the North American Treaty Organization (NATO) alliance and North American Aerospace Defense (NORAD), even if the Canadian public and Canadian political leaders often have given less weight to the priority of these defense and security questions and even if Canadian foreign policy preferences reflect a widespread domestic consensus on the importance of diplomacy over defense.

Another important development not adequately anticipated in the earlier volume is the increased importance of environmental issues on the bilateral agenda. In chapter 6, Lynton Caldwell argues that the growth of an ecological perspective in both countries may provide for a shared political culture that will redefine the meaning of sovereignty, now interpreted in what he calls the prevailing "political-economic" perspective.

In the prevailing political-economic perspective, environmental issues are decided by governments in response to cost-benefit calculations and pressures from their own populations. Caldwell warns that conventional politics and diplomacy, based on trade-offs and bargaining, may not be able to handle problems such as acid rain where environmental damage extends over wide areas and where environmental change may be unacceptable to large numbers of people on both sides of the border. For an ecological perspective to be effective politically, there would have to be a wide change in values on the part of substantial elements in the population of both countries. Where differences in values are added to the usual conflicts of interest, strong cleavages are likely to emerge. Caldwell's image of a new form of continentalism based on binational responsibility for protection of the environment is a long-term one. The short-term outlook is for sharply increased controversy in managing domestic politics, particularly in the United States. This will in turn continue to complicate the U.S.–Canadian diplomatic agenda in trying to resolve environmental problems. Caldwell argues for more institutional innovation beyond the International Joint Commission in anticipating and avoiding future conflict on these difficult environmental issues.

In the final chapter, the editors attempt to set out the factors of continuity and change that will influence the binational agenda in the years ahead. Foremost among these is the challenge that a rapidly changing international environment, both threatening and promising, presents to Canada and the United States. Many bilateral problems, such as redrawing maritime boundaries, now arise because of decisions made in multilateral settings. How Canada and the United States manage the impacts of change from outside North America largely will determine the success of the bilateral relationship in the remaining years of the twentieth century.

Gordon Robertson

1

The United States
and
Problems of Canadian Federalism

When a Canadian observes the degree of concern that the United States directs toward events in the Caribbean and Central America and to the security of its southern approaches, it is difficult to decide whether to be flattered or offended by the lack of interest it displays in its neighbor to the north.

The casual acceptance of Canada is undoubtedly more compliment than insult. If the country is taken for granted, it is probably because it has been peaceful and friendly since 1812. During and since World War II it has been an active and reliable, if junior, partner in North American defense. The assessment by Americans that Canada can be relied upon and be expected to handle its own problems is not inaccurate. However, a lack of understanding by the United States of some of the underlying

THE HONORABLE ROBERT GORDON ROBERTSON *was, until retirement in 1984, the president of the Institute for Research on Public Policy in Ottawa, Ontario. Dr. Robertson has received seven honorary degrees from Canadian universities and one from Oxford. He has had an extremely distinguished career in the Canadian government, including deputy minister of northern affairs and national resources, commissioner of the Northwest Territories, and secretary to the Canadian cabinet, the senior position in the Canadian public service. He was also sworn as a member of the Queen's Privy Council for Canada. Dr. Robertson is chancellor of Carleton University.*

problems that do exist in Canada, as well as the reasons for measures taken by Canadian governments to cope with them, has led in the past to misinterpretation and resentment; it could well lead to more in the future. Problems in Canada are usually undramatic and mercifully nonviolent in their expression, but they are nonetheless real. Unless they are comprehended by Americans, Canadian actions that are domestic in purpose may appear aggressive and anti-American. A better U.S. understanding of the Canadian federation and of Canada's underlying forces could contribute to better Canadian-American relations.

The Recent Years

On rare occasions in the last ten years Americans were jolted into an awareness that something unusual, perhaps even disturbing, was happening in Canada. On November 15, 1976, the Parti Québécois came to power in Quebec with a program calling for the separation of Quebec from Canada. A few months later Premier René Lévesque visited New York and, in a dinner address, drew a parallel between the position of his province at that time and the situation in the thirteen colonies immediately before the American Revolution. The ringing exhortation by President Charles de Gaulle some ten years earlier, on a state visit for Canada's centennial in 1967, had perhaps persuaded Premier Lévesque that foreign aid would be available to them as it was to the young United States after 1776. ("Vive le Québec libre," the slogan of a separatist group, thrown by de Gaulle into the excitement of a Montreal crowd, had overtones of revolution.) Lévesque's New York audience in 1977 was probably more disposed to draw a parallel with the position of South Carolina immediately before the Civil War; it was secession from the Canadian union that was threatened, not liberation from an oppressive imperial regime.

Either parallel was disturbing. For probably the first time since the 1867 establishment of Canada in its present form, the United States had to consider what the consequences would be if the peaceful country of mounted police and maple leaves were to break up. The American government, in the most discreet way, made it apparent that the United States did not regard this as a pleasant prospect. Relief was obvious when Prime Minister Pierre

Trudeau, another French Canadian, assured a joint session of Congress of his confidence in both Canada's continued unity and his government's capacity to cope with the new threat.

While there was no doubting Pierre Trudeau's resolution, it was equally certain that the Parti Québécois, firmly in power, had the support of a considerable part of the province's French-speaking population for its plan for Quebec's independence. A referendum was promised on the issue, and it came to be thought of as the ultimate battle between the "separatists" and the "federalists." The prospects appeared more ominous because discussions within Canada on constitutional change, which had started in 1968 in response to demands by the previous Liberal government of Quebec, had produced no progress whatever. Even Quebec federalists were discontented. The "status quo" was unacceptable, but reform appeared impossible. René Lévesque's proposal for Quebec's political independence, combined with an economic association with what would be left of Canada, appeared to many in Quebec as the only solution.

In any event, the referendum of May 20, 1980, went against the Parti Québécois. Many of the 59 percent who voted *non* did so after assurance by Prime Minister Trudeau and English-speaking leaders that a vote against separation would not be a vote for the status quo. There would be "renewal" of Canadian federalism.

Indeed, there was an effort immediately after the referendum to achieve agreement on a dozen areas of importance. The constitutional discussions, which had been fruitless in the years before the referendum, were resumed in June 1980 with new determination. They culminated in the following September in a televised wrangle between the prime minister and the provincial premiers, and no agreement was reached on anything. Announcement by the prime minister in October that the federal government would "go it alone" on constitutional change, with or without provincial agreement, produced a year of crisis.

A disadvantage of the Canadian taste for "evolution, not revolution" was that the Constitution of 1867 contained no amending procedure. (The assumption of that day had been that the British Parliament would, as in the century before, make any changes that seemed necessary.) Like the least of colonies, the independent Canada of 1980 was in the ludicrous position of having to go to London for amendment of its own Constitution. When the federal

plan for change was unveiled, it found support from only two provincial governments, New Brunswick and Ontario, although together they represented more than 40 percent of the Canadian
population (Ontario alone contains over 33 percent). The federal
government was, therefore, seeking an amendment against the opposition of eight of the ten provincial governments, and in many
of the eight provinces, including Quebec, feelings were very
strong. Indicative of this depth of feeling, only a few months after
the Quebec referendum the majority of the provincial governments were in alliance with the separatist government against the
proposals of the government of Canada.

The fact that the defeat of the separatist side in the referendum
of May 1980 had not ended the crisis in Quebec was made apparent in April 1981—just eleven months later. Premier Lévesque's Parti Québécois, playing heavily on the federal government's declared intention to go ahead with constitutional change
without Quebec's agreement, scored a stunning victory in the provincial election. There was nothing to indicate that their long-
term objective of separation had changed.

By agreement among "the gang of eight" opposing provinces,
three launched court actions in Canada challenging the constitutionality of the federal proposal for action by the British Parliament. Furious lobbying also was mounted in London to convince
British legislators that they had a responsibility *not* to do what
the Parliament of Canada would ask them to do when it passed
the government's resolution. The Conservative opposition in the
Canadian House of Commons used every device to oppose and delay the government's proposal. In the end, in September 1981, the
Supreme Court of Canada delivered a judgment worthy of Solo-
mon. The unilateral action the federal government proposed
would be legal in the strict sense of the law, but it would be unconstitutional in the sense that it would be contrary to fundamental conventions of the Constitution. The court also stated that it
did not have the power to enforce constitutional conventions: that
was something for the political process, not for a court of law.

The judgment could not have been better designed to impose
reason and good sense. The federal government and the ten provinces came back to the conference table in November 1981. In the
late night of November 4 an agreement did emerge, a compromise
in the nature of so many solutions to problems and issues in Can-

ada. But in this case there was a difference—the compromise did not include Quebec. Indeed the representatives of the government of Quebec were not invited to the informal sessions at which a "deal" was worked out. The province whose discontent started the whole constitutional discussion in 1968 and which had been promised "renewal" in 1980 was isolated and alone. These facts and the arithmetic of "ten to one" would be bad enough. What made the triumph of "agreement at last" on a measure of constitutional change the more ominous was that the excluded government was the only one in Canada elected by a French-speaking majority. French Canadians make up about 26 percent of Canada's population, and 85 percent of them live in the province of Quebec. French Quebec, federalist as well as separatist, felt its isolation from the rest of Canada more sharply, perhaps, than at any previous time.

Despite these unpleasant truths, a much relieved British government was off the hook. The resolution of the Parliament of Canada, supported by nine provinces, was passed into law in London, the last law the British Parliament will ever pass for Canada. The Canadian Constitution "came home" on April 17, 1982, nearly 115 years after it had been passed. But the changes embodied in this "new" Constitution effected none of the reforms that Quebec governments had been demanding. Also, it was a Constitution that was "imposed" on Quebec against the will of its government. Quebec's legislature passed a resolution of condemnation.

Nor did the support of the nine provinces other than Quebec for the "new" Constitution of April 1982 mean that other basic problems of the Canadian federation had been resolved. The "alienation" of the western part of Canada from the central government had been demonstrated in the federal election of 1980. No supporter of the Liberal party of Prime Minister Trudeau was elected in the 2,000 miles west of Winnipeg—and only two in the entire four western provinces. The sense of domination of the West by the central provinces and of unfair treatment by "Ottawa" remained unabated.

The four Atlantic provinces of Canada are the perennial "poor relations." The poorest, Newfoundland, far exceeds the rockbound coasts of Maine in the austerity of its landscape and the poverty of its resources. It is off shore that hope is seen in development of oil and gas in the continental shelf and of the rich fisheries above it. But these areas are under federal jurisdiction—a jurisdiction confirmed by the Supreme Court of Canada in 1984 in the case of offshore resources. The province is intensely dissatisfied with its lack of control of what appear to be the only resources that provide any prospect of economic development or even modest prosperity. The constitutional amendments of 1982 did nothing to meet these difficulties.

It would be unfair to be too critical of the results of the federal-provincial meeting of November 1981. Thirteen years of constitutional discussions and many decades of frustration in attempts to work out an amending formula had shown all too clearly the "limits of the possible" in this exercise of high politics. But it would be unrealistic and naive to accept the rhetoric that surrounded the celebration of the "new Constitution" of April 1982. It was not new; the "patriated" document was a limited amendment of an old one. It did not herald a new era in Canadian federalism and left unresolved many of its most serious problems.

The Underlying Problems of Canadian Federalism

The existence of any federation is testimony to differences and divisions too important to permit the establishment of a single government such as is normal in most European countries, Japan, and the majority of states of the world. The thirteen colonies had difficulty enough agreeing in 1787 on a central government at all, even though the powers left to the states were intended to be large. The choice of the federal system in other countries equally reflects the compromises needed to bridge underlying differences. What is unusual in Canada in this respect is the depth and sharpness of the regional divisions it contains; more than a century of history as a country has not done as much to reduce them as national existence has done for other federations.

The United States is a much more unified country than when the American Constitution came into force in 1789. A civil war was a major factor, but the increasing bonds and sense of common identity after more than 200 years of existence have removed any idea of fundamental competition in loyalties between state and nation, as was possible in 1860. In Australia, too, the national dimension has asserted itself above those of the states much more strongly than in Canada and after a much shorter life as a country. A difference in Canada undoubtedly has been the fact that one province, Quebec, contains so large a part of the people of one of Canada's two basic linguistic groups. For them the powers of the provincial government are fundamental to the preservation and development of their French society and culture. The sense of loyalty to the province is the stronger when they contemplate not only the 19 million English-speaking Canadians around them, but the vast sea of English-speaking North Americans whose culture could submerge theirs so easily. Quebec is a permanent, built-in force for provincial rights in Canada. Its existence and the sensitivity of the Quebec people about their language and culture undoubtedly impose limits on the degree to which unifying forces in Canada can be expressed in federal power.

It is the combination of geographical distance and the sense of exploitation by a more populous "East" that fuels the sense of western identity and remoteness in Canada. Despite the increase in the economic weight of Alberta and, to a lesser degree, of Saskatchewan during the energy boom of the 1970s, there is not yet a California or Texas that would provide the sense of a clear shift in power from the East. There is no prospect of any significant population tilt in the years ahead. Divisions and resentments are not those of the postbellum South, but they are deep and enduring.

There are other problems than language and geographic separation. The institutions adopted in the Canadian Constitution of 1867 were not well designed to cope with the divisions of a continent-wide federation. For colonies in which the parliamentary system was well established, it was natural to adopt it for the new federal government. It is a system that provides democratic sensitivity in combination with internal coherence of policy and action. But it is also a system that concentrates power in a prime minister and cabinet without the "checks and balances" of the congressional system. Its nature requires a degree of party discipline that leaves little scope for the regional flexibility and the public debate of regional interests that characterize American parties. The House of Commons cannot be a chamber for reflection of regional views because it has an overriding role: it is the chamber in which a government can be defeated and thrown out of office at any time—and in which, therefore, a government must be defended if it is to continue in power. The battle of the "ins" and the "outs" is the plot and the purpose of action in the House of Commons. Regional views that cross these basic lines of force get little hearing.

Such problems arising from the parliamentary system would not be so serious if Canada had an effective "second chamber." In the United States this was the essential offset for the small states in the "Great Compromise" of 1787. The two members from every state were to be chosen by the state legislatures, until this was changed in 1913 to direct election. They were to be the voices of their states against the population dominance of the great centers and against the federal government itself. The founders of the Canadian federation, meeting at a time when the too-powerful American states were engaged in a war of secession, were not prepared to take the risk of so strong a second chamber. Canadian senators were to be appointed by the national government of the day and appointed for life—no check or balance there, no authoritative independent voice for any region. It is a defect that most Canadians only dimly recognize because they have never experienced a second chamber designed to give effective voice to the underlying reasons why their government is federal. The lack is, however, an undoubted factor in the sense of powerlessness felt by the small provinces, both western and eastern. It is a factor in the resentment and division that are its product.

A more serious consequence on the operation of Canada as a country is that the provincial premiers have moved into the vacuum created by the lack of a second chamber for regional representation. They have increasingly become the voices of local interest, not merely on matters under provincial jurisdiction, but on federal policies as well. Federal-provincial conferences in Canada have tended to become televised battles in which it is all too easy for a provincial premier to find political profit in "bashing" the federal government. It is not surprising that Canadian viewers gain the impression that every province is strongly opposed to a "Canadian" government that appears, from the testimony of the premiers, to be doing nothing but ill to the country at large. The public wrangles are to a degree misleading. There is a good deal of cooperation between the two orders of government, usually achieved through quiet discussion that attracts little attention. However, it remains the case that cooperation is much more difficult in Canada than it would be if there were a forum other than federal-provincial meetings where the deep divisions of the country could be expressed.

An additional factor adding to the extent and sharpness of federal-provincial division is that the powers of the respective governments have not worked out as was intended in 1867. Canada was to have been a highly centralized federation. To achieve this—and to avoid the dangers of "states rights" in the United States—the federal government was given many unusual powers in addition to that of appointing senators. It was to appoint the lieutenant governors of the provinces, who were to act in the provincial capitals as built-in agents of the federal government. They were given the power to reserve any enactment of a provincial legislature for federal review—and the federal government had the unfettered power to "disallow" a provincial act for any reason it saw fit. The federal government also was to have the power to take over any provincial "work" if Parliament judged it "to be for the general advantage of Canada." All unallocated powers of government were to go to Parliament, not to the provinces.

The Constitution has not worked out that way. Judicial interpretation in the first decades of the federation substantially limited federal powers. But another factor undoubtedly has been that the degree of centralization planned in 1867 was out of balance with the deep divisions within the country. The unusual federal powers, except appointment of senators, have atrophied because when resorted to after the early years of the federation, they were found to be repugnant to the views of voters in different areas. Activities of government also have tended to grow more in provincial areas than in federal ones. So long as the federal government had ample funds it could and did influence provincial actions by the conditions it attached to grants of federal money. However, the loss of the intended federal dominance and the growth of the role of government outside the neat compartments designed in 1867 have produced a contested and quarrelsome relationship. There are few things on which governments in Canada can act alone, and there appear to be even fewer on which they can act in concert without a good deal of dispute about policy and action. This is not to say that agreed policies and effective programs do not emerge. Normally they do. But the process and the agony can be protracted and noisy.

The "Quiet Revolution" in Quebec

The underlying divisions of Canada, the problems inherent in some of its governmental institutions, and the increase in the role of government would undoubtedly have led to some growth of difficulty and dispute. However, what brought problems to a head in the mid–1970s and what gave the arguments the character of crisis was the "quiet revolution" in Quebec that started in the 1960s.

From the time of the conquest of the French possessions in North America by the British in 1759, the prime concern of the French colonists and of their descendants was to preserve their French culture and society, as adapted to the new world, and the Roman Catholic religion that largely distinguished them from the English-speaking population. After the federation of Canada came into being in 1867, Quebec continued to reflect these basic concerns, with the church being the primary influence in preserving a society and system of education tending to shun the world of commerce and industry. It was not until after World War II that pressures became strong for a complete revision of Quebec society and attitudes to turn them from a defensive focus on the past to a greater acceptance of outside influences and future needs. The death of Premier Duplessis in 1959 and the subsequent defeat of his Union Nationale party, in power with only one break since 1936, brought in a new era of total change.

To achieve the needed revolution in virtually every aspect of life, the provincial government was both the symbol of the new Quebec and its critical instrument. For the first time government in Quebec would take over education, hospitals, and social services from the church. It was to train a new generation for the world of industry. It determined to create the means by which the commercial and industrial life of Quebec could be transacted in French and controlled by the French-speaking majority. Previously, the English-speaking minority had dominated both and almost exclusively controlled business and finance, partly through their own initiative and partly through French abstention from those worlds. The structures, activities, and life of the Quebec of the future were to be modern in every respect—and were to be in French. It was apparent that the powers of the provincial government had to be adequate to the task. In the early 1960s this need and determination led to confrontation with the federal government. By 1968 it was accepted by the federal government that the entire Constitution would have to be reviewed to see if changes could meet the demands of the Quebec government while still being consistent with the needs of the federal system as a whole.

The whirlwind in Quebec was not easy for politicians to ride.

A variety of parties and organizations arose determined to remove Quebec from the federation. By 1966 the political party that had given birth to the "revolution," the Liberal party of Premier Jean Lesage, had been defeated by Mr. Duplessis's old party now demanding "Equality or Independence." In 1968 the new Parti Québécois arose spurning "equality" and dedicated to sovereignty for Quebec. Against this background of activity within the legitimate democratic parties, fringe groups in Quebec took to violence. During the 1960s, street demonstrations and bombs in letter boxes shook Canadian perceptions about their peaceful society. In 1970 a mysterious organization calling itself *Le front pour la libération du Québec* (FLQ)—the "Quebec liberation front"—kidnapped a British diplomat and murdered a Quebec cabinet minister. The government of Quebec appealed to the federal government to invoke the War Measures Act and to move in troops to ensure order and preserve government. For a few dramatic weeks the Canadian armed forces took on a visibility and role hitherto unknown in Canada.

The Constitutional Discussions, 1968 to 1979

Constitutional discussions had begun in February 1968, more than two years before the FLQ crisis in Quebec, but no agreement of any kind had been achieved despite five meetings of the prime minister and the provincial premiers. The review of the Constitution was intended to be total since the demands of Quebec governments called into question virtually every aspect of the Canadian Constitution: the powers of the federal and provincial governments; the parliamentary, judicial, and other institutions of the country; the status of the English and French languages in Canada; the procedure for amending the Constitution; and other matters. The federal government gave high priority to the perennial problem of language in Canada and established a royal commission of inquiry in the early 1960s. To define language rights, but also to establish in the Constitution basic rights of a more general kind, it sought agreement on a Charter of Rights of a comprehensive character. The interest of the other provinces was minimal. For them the long and arduous conferences, with meetings of officials between, were a nuisance that took time and attention from "real" problems.

Spurred by the FLQ crisis of October 1970 and in the hope of eliminating the time-consuming albatross of constitutional review, a major effort was made at a conference in Victoria, British Columbia, in June 1971 to achieve agreement on a limited "package" of the most essential areas of change. Ostensibly because of disagreement on one specific issue, the government of Quebec withheld its acceptance, although its refusal was probably based on the fact that the package fell far short of its original goals. Three years of effort, seven meetings of the prime minister and premiers, and dozens of meetings of ministers and officials thus ended in failure. No change of any kind emerged.

While up to this point it had been the discontents of Quebec that provoked the search for constitutional change, the western provinces found in 1973 that they too had cause to be dissatisfied. The first Organization of Petroleum Exporting Countries (OPEC) oil crisis and the sharp rise in world prices of petroleum led the federal government to adopt policies designed to keep the price of oil and gas in Canada below world levels. Measures taken to secure increased revenues from Canadian production outraged the petroleum-producing provinces of the West. At last the Constitution and federal powers under it became real and important for them. The offensive action by Ottawa in the interest of the oil-consuming provinces of the East heightened the western sense of grievance at the way government appeared to work under the Canadian federal structure.

The failure in 1971 of the effort to achieve constitutional reform left Canada's political leaders exhausted and dispirited. In Quebec the separatist thesis appeared to be proven—federalism in Canada could not be reformed; it could only be ended. In the West the trampling on their economy and on their resource ownership and jurisdiction produced a legacy of bitterness that strongly alienated both governments and people from the national government in Ottawa. The final shock was delivered on November 15, 1976, with the election that has been referred to earlier in this chapter of a separatist government in Quebec. For the first time in their history, the Canadian people had to consider seriously whether or not the union would disintegrate with the departure of Quebec, which contains about 25 percent of the Canadian population.

In July 1977 the federal government appointed a "Task Force on Canadian Unity," directed to "hold public hearings" and to "assist in the development of processes for strengthening Canadian unity and be a source of advice to the government on unity issues." Provincial governments and organizations throughout the country turned their attention to devising recommendations as to changes that could, in their view, strengthen the national structure in which so many cracks seemed to be appearing.

Since agreement with the provinces on reform seemed impossible, the federal government introduced legislation in the Canadian Parliament in 1978 to make as much change in governmental institutions as it could by the use of federal powers alone. But this too brought provincial opposition. The premiers, at their annual meeting in August 1978, opposed "any unilateral change by the federal government." They went on to "express doubt that the federal government has the legal authority to act alone."

The federal government appeared to be blocked no matter what process of reform it attempted. The prime minister's frustration was reflected in a letter of September 13, 1978, in which he said:

> We have done everything we could to make clear that we want a full exchange of views with the provinces and as much agreement as can be achieved. The question is not whether agreement is desirable: it is. The question is whether, if the complete agreement of all provinces cannot be achieved, nothing whatever can be done—as nothing has been done in eight previous efforts to achieve major and far-reaching agreements on constitutional change, undertaken by six Prime Ministers of Canada, starting in 1927. The federal government believes that a continuation indefinitely of that total incapacity to act is not something that can or should be accepted as the inevitable result of a possible failure to get the agreement of each and every government.

The prime minister's frustration with the provincial governments was of no help in the House of Commons. The parliamentary opposition attacked the legislation to effect limited change by federal action and challenged its constitutionality. A reference to the Supreme Court of Canada on the matter produced a judgment in 1979 that some parts of the legislation—those dealing with Senate reform—did indeed exceed the constitutional powers of Parliament. Another effort at change was dead.

With all the opposition, and with a national crisis impending, there was no alternative but a return to the federal-provincial conference table. The new series of constitutional meetings, which ran from October 1978 to February 1979, went further than any previous ones in exploring possible changes in the distribution of power between the federal and provincial governments, as well as other fundamental matters. Like Dr. Johnson's proposition about knowing one is to be hanged in a fortnight, so the knowledge that a referendum on the separation of Quebec was looming wonderfully concentrated the minds of the political leaders. But to no avail. Again, agreement proved impossible to achieve. The final seal of failure of a great effort was given when Prime Minister Trudeau, who had led the discussions through eleven years of frustration, was defeated in the federal election of May 1979.

Crisis Dispelled and Renewed

There was no time to discover what Prime Minister Joe Clark and his new Progressive Conservative government might have done about the constitutional puzzle. His party had only a minority in Parliament and was defeated after a few months in office. A new election early in 1980 brought Trudeau back to power.

The outline earlier in this chapter of the main events of "The Recent Years" has described the defeat of the separatist proposal in the Quebec referendum of May 1980. There is no doubt that the defeat was of critical importance. From 1976 to that moment, favorable winds had filled the sails of Premier Lévesque and his party, just as those of the federal ship hung limp in frustration. But now it was the Parti Québécois that had lost its momentum.

With a new majority behind him in Parliament, and with his great Quebec opponent discomfited, Prime Minister Trudeau was much tougher in the constitutional discussion of 1980–81 than he had been in 1978–79. It was because of the strength of his new position that he could announce, after the failure of the conference of September 1980, that the federal government would proceed on its own course for constitutional change, with however much or little provincial support it might find. It was also because of the repeated frustrations over many years—and the suspicion that a Quebec government dedicated to separation would never agree to anything that would improve the federation it wanted to leave—that this dramatic course received as much support as it did, both in Quebec and in Canada generally.

When the Supreme Court judgment of September 1981, referred to earlier in this chapter, made the "unilateral course" too dangerous for the federal government politically but equally made continued opposition by the provinces too dangerous for them constitutionally, the need for some kind of agreement was heavy on both sides. As a result, the federal government accepted a formula for amending the Constitution that it did not like, but most provinces wanted, in exchange for a Charter of Rights it very much wanted, but most provinces disliked. The amending formula requires that changes to the Constitution have the agreement of the Parliament of Canada and seven provinces representing 50 percent of the population of all the provinces. The western provinces got a clause to establish and define their jurisdiction over natural resources. The Atlantic provinces got a constitutional commitment to further "economic development to reduce disparity in opportunities." The aboriginal people got recognition and confirmation of their "existing aboriginal and treaty rights." Only the province of Quebec, which had been unhappy with confederation as it was and which had started the whole exercise of constitutional review in 1968, got nothing. The seven English-speaking provinces that had joined with Quebec in opposing the federal course in 1980 and that were in alliance with it right up to the climactic night of November 4, 1981, finally decided that they could no longer be associated with a separatist government in yet another frustration of constitutional change.

For Quebec the result was traumatic—a trauma lessened only by the fact that the leading federal actors were French Canadians from Quebec: Prime Minister Trudeau and Minister of Justice Jean Chrétien. It was not just that Quebec had gained none of the objectives that its governments, both federalist and separatist, had sought over twenty years. Its position was worse than at the outset—and this after the promise of a "renewal of federalism." The new amending procedure provided no veto on possible changes in the Constitution nor any special position to protect French Quebec against the English majority in all other provinces and in Ottawa. Far from having more power, the legislature of Quebec, in common with all other legislatures in Canada, had less because of the Charter of Rights. But all the other provinces had agreed, however reluctantly, to the limitation. Quebec alone had the charter imposed on it.

Paradoxes of the Canadian Polity

In most countries of the world, events comparable to those in Canada from the mid–1960s to 1981 would produce an explosive situation. Almost exactly half of the French-speaking majority in Quebec had voted in favor of negotiating separation from Canada; the other 50 percent thought they had been promised a better deal if they voted to stay in Canada. Neither got what it wanted. There was neither separation nor reform for Quebec. In the first shock after the Conference of 1981, all it seemed to have for thirteen years of effort was betrayal and a slap in the face from Canada's other ten governments—all dominated by English-speaking majorities. Such results might be expected to set the stage for trouble and confrontation, but that has not been and almost certainly will not be the result.

There has been no suggestion, even among the most fanatic adherents of independence for Quebec, of recourse to violence. Fundamentally this must rest on the recognition that it would not succeed. Canada is a society deeply committed to the rule of law. Despite the tragicomic rebellions of 1837 in the area now comprising Ontario and Quebec, a quickly suppressed rising of plainsmen of mixed blood on the western frontier in 1885, and the brief episodes of terrorism in Quebec in the decade from 1960 to 1970, there is no tradition in Canada of violent change. Public support of any significance has never been available for resort to violence to achieve political objectives. Canada has experienced no revolution. Indeed, a profound part of its social character is attributable to its refusal to become "the fourteenth colony" and to its rejection of the American Revolution. There has been no "man on horseback" in its history. No military hero has become prime minister or leader of a political party. The fundamental Canadian reaction to violent solutions was revealed in the 85 percent support for the federal government's invocation of the War Measures Act to crush the terrorist FLQ in 1970.

Along with the commitment to the rule of law is a profound belief in the political process. It is doubtful if in any other country in the world there would be general public acceptance of the right of people in one part of the country to vote whether to separate from it. Isolated suggestions in Canada before the Quebec referendum that it was illegal, treasonable, or should be stopped got no support. The idea of using force to preserve the Canadian union was not seriously raised. And the same adherence to the democratic process was shown in the totally peaceful, if bitterly disappointed, acceptance by the Parti Québécois of the referendum result. No more in the future than in the past are Canadians likely to depart from the path of democracy and law.

A related, but somewhat different, factor is the Canadian distrust of drastic solutions or of carrying almost anything to "the logical conclusion." The nature of Canada, its two linguistic groups with differing interests and points of view, and its deep regional divisions have imposed accommodation and compromise as the price of national existence. Compromise produces muddy second bests that logic can find repugnant. However, it is unlikely to drive citizens to the barricades.

A final factor weighing against any extreme reaction in Canada is the paradox of deep attachment to the country along with the equally deep divisions within it. Quebec presented the most dramatic demonstration in the period shortly after the referendum of 1980. While 40 percent of its people voted for "sovereignty-association," public opinion polls showed 73 percent expressing a "strong attachment" to Canada. In Alberta, where western alienation reached its most extreme bitterness, the attempt to form a western separatist party collapsed in humiliation. For most Canadians the attachment is emotional. It is an attachment to an undefined "Canada" meaning different things to different people, and one that often conceals profound differences that any analysis quickly would reveal. Yet for all the underlying differences, the emotion is real and constitutes a powerful force that conditions the attitudes of all.

Economic Concerns and the Climate in Quebec

After the defeat it suffered in the constitutional conference of November 1981, Quebec's government tried to turn the "isolation of Quebec" into a new crusade against the treatment of the province within the Canadian federal system. The effort failed, despite a substantial majority in the legislature for a motion of condemnation of the new constitutional arrangements.

In part the failure was because Quebec had two heroes and two leaders. One of them, Prime Minister Trudeau, proclaimed the virtues of the new arrangements and especially the importance of the Charter of Rights for the French language and culture in all the provinces. In part, however, it was because the economic recession of 1981–82 gave the people of Quebec, and particularly a new and younger generation, a greater concern about unemployment and economic performance than about the sovereign state into which Premier Lévesque would lead them. It was no time for risks, and clearly the well-known federalism seemed safer than an untested and possibly precarious independence. The economic difficulties, and especially protracted contests with organized labor, diminished the glamour of the Parti Québécois government. What had, in 1976, the status of a national movement, celebrated by the leading singers, poets, and authors of French Canada, had become just another political party. The government it provided was as fallible as every other. Disillusion blunted its appeal to rally round the great objective of an independent French "nation" in Quebec.

A possible irony is that the success of one of Premier Lévesque's most popular measures, the Quebec language act, may have contributed to the decline in separatist fervor. The act made French the official language of Quebec and imposed strict and detailed restraints on the use of English. Businesses in Quebec were required to achieve set standards in their internal use of French. Exterior signs could not be in English nor could they be bilingual. Only children of a parent who had gone to an English-language school in Quebec would have the right to be enrolled in an English school. The children of English-speaking parents coming from other provinces could get temporary permits to attend an English school, but only for three years. Neither immigrants nor French-speaking Québécois had the option of having their children educated in English. As a result of the legislation and general pressure by the government, the use of English in industry and commerce has sharply declined. Careers in business in French are now possible for young French Canadians. The income advantage of the English-speaking has almost vanished. French cultural activities are vigorous in every field. In short, the Parti Québécois has provided a convincing demonstration that its own thesis is untrue. Quebec *can* be French; its culture *can* grow and expand; and all of this *can* be done within the Canadian federation.

By 1983, instead of leading a new crusade, Lévesque found himself having to reassure his most fervent supporters that "independence" would not be dropped as the objective of the party. He committed himself to holding the next provincial election on the issue despite general agreement that it presented no chance of gaining majority support. The most rational explanation was that his party regarded defeat as inevitable and would rather lose the next election on an issue of principle than on the record of the government.

The federal election of September 4, 1984, however, created a situation in which all prospects have to be reexamined. The Liberal party, in power since 1963 with the brief interruption of Clark's regime in 1979–80, suffered the worst defeat in its history and won only 40 seats in the House of Commons, while the Progressive Conservatives took 211. In popular vote, the Liberals received 28 percent, the Conservatives, 50 percent. Much more astonishing, and probably more significant in the long run, were the results in Quebec. While the Liberals claimed 74 of the 75 seats in the 1980 election, in 1984 they won only 17. In 1980, they received 67 percent of the vote, in 1984, only 35 percent. The Conservatives scored an unbelievable gain in votes from 12.7 percent in 1980 to 50.3 percent in 1984.

Led by Brian Mulroney, a fluently bilingual Quebecer, the Progressive Conservatives convinced the voters of the province that the needs, aspirations, and problems of Quebec were understood and could be better handled by the Conservatives than by the Liberals under their new leader, John Turner. The rejection of the Liberals and the decisive swing to the Conservatives constituted a political revolution comparable to that in 1896 when Quebec dropped its adherence to the Conservatives of that day and swung its support to Sir Wilfrid Laurier's Liberal party. Apart from a brief and disillusioning fling with the Conservatives under John Diefenbaker from 1958 to 1963, Quebec's transfer of allegiance to the Liberal party lasted eighty-eight years. Almost certainly a new era was ushered in on September 4, 1984. Only future developments will disclose whether it will be a shift of block support from Liberals to Conservatives or a more healthy situation in which no political party will be able to rely on the unwavering and uncritical vote of Quebec. Whichever it is to be, new prospects emerge for the province and the federation.

In his election campaign, Mulroney presented his party to the voters of Quebec as the party of conciliation. If elected, he would endeavor to make it possible for Quebec to accept the Constitution of 1982 "with honor." Just what that implied was not defined, but the prospect was balm to the wounds of those who still suffered from the defeat and rejection of November 1981. Mulroney's conciliatory attitude attracted the support of a broad coalition of Québécois—people for whom the federal orthodoxy and constitutional intransigence of Pierre Trudeau still rankled—members of the Parti Québécois, old supporters of the defunct Union Nationale, and even organizers of the provincial Liberal party. Mulroney sensed and responded to a broadly felt desire to end the wars of argument and ideology that had riven Quebec for twenty years. The voters were weary of contests over status and wanted to turn energy and attention to problems of more immediate concern.

The most convincing indication of the mood and the consequences of Mulroney's astute appeal came two days after the election. Premier Lévesque announced that Quebec would end immediately its boycott of federal-provincial meetings; henceforth it would participate fully and completely. He added that Quebec rejoiced "that Mr. Mulroney is of the opinion that the constitutional dossier eventually should be reopened in a manner that could satisfy Quebec." It was significant, however, that Lévesque did not let his joy at that prospect deflect his keen political sense. He noted that "the first priority of the voters and of governments does not lie with the Constitution but with the economy and the stimulation of employment." As to the formal resolution passed by his own party some months before that stated that a vote for it at the next provincial election would be a vote for the sovereignty of Quebec, Lévesque said that "for the moment, there is no question of reopening that can of worms." Constitution and sovereignty could wait. The economic problems of Quebec come first, and Quebec would participate with the other governments of Canada to help resolve them.

While Lévesque might have wished it, the "can of worms" would not stay closed. Just six weeks later, the Parti Québécois found itself questioning openly and directly whether it should continue to hold to its fundamental goal of independence for Quebec. In a letter published on October 25, 1984 in *La Presse* of Montreal, the most widely read French newspaper in Quebec, the program advisor of the party, Jules-Pascal Venne, said bluntly that the P.Q. had been wrong in its objective of trying to achieve sovereignty by the referendum-election process. The effort had broken down. He called instead for a "historic compromise" between Quebec and "Canada" within the Canadian federation. The following day, Pierre-Marc Johnson, the minister of justice and of intergovernmental affairs in the Quebec government, expressed views less direct but equally clearly at variance with the official position. He wanted the "affront" to Quebec in the 1982 Constitution remedied, the amending formula changed to provide a veto for Quebec, and constitutional recognition that Quebec is a "distinct society" within Canada. He was, however, opposed to having a new vote in Quebec on sovereignty because it would again be lost. He argued that Quebec should take advantage of the new political situation in Ottawa to negotiate changes important in its place within Canada. Such heretical views plunged the party into public soul-searching and debate about the most fundamental articles of its creed. A group of Quebec ministers on the other side of the issue met to develop the arguments in favor of continued adherence to the orthodox objective of sovereignty. Premier Lévesque led a three-hour discussion in his cabinet on the party's goals in which ministers were said to be equally divided among federalists, "independentists," and undecided. Lévesque preserved his uncommitted position but made clear that the cabinet and the party would have to settle the issue before the next provincial election.

It is apparent that 1984 marked a fundamental change in the political balance in Canada. Just what it means for the future will not be certain for some time. The Parti Québécois seems likely to draw back from its strong commitment to "sovereignty" for Quebec but, if it is to do so, the risk of a split within the party will be great. Whether it, or a possible new Liberal government in Quebec, can work out an agreement with other governments for changes in the Canadian Constitution that will be acceptable to Quebec is another matter. The Speech from the Throne on November 5, 1984, opening the first session of the Canadian Parliament under Prime Minister Mulroney's government, declared that "the constitutional agreement is incomplete so long as Quebec is not part of an accord." It committed the federal government to work "to create the conditions that will make possible the achievement of this essential accord" and called for "the cooperation of all partners in Confederation." It is clear that the constitutional battle is not over in Canada.

Whatever the contending parties in Quebec may adopt as their programs and objectives, unless the federal government can devise means, acceptable to the other provinces, to give recognition to Quebec's "difference," no government of Quebec will long be able to acquiesce in the Constitution "imposed" on Quebec in 1981–82. It will not be easy to contrive a solution. There is little or no prospect of restoring the veto Quebec once thought it had over constitutional change. It will require the unanimous consent of the federal parliament and all the provincial legislatures to change the amending formula. Major change in the Charter of Rights, which invalidates part of Quebec's language law, is highly improbable. The distribution of powers has shown that it is a morass that can engulf whatever legions of politicians or constitutional lawyers try to wade through it. It is by no means clear how the results of the agreement of November 1981—the agreement in which Quebec did not take part—can be qualified or softened so they will not become festering sores and sources of grievance to be rediscovered by a new generation of Québécois. However, if necessity has imposed on Canada one great talent it is that of political ingenuity and compromise. Canadian political leaders probably will prove equal to the task. It is among their most critical challenges in the next few years.

Containment of the Risks to Canadian Unity

The real risks to Canadian unity in the future remain what they have been in the past: the division between the two languages and cultures, the way rights of the French minority are treated in provinces other than Quebec, and the struggle to develop satisfying roles for Quebec and Québécois within confederation. The other problems of a resentful West and a frustrated Newfoundland are difficult, irksome, and must get imaginative attention—but they are not threats.

The psychology of French Quebec is complex, with a wide range of interpretation and explanation by Quebec leaders and intellectuals themselves. Quebec nationalism has been a constant factor since well before confederation in 1867. It was an element in the rebellion of 1837 and has become a powerful force at recurring points in Canadian history: the hanging of Louis Riel for treason after leading the western rebellion in 1885, the opposition to military conscription in the two world wars, and the latest separatist crisis of 1970–80. The nationalist sentiment is not homogeneous in intensity, expression, or objectives. For virtually all Québécois it is strongly cultural, attached to the preservation of the French language and culture as the basis of Quebec society. For most Québécois accommodation within Canada is the objective, provided the French language and culture are dominant in Quebec as English is in other provinces. A complex part of the question is the extent to which the treatment of French in the rest of Canada is important to people and parties in Quebec.

In 1965 the Royal Commission on Bilingualism and Biculturalism warned Canadians that, without fully realizing it, they were passing through the greatest crisis in their history. The cause of the crisis, in the opinion of "B and B" commissioners was that "the state of affairs established in 1867, and never since seriously challenged, is now for the first time being rejected by the French Canadians outside Quebec." The commission recognized that much of the problem both in Quebec and elsewhere was, as they put it, "the product and consummation of all the past resentments" against the treatment of the French reality *in Canada generally.* The commission was undoubtedly right. However, many separatists in Quebec in recent years have justified their readiness, if Quebec left Canada, to abandon the 15 percent of French-speaking Canadians in other provinces by arguing that they are "write-offs" anyway, bound to be assimilated by the English-speaking majority.

The apparent implication that separatist Québécois do not care what happens to French or to the French-speaking in Canada *outside Quebec* is not correct. Few Québécois, whether federalist or separatist, do not resent any unequal treatment for French or any lack of respect for the French-speaking community in other provinces. There is little question but that the improved treatment of French at the federal level and in Canada generally through the Official Languages Act of 1969 and the Charter of Rights of 1982 has diminished resentment in Quebec as well as in the rest of Canada. New Brunswick, with 33 percent of its population French-speaking, has become officially bilingual. Ontario has greatly improved the treatment of French and its French-speaking population of nearly 500,000, who comprise just under 10 percent of Ontario's total, although it has declined to accept the kind of constitutional guarantees for the French-speaking that are provided for the English-speaking population of Quebec—now reduced to some 12 percent. The Charter of Rights has become a factor in the better treatment of French in Ontario. The Court of Appeal of the province in June 1984 held that the charter gives French-speaking Ontarians the right to education in French anywhere in the province and the right to control their own schools. A bitter contest in Manitoba in 1983–84 over the reestablishment of rights for the French-speaking there, dating from 1870 but removed by legislation in 1890 that was found unconstitutional only in 1979, showed that the fire has not died out of the language issue entirely. However, the attitude of English-speaking Canada is much more understanding than in 1965. Language problems are diminishing as sources of division and serious difficulty.

It is only for a minority in Quebec that Quebec nationalism extends beyond the protection of language and culture and includes support for political separation from Canada. A poll in early 1984 showed that support to have dropped to 19 percent, even if independence was accompanied by economic association with the rest of Canada. The party that had won the election of 1981 found in a poll of its own that only 22 percent of Quebec voters would vote for it in 1984. Because of the underlying attachment of most Québécois to Canada, the minority favoring any form of separation is not likely to become the majority, provided there is understanding of Quebec and of the legitimate place of French in the rest of Canada. Prime Minister Mulroney's understanding of the importance of the language issue to Quebec and to French Canadians generally will help greatly. The authority of his enormous majority and his demonstration of the political dividends that conciliation and understanding can produce in Quebec will mute and perhaps diminish the traditional resistance of many English-speaking Conservatives to language equality. There is no prospect of removing the language issue entirely, but it may cease to be seriously divisive.

French Quebec is proud of its leading political role in Canada. Since confederation, it has provided Canadian prime ministers for over one-third of Canada's history. "French power" dominated the government of Canada from 1968 to 1984, the period of the most intense challenge to Canadian federalism since its beginning. French Canadian thinkers provided a disproportionate share of the intellectual energy and ideas of the period.

The problem of French Quebec today is the other side of the

coin. Its culture and language are probably more secure than ever before, but it sees its population proportionately diminishing as a part of the national total. Its birth rate, once one of the highest in the world, is now the lowest in Canada. Its economy is not healthy, and it has suffered a net emigration of French-speaking people to other provinces in recent years, although the emigration of the English-speaking has been much greater. Quebec has become more French in population, language, and culture, but it has become a smaller proportion of the total Canadian entity. That diminution adds to the unease with which it regards the unsatisfactory results of the constitutional provisions of 1981–82. An adequate sense of security for a smaller Quebec within a growing Canada has yet to be established.

French Quebec, which comprises about 87 percent of all Quebec, is determined to retain its French character and language. A second concern, less in order but still vital, is ensuring full respect for French outside Quebec. If those concerns can be assured, and if some means can be devised to give a more satisfying expression, constitutionally or less formally, to the unique quality and character of Quebec within the Canadian family, Canada will never again encounter as great a risk to its unity as that of the last decade.

The Strains and Strengths of Canadian Federalism

One of the differences between the Canadian and American versions of federalism today is the much greater power of the Canadian provinces than of the American states. It is a paradox that this should be so since, as already mentioned, the Canadian design of 1867 was strongly influenced by a desire to avoid the degree of state power that was thought to have been an important factor leading to the American Civil War. As suggested earlier, increase in provincial strength has come about in part through judicial interpretation and in part as a product of the basic facts of a country of deep regional divisions. It is also a national generalization of the restraint federal governments in Canada have had to exercise in dealing with Quebec. Whenever a federal policy was unacceptable to Quebec and opposed by its government, that opposition tended to rally the support of other provinces for whatever restriction of federal activity Quebec might be seeking.

It would be wrong, however, to think that the federal govern-

ment has been without instruments of power and has not used
them. During the postwar years, as the welfare state developed, it,
like the federal government in the United States, used its financial
resources as an instrument of policy to attach conditions to money
it offered to the provinces under its "spending power." Social support, health, and welfare come normally under provincial jurisdiction, but the federal government tried, usually with success, to
achieve national objectives through its design of the purposes for
which its grants could be spent. The resentment of Quebec over
this use of federal power to impose policies and priorities in areas
of provincial jurisdiction was shared in varying degrees by other
provinces. There was increasing and more general opposition to
federal "intrusions" into provincial fields. Such stresses, together
with the constitutional and resource disputes of the 1970s, produced great strain in federal-provincial relations from the mid–
1960s into the 1980s. The culmination of these strains frequently
emerged in conferences of the prime minister and the premiers,
which became increasingly public as the years passed and were increasingly marked by a greater capacity for noisy disagreement
than for cooperation.

Federal-provincial conferences in Canada have no parallel in
the United States. The president does not sit down with fifty governors to attempt to hammer out agreement on joint policies or
programs. The number of states would make it impossible, but
equally would the disparity in status and power between the president and the governors with whom he would be dealing. No
American would suggest, as has been done in Canada, that there
is an equality of role between the heads of the national and state
governments or that there is a "national interest" that is not
achievable by the American government and that requires the
participation of the states with the central government for decision or accomplishment. There has been more cooperation between the federal and provincial governments in Canada than
the viewers of the televised conference spectacles would believe,
but the impression left has been one of pervasive conflict and
dispute.

The frequency, prominence, and stress of the constitutional
meetings from 1968 to 1981 undoubtedly added to the tensions of
recent years. The contests over power and jurisdiction exacerbated
personal differences between the prime minister and some provin-

cial premiers that would have been severe in any case. The stridency of argument may well be less in the future, but the Canadian system of government is more calculated to provide the basis for intergovernmental dispute than is the American congressional system. Canadian heads of government can negotiate as independent powers, each of whom controls a majority in his legislature. It is a condition of existence for a government under the parliamentary system. A genuine and certain power base is thus available to all, and that base can be used to disagree or to block action if either the interest of a province or the political advantage of a party make that course attractive. As long as seven provincial governments continue to be of Prime Minister Mulroney's party, political incentives will favor agreement if it is reasonably possible to achieve it. However, the differences between the interests of the "have" and the "have-not" provinces, between the consumers and the producers of oil and gas, and between the needs of a province and of the country as a whole will not have vanished. They will gradually reassert themselves in federal-provincial meetings, especially because of the lack of any forum at the national level for their effective expression.

There has been a growing interest in the West, which is conscious of the weakness of its permanent minority situation in Canada, in correcting some of the imbalance of power through an elected Senate. As it found in the dispute over the National Energy Program, there is temptation for national governments, if they must choose, to prefer the interests of 62 percent of the population in the center of Canada (Ontario and Quebec), to those of 29 percent in the West. The western interest in a new Senate will probably diminish in the immediate future since the West is now represented strongly in the Progressive Conservative government. However, its representation will continue to be drastically less than that of central Canada. Prime Minister Mulroney's glorious victory in Quebec will not be without its problems for the West. Whatever the party distribution may be at any particular time, the House of Commons reflects that population imbalance, so it is of little help to the smaller provinces. Western advocacy calls for a Senate modeled along American lines so that every province would be equally represented. The "three E's" are its symbol: elected, equal, and effective. A resulting problem is that this plan would reduce Quebec from its current 22 percent of Senate seats to only 10 percent. The Senate in Canada was supposed to provide overrepresentation and, thus, a degree of protection to the French-speaking minority whose heart and center is in Quebec. A solution may be to increase western representation greatly, stop short of provincial equality, and make special provision for areas of prime importance to the French-speaking minority. It will not be easy to achieve any such change. There are too many conflicting interests—including vested interests in the appointed Senate as it now stands. However, it seems to be the only change likely to do anything effective and enduring to reduce some of the regional insecurities and inadequately vented frustrations that now plague federal-provincial relations.

The strengths of Canadian federalism are less obvious than the difficulties; they are not news. If negotiated agreements must be achieved because federal power usually cannot dominate, once reached, they are apt to be more lasting and less troublesome than imposed arrangements. With the exception of Medicare, present problems with respect to welfare, health, and social security programs largely concern finance, not differences of policy. The system is costly, but few Canadians would be prepared to see it significantly reduced or seriously changed. The much greater understanding about language policy, after twenty years of debate and difficulty, together with the new constitutional Charter of Rights, probably have put the Canadian union on a more sound basis than has existed since 1867 with respect to its greatest single source of difficulty.

Religious differences, once sharp in Canada, virtually have ceased to be a source of political concern, and only a cynic would attribute the change entirely to religious indifference. It is symbolic of the greater tolerance characteristic of an increasingly temperate society.

In other important ways social and policy changes have tended to blunt the sharpness of Canadian differences. French-speaking cultural leaders deplore the "Americanization" of Quebec's values, attitudes, and language through pervasive American television and films. Whatever the cultural loss may be, the process brings Québécois a bit closer to their English-speaking compatriots who are being "Americanized" at a faster rate by the same process. There was a time when cultural differences and historic traditions produced strains much more tense than those today. Few English-speaking Canadians now look to London for leadership or with political loyalty. Few French-speaking Canadians look, as they did in the nineteenth century, to Rome in their search for leadership and guidance on social and sometimes political issues. All Canadians, French-speaking and English-speaking, are North Americans—with differences but with much less distance between them now than used to be the case.

Similarly, the federal policy of "equalization" (which provides money to provincial governments to deliver essential public services of comparable standard to their citizens without unduly different costs to their taxpayers) has taken some of the edge off regional disparities. There are still substantial differences in tax levels and in services among the provinces. Newfoundlanders pay more for inferior services than do the people of Ontario or Alberta for better ones, but the disparities are less than they were.

Canadian federalism, with all its difficulties, has produced a society characterized by more humanity and social justice than is found in most nations. It is a significant element of national strength. It gives substance and practical value to the emotional attachment to the country that most Canadians feel.

Canadian politics tend to reflect national realities. There is little of ideology to distinguish the parties—and sometimes not too much of policy. To achieve power, each must try to attract support in all regions. The parties tend, accordingly, to be shapeless, pragmatic coalitions that look for an elusive "greatest common factor of agreement" across the land. A problem of recent years has been that the Progressive Conservative party has had virtually no support in Quebec and the Liberals have almost as completely lost strength in the West. The first half of this problem has been remedied, quite possibly in a permanent way; the second has not. The Liberals' problems in again becoming a national party are not just with the Conservatives; they also will have to displace the New Democratic party as the "alternative" in the West. It will be extremely difficult. Geographical polarization in Canada assumed a new guise with the election of 1984 and, mercifully, was removed as an immediate problem within Mulroney's government and in his following in the House of Commons. The completely national quality of his support, together with the undoubted efforts of the Liberals to reestablish themselves in the West, almost certainly means that both polarization and its consequences will be less in the years ahead than they have been for a long time.

Strength and Unity in the American Shadow

While these elements of strength are real, a sparse population, divided into two language groups, scattered across 4,000 miles, and burdened with still diverging pressures and interests unfused by any great historic experience of revolution or liberation would have difficulty in finding a general sense of unity and coherence in the most favorable of circumstances. In the shadow of the United States the problem is even more difficult. In economic, political, and cultural life the proximity, scale, and vitality of the United States inhibit the establishment of a sense of common identity and significant difference in a much smaller neighbor.

Canadians look at far more American than Canadian television programs. It requires a stoic acceptance of small returns for Canadian magazines to survive against the flood of American periodicals crossing the border. French-speaking Canadians have some degree of "protection," but it is by no means complete. They enjoy American programs, too. Canadian culture fights for its existence under the benign and unconscious aggression of American artists, authors, broadcasters, publishers, and film makers.

It is not easy for Canadian governments to know what they should do or what they can do to meet such problems. While Canada is proud of the pluralism of its cultural mosaic that its open and free society makes possible, many Canadians are aware of the difficulties that arise from the tenuous sense of identity and the frequently elusive common purpose that are features of Canada. Measures taken to strengthen and enhance them are often unpopular and adopted in the face of criticism and opposition. Occasionally such measures may injure specific American interests, but they are almost never anti-American in purpose or intent. It is only a very small minority in Canada for whom anti-Americanism is an accepted attitude.

The National Energy Program of the Trudeau government, introduced in October 1980, provides an excellent example of action to meet a problem of Canadian autonomy—an action that has been perceived in the United States as anti-American. That was not its intent. It was designed to accomplish a variety of purposes relating to the development of petroleum resources in Canada. Among these, one of the most important was to reduce the extent of foreign ownership and control. Limitation of foreign ownership is a policy not unknown in the United States in a variety of sensitive fields, but in no case have Americans had to contemplate the degree of foreign domination found in the Canadian petroleum industry in the 1970s or at present.

The first OPEC oil crisis of 1973–74 made very clear the risks for any country in too great a reliance on foreign oil sources. Another moral for a country with domestic energy sources was the folly in having too little control in so sensitive an area. By 1980, when the National Energy Program (NEP) was adopted, foreign ownership of the Canadian industry, on the basis of control over the oil as it came out of Canadian ground, was 72 percent. The Canadian government had come to the conclusion that such a degree of foreign domination was not acceptable to the national interest. It is doubtful if any American government would come to a different conclusion about that degree of foreign ownership of far less sensitive activities, resources, or products in the United States.

The NEP gave a preference to Canadian companies and Canadian investment in order to increase the degree of Canadian control. In this respect the policy succeeded. By 1982 the degree of foreign ownership had dropped to 62 percent—a figure that is still very high and seems not to have changed much since.

Virtually all of the foreign ownership and investment in the Canadian oil industry is American. There is some British, some French, but, overwhelmingly, it is American capital and enterprise that is involved. The policy affected American investors and companies far more than any other and, therefore, seemed anti-American. It is, perhaps, the most striking recent demonstration of the problem a Canadian government may encounter with a policy designed to strengthen Canadian autonomy against a "threat" that Americans do not see as a threat at all.

It is also a striking example of a Canadian dilemma. The policy sharply reduced the flow of American investment. This, along with other changes in the world petroleum scene, severely hit the level of economic activity in western Canada. The policy is intensely unpopular there for a variety of reasons and has sharply worsened the already weak position of the Liberal party in the western provinces. The costs, both political and economic, have been high. "Canadianization" can hurt, and if it hurts too much, Canadian governments have to consider the nice balance of objectives and consequences that can be involved.

If cultural development is important for the attainment of a greater sense of common identity in Canada, and if Canadian control of vital resources is thought necessary for Canadian independence, of equal importance and difficulty is the transition of the Canadian economy from its traditional reliance on raw materials and staples to a more mature industrial base. Canada is unique among the seven countries of the economic "summit" in being at the same time a developed and an underdeveloped country. Again the United States appears in the dual role of problem and solution. The United States accounts for 70 percent of Canadian exports. The market is vital to Canada, and, yet, too great a dependence again raises the question of identity and independence.

Canada is conscious that it has not done well in the last few years in the transition to a new industrial structure. The former government was reproached for having no "industrial strategy," yet it is not at all apparent what this should be or whether or not it would be feasible in a country as divided as Canada and with so much external trade concentrated in one country. Again the problems of regional differences, disparate interests, and uncertain federal powers are part of the picture.

Impacts of Canadian Federalism on Canada–United States Relations

Two features of Canadian federalism produce a situation in which the Canadian provinces have a role in Canada–United States relations far greater than do the American states. One is the extensive powers and jurisdiction of the provinces, to which reference has already been made. Of particular importance is their jurisdiction over natural resources. The other is that there is, under the Canadian Constitution, no treaty-making power comparable to that in the United States Constitution. An American government, in the exercise of its powers over foreign relations, has within its capacity the power to enter into and carry out international obligations not limited to its own internal areas of jurisdiction. It can override, for such purposes, the powers that reside in the states. The Canadian government has no such power. If an international arrangement, whether bilateral or multilateral, involves commitments or actions in areas under provincial jurisdiction, the province or provinces concerned must agree and be prepared to act or the Canadian commitment cannot be implemented.

As with the lack, until April 1982, of an amending clause in the Canadian Constitution, the limitation of Canadian federal power in international affairs is the unplanned result of the fact that Canada was not fully independent in 1867. It was a new thing—a "dominion"—more than colony but less than country. It was still a part of the British Empire, and foreign relations for the entire empire were controlled in London. It was realized that the powers of the provinces in the new dominion, which was also the first federation established in the empire, could cause problems. So a clause was inserted, Section 132, which provided that

> the Parliament and Government of Canada shall have all Powers necessary or proper for performing the Obligations of Canada or of any province thereof, as part of the British Empire, towards Foreign Countries, arising under Treaties between the Empire and such Foreign Countries.

By the 1930s Canada had evolved to independence and handled its own foreign relations. If the government of Canada entered into an international obligation, did Section 132 give it the power to fulfill it, regardless of provincial jurisdiction, as it had been able to do when such obligations were incurred as part of the British Empire? Ontario and several other provinces challenged the federal government on the question over some international conventions it had signed. The issue came to final judgment in 1937. The answer was that the federal Parliament and government had no such power to override the provinces. After considering the new status that Canada had achieved, with full capacity to enter into international relations and incur obligations toward other countries, the judges crushed the federal hope that it had the power to fulfill such obligations, even if the subject matter fell within provincial jurisdiction. They said:

> It must not be thought that the result of this decision is that Canada is incompetent to legislate in performance of treaty obligations. In totality of legislative powers, Dominion and Provincial together, she is fully equipped.

But the legislative powers remain distributed and if in the exercise of her new functions derived from her new international status she incurs obligations they must, so far as legislation be concerned when they deal with provincial classes of subjects, be dealt with by the totality of powers, in other words by cooperation between the Dominion and the Provinces.

The serenity of the judicial perception was not affected by the obvious difficulties in the 1930s of achieving federal-provincial cooperation. Nor would it be altered by the equally disputatious situation the 1980s have shown thus far. The law remains as the judges declared.

The importance of this situation for Canada–United States relations can be better appreciated when one considers important areas of interest or concern between the two countries. Provincial jurisdiction, and, therefore, the need for provincial cooperation, is or can be a factor in a great number of them. It was involved in negotiating the Columbia River Treaty, and the policies and attitudes of the British Columbia government fundamentally affected the treaty itself. No American state played any role; the U.S. government had adequate powers. The raising of the level of the High Ross Dam to provide more power for Seattle was blocked for years by British Columbia's jurisdiction over lands and resources. It objected to the increased flooding of the Skagit River Valley, and the treaty, ratified by the American Senate in June 1984, had to yield to that objection. On the Atlantic coast, the contentions of the government of Newfoundland about offshore jurisdiction held up investment in oil development until the Supreme Court of Canada ruled against the province. Provincial jurisdiction will be a major feature in whatever arrangements can finally be worked out to deal with the problems of acid rain. The Garrison Dam and the diversion in North Dakota create a problem in which the jurisdiction of Manitoba over provincial resources brings it squarely into the question. Even when provincial jurisdiction is less certain, the control over resources can bring provincial governments into the picture—Quebec on the export of electric power from Newfoundland to the New England states, Alberta and Saskatchewan on the pricing and level of gas exports, and all the coastal provinces on the complex problems of Atlantic and Pacific fisheries. A question for the future will almost certainly involve the supply of fresh water for parts of the United States that look ahead with apprehension to growing shortages.

Water within a province is either under, or involves questions of, provincial jurisdiction. In a great many cases that jurisdiction cannot be overridden by the federal government no matter what may be its interest or concern.

Canadian federalism and the role of Canadian provinces under the Constitution will inevitably be a substantial factor affecting Canadian-American relations in a host of issues of major concern to both peoples.

The United States Interest in a Strong and United Canada

The United States has become increasingly aware of the importance of the stability of the Western Hemisphere. Its responsibilities as leader of the Western democracies and as the ultimate determinant of their peace and security are enormous. They cannot be effectively exercised without the support of friendly countries. Nor can attention be fully directed to them if there is insecurity in America's back yard. Canada is democratic, orderly, economically stable, strongly committed to human rights and freedom, and dedicated to the establishment of a peaceful international community. It has shown in two world wars that it is prepared, in case of need, to carry its full share. It has played a role beyond its numbers and power in the creation of the United Nations and NATO, in peacekeeping in many troubled areas, and in aid to the Third World. It is militarily allied with the United States to protect the security of North America. In short, Canada *now* provides, in a more critical location, what the United States would like to achieve in Central America and the Caribbean. It is difficult to imagine anything that could be more injurious to U.S. policy or interest than a troubled, ineffective, or unfriendly country to the north.

Successive governments in the United States have demonstrated awareness that they must not intervene in Canadian affairs. They have also, on many occasions, shown a willingness to try to meet Canadian interests and to help in the solution of problems raised by Canadian governments. It is not surprising that the awareness is not constant and even less surprising that Canadian problems should be remote from the concerns or knowledge of senators, representatives, or the American public. The constant task for

Canada is to achieve a hearing in the many centers of interest and influence in the United States about the nature of its economic, cultural, and political problems; about the need for effective measures to meet them; and about the U.S. interest in being as cooperative as it reasonably can when American action or acceptance may help.

Canadian policies are almost never directed against the United States or its interests. They are directed toward strengthening a country of middle rank, not yet fully industrialized and competing with difficulty with both much larger and more integrated economies and much smaller and less costly ones.

It is vital, too, that the United States should understand the reality that Canadian policy and attitude in foreign relations cannot be blindly supportive of its own. The attitudes and concerns of a power of modest scale are bound to be different from those of a superpower aware of its might and its world responsibilities. At times the absence of real power may lead to apparent irresponsibility, but, equally, at times the possession of great strength may lead to overly aggressive and combative positions. Canadian policy will inevitably reflect the values of the country from which it emerges. It will have to bridge many internal differences and be seen as validly expressing the general Canadian interest. If history and the logic of physical facts and human sympathies are any guide, that interest on the great issues of world affairs will not be in conflict with the fundamental concerns of the United States.

The periodic noises in the North American attic do not indicate that the roof is about to come off. The family upstairs has its problems from time to time, but it will manage them as it has in the past. It may, however, once in a while require a special degree of understanding and an extra bit of accommodation from the householder below.

J. L. Granatstein

2

Cooperation and Conflict:

The Course of Canadian-American Relations since 1945

The relations between Canada and the United States are as close as those between any two nations on earth. Citizens of the two countries travel freely in each other's territory, eat the same food, read the same magazines, watch the same movies, and wear the same fashions. The economies are intertwined in a thousand different ways, and each is the largest customer of the other. On a personal level, relations are invariably close and warm. But on a government-to-government level, there are inevitable frictions and concerns, and sometimes they create substantial irritation. This chapter will focus on the difficulties in the relationship in the four decades since the end of World War II.

1940 to 1945: The War Years

"There has been the open exchange of confidence between the Americans and Canadians," two Ottawa officials who had spent much of the war working on North American defense and eco-

JACK LAWRENCE GRANATSTEIN *is a professor in the Department of History at York University, Toronto. Dr. Granatstein has written many books on Canada's political history, foreign policy, and the civil service. He was recently the co-author of* Twentieth Century Canada. *He has also written many articles and reviews for prestigious international journals and periodicals. A noted lecturer, Dr. Granatstein is also the recipient of numerous awards and fellowships.*

nomic questions wrote in an academic journal in September 1945, "the warm welcome, the freedom from formality, the plain-speaking, and the all-pervading friendship." There had been such a high degree of cooperation between the two countries during the war, they suggested, because of "commonsense, a common background of language and culture, and the close trade and industrial relationship." Ultimately, however, the real reason things had gone so well was that "our approach to problems is similar."

In the afterglow of victory, such a rosy view of the North American partnership across the undefended border was more than the stuff of after-dinner speeches; it was, in fact, a largely accurate description of a wartime relationship that had erased a century or more of occasional bitterness and frequent misunderstanding. The Ogdensburg Agreement of 1940, signed on an August day by President Franklin Roosevelt and Prime Minister Mackenzie King, created a permanent defense relationship; it was an event whose significance few failed to notice. In the perilous days after Dunkirk, Canada had recognized that Britain might be defeated and could no longer guarantee Canada's safety against hostile empires. In the circumstances, Canada had no choice other than to look to the United States; for Washington, with the future of the Royal Navy in doubt and North America in potential peril, securing the northern approaches to the United States was essential. The next year at Hyde Park the two nations effectively agreed to pool their war production. This was a far greater boon to Canada, desperately short of American exchange, than it was to the still-neutral United States.

For a brief time in 1940 and 1941 Canada seemed to be Roosevelt's most important friend. But Pearl Harbor put that to an end, and Canada's status slipped as the Great Coalition took shape. Even so, when Canadians wanted something—a seat on some of the combined boards, a role in the Chicago air transport meetings, or adjustments in exchange holdings—ordinarily there was little difficulty in securing a hearing at the highest levels and a willingness to resolve matters to Canadian satisfaction. In part this was because of the general mood accurately described by the Ottawa officials at war's end. Even more, it was a product of the genuine working relationship between "Franklin" and "Mackenzie" and between Canadian diplomats such as Hume Wrong, L. B. Pearson, Norman Robertson, and Escott Reid and their counterparts in the State, Treasury, and War Departments and in a host of wartime agencies. The Canadians knew how the Washington bureaucracy operated; they understood the system; and they had the sympathy and support of the Roosevelt administration as they strove to ease the inevitable frictions that war produced.

From the president on down, the Washington word was that Canada was "okay," and in Ottawa the reciprocal spirit prevailed, although perhaps with a shade more caution and occasional testiness understandable in a sensitive junior partner. For the Canadians, always fearful of Congress and always seeing the Senate and the House of Representatives as uncontrollable wild cards on every issue, administration support was critical. If Ottawa's politicians and officials favored the strongest possible executive branch in the United States—and they did—it was out of simple practicality. In Canada, where the power resided with the prime minister and the cabinet, United States concerns generally were easier to resolve.

1945 to 1957: Cooperation with Caution

Within two years of the peace, Canada was in economic difficulties. The country had offered loans to Britain and to European trading partners out of a combination of altruism and a desire to continue trade. The postwar rush by Canadians to acquire luxury goods, such as refrigerators, automobiles, and jukeboxes from the south and the desire to go to Florida for winter holidays, drained the foreign exchange reserves by late 1947. The result was imposition of stringent dollar-conservation measures, ironically announced the same day that Canada accepted the General Agreement on Tariffs and Trade (GATT), negotiated in Geneva, that produced a general lowering of tariff barriers. The dollar crisis had forced Canada to put restrictions on luxury imports and travel, and a stand-by credit of $300 million had been secured from the Export-Import Bank. Bad as it was, the package of restrictions that was to fall on American exports to Canada was mild compared to "Plan B," which the Canadians had refrained from imposing only on the clearest of understandings from Washington.

These understandings were twofold. Canada had sought and been given assurances that the Marshall Plan, then working its way through a dubious Congress, would include provisions for "offshore purchases." In other words, should Congress so dispose, American funds given to France, for example, could be used to purchase not only American goods and products but also those from offshore countries such as Canada. In this way Canada could export to Europe and be paid with the scarcest of all hard currencies, U.S. dollars. Without such assurances, Canada, a nation that had to export to live, could only lend its overseas customers the money to buy Canadian wheat and minerals, something that worsened the Canadian economic difficulties because of the perennial Canadian balance of payments deficit with the United States. The Marshall Plan understanding, therefore, was crucial to Canadian economic recovery, even though all that Canada had, and all that she could get, was a pledge of administration support. That was worth something, but it was no ironclad guarantee of congressional support. In the end, thanks to the fortuitous spring crisis of 1948—President Harry Truman's request for universal military training, the Czech coup, and alarming messages from Germany—the Marshall Plan and the offshore purchasing provisions whipped through the House and Senate. The Canadians had watched the Truman administration stir up fears about the Soviet Union, and they said nothing, understanding the American motives and knowing full well that their interests could only benefit if the administration prevailed. And Canadian interests did benefit. Marshall Plan dollars, to the tune of more than $1 billion, came to Canada by mid–1950, greatly easing the Canadian dollar shortage.

The second undertaking Canada won from the United States in November 1947 was for a new round of trade talks to go beyond the GATT agreements in reducing tariffs between the two countries. "The intention in Ottawa," John Deutsch, the chief Canadian trade negotiator, wrote to a colleague, "is to try to work out further tariff cuts, particularly in the manufactured goods field, which would make possible a better balance in the enormous one-way trade associated with our branch plants." And as the Americans who attended the first meetings on the trade talks noted, Canada was willing to enter an agreement "even if it necessitated a major readjustment and reorientation of Canada's international economic relations. They feel that Canada must either integrate her economy more closely with that of the United States or be forced into discriminatory restrictive policies" that could cause problems with her major trading partner, the United States.

The Canadian view, as expressed by Deutsch, was that a customs union was politically impossible. As he told the American negotiators and said to a friend, a customs union meant that Canada would "inherit a vast structure of American government policy. . . . Policy would be shaped in Washington. . . ." That would not fly in Ottawa, he believed, whereas a much greater measure of free trade would link Canada to the one powerful economy in the world while still letting it set its own policies. With Europe still in ruins, the only alternative to freer trade with the United States was oligopoly, but that meant turning Canada into a high-cost restrictive economy, and that was a road to disaster.

To Deutsch's surprise, however, the American team proposed a modified customs union, one that would allow each country to maintain separate tariffs against third countries and one that would give both Canada and the United States a special transitional period of five years to prepare their economies for free trade. Canadian manufacturers, in other words, would have five years to modernize and become ready to meet American competition. Deutsch liked this idea, and so did the ministers and officials in Ottawa he secretly briefed. The Americans who proposed the scheme admired their handiwork, one noting that the Canadian government was tending "to the view that Canada's ultimate destiny is inevitably linked to ours and that the integration of the economies which was effected during the war should be continued and developed further." In addition, Woodbury Willoughby of the Department of State added, "The psychological factors favor immediate action. The widespread popular concern over Russian policy will undoubtedly lead to an acceptance of the international political and strategic implications. . . ." As late as mid–March 1948 (although the highest levels of the U.S. administration had yet to be informed of the plan), everything seemed to favor the establishment of the Canadian-American customs union.

But it would not come to pass; fate was against the continentalists. Mackenzie King had been alarmed by a *Life* magazine editorial favoring a customs union, and he began to fret about the political implications. He picked a book off his shelf, Sir Richard Jebb's *Studies in Colonial Nationalism* (London, 1905), and found a chapter called "The Soul of Empire." Would it not destroy the regard in which he was held by Canadians if he agreed to a customs union? Would it not allow the Conservative party to charge that King was selling Canada to the hated Yankees? "I would no more think of at my time of life and at this stage of my career attempting any movement of the kind than I would of flying to the South Pole," the prime minister wrote in his diary. The customs union was dead, shelved with vague words about the possibility of including it under some wider arrangement that might be negotiated into the North Atlantic Treaty, then under discussion. Hence, the zealous concern of Canadian officials for Article II of the treaty, which promised greater economic cooperation among the Atlantic partners. For Mackenzie King, there could be cooperation with the United States, but too close an embrace had to be prevented.

Free trade would not emerge as an issue in a serious way again until the 1980s. To Deutsch, Willoughby, and those who thought as they did, a historic opportunity had been lost. But for Mackenzie King, Canada had been snatched from the brink of the abyss. It is striking that King, at the fag end of his career, still had the power to arrest a movement that seemed to many to serve Canadian economic interests. The cooperative thrust engendered by the war was powerful, but it still could be derailed by King's combination of sentimental Britishism and shrewd political calculation.

But the processes of continental integration proceeded all the same, under both King and his successor, Louis St. Laurent. The shortage of American dollars was perennial, and the integrative effects of Hyde Park and the 1947 agreements were clear. To get dollars, the Canadian government actively encouraged American investment. And the United States, concerned about its diminishing stocks of strategic minerals and metals, particularly after the beginning of the Korean War, looked eagerly to Canada. The result was a massive inflow of American development capital—total American investment in Canada roughly doubled each ten years after 1945—and the great Canadian economic boom. The customs union was a nonstarter but, for all practical purposes, in the era of cooperation, North America was already one economic unit.

1957 to 1963: Anxiety

There always had been economic problems between Canada and the United States. What differed after the war was that defense also became a major subject of discussion and action between the two governments. The Ogdensburg Agreement, perhaps to everyone's surprise, did seem to create a permanent defense relationship. Increasingly, there was cooperation between the armed forces, most notably between the Royal Canadian Air Force (RCAF) and the United States Air Force (USAF), and in the two decades after 1945, training methods, equipment, and attitudes in the Canadian services began to move away from the British style, on which Canadians had been raised and with which they had fought the war, toward the more highly technical and sophisticated American models. The United States had the most up-to-date equipment and methodology, and the Canadian forces wanted both.

But there was also some caution on the political level in Canada. All the U.S. installations built in Canada during the war were purchased at full cost by the Canadian government, anxious lest there be any misunderstandings. There was continuous concern that the Pentagon's defense pressures on Canada were too heavy. There were proposals for a massive air defense scheme in the immediate postwar years even before there was any credible threat to the continent; and in the 1950s, there was a recognized need for massive, expensive radar networks to warn of approaching Soviet bombers. The Americans looked to Canadians as friends but saw them as essentially undefended, and in the nuclear age, understandably enough, Pentagon planners could not accept this. If the Canadians would not defend their own air space and the route to the United States, then Americans would. The result was that Canadians, ordinarily casual about their Arctic territories, found themselves dragged into the modern era. This meant massive expenditures (in Canadian terms) for radar lines, a very large peacetime air defense network (again by Canadian standards), and the ultimately unsuccessful and very costly attempts to produce an all-Canadian supersonic interceptor aircraft—the CF-105 Avro Arrow.

The costs were begrudged, but the Canadian government and people accepted them because they agreed with the basic picture of the world painted in both Washington and Moscow. The Soviet Union was a threat to North America, and North America had to be defended. Even so, the major threat to the free world was through Europe, and Canada would do its part there, too, to the extent of sending a brigade group of infantry and an air division of interceptors overseas to serve with NATO in the early

1950s. Indeed, Canadians tended to believe that they had seen the threat as early or even earlier than the United States. Certainly the first public expressions of the need for a North Atlantic military alliance were made by Canadians. For economic and political reasons, as well as for broad strategic ones, there is no doubt that the Canadian government wanted to see the United States bound to the defense of Western Europe. There was no worry in Ottawa about the Truman or Eisenhower administrations' desire for this; as always the concern was with Congress.

The new Conservative government that took power in Ottawa in 1957 shared some of its Liberal predecessor's views of the world. Prime Minister John Diefenbaker saw the Soviet Union and its allies in demonological terms, had a high regard for President Dwight D. Eisenhower and the United States, believed fervently in the British connection and, if his party's rhetoric in opposition could be believed, would have supported Britain and France during the Suez crisis of the fall of 1956. But Diefenbaker and his party were also nationalists, concerned about the extent of American investment in Canada, troubled about the implications of living in a branch-plant economy, and prickly and sensitive about being manipulated by the Pentagon.

There was a certain irony, therefore, in the way Canada agreed to sign the North American Air Defense Agreement in July 1957. The idea of integrating the air defenses of the continent had been discussed between the two forces since February 1953 when Canada had proposed that a joint military study group be set up to consider the question; after all, that made sense. The Soviet bomber fleet could strike at North America with nuclear weapons, and the defense of the continental heartland was a common problem. By the end of 1956 a plan for an integrated air defense command was ready, one that seemed to take cognizance of Canadian concerns by stressing that the deputy commander would always be from the nation not providing the senior officer. In addition, the overall commander was responsible to the chiefs of staff of both countries, and the chiefs were charged with keeping their governments informed. Canadian governmental concurrence to the agreement was delayed because of the 1957 election and, as the new Conservative minister of national defence recalled, "from the moment I took over," the military "pressed the urgency of getting a decision." An old soldier sensitive to military concerns, George

Pearkes agreed and secured the new prime minister's agreement to North American Air Defense (NORAD), without consideration in the cabinet's defence committee (still not formed in July 1957) or discussion in the cabinet as a whole. So quickly was the decision taken, in fact, that the Department of External Affairs learned about it from the American ambassador in Ottawa and spent the next several months scrambling to catch up.

But if the NORAD decision suggested to Diefenbaker that defense decisions could be taken quickly and easily, there was still much to learn. The Avro Arrow had been under development since the early 1950s. The CF-105 was a highly advanced two-seater interceptor designed to operate at supersonic speeds in the Canadian north and intercept attacking Soviet bombers before they penetrated to populated areas. But the Arrow's development costs escalated alarmingly—estimates by the late 1950s were that the aircraft would cost $12 million each, in contrast to about $2 million for a roughly comparable American aircraft—just at the time that defense strategists were turning their attention to intercontinental missiles and their associated problems. For the Diefenbaker government, there was the certainty that to proceed with the Arrow would cost billions of dollars and would probably vitiate the rest of the country's defense program, which could not afford reequipment of the army and navy if the RCAF's new interceptor drained all the money. On the other hand, there was still need for defense against bomber attack, and, if the Arrow were scrapped, there would be the politically unpalatable but necessary decision to buy American aircraft for the 1960s. Finally, the Arrow project had brought together a highly skilled concentration of engine, airframe, and electronics specialists. If the CF-105 were cancelled, these experts might be lost to the country and more than 25,000 jobs in Toronto would disappear, a serious matter in a time of high unemployment and economic turmoil. The Canadian government tried to sell the Arrow to the USAF and to NATO countries, but there were no takers, and as a result Diefenbaker finally grasped the nettle and closed down the Arrow project. There were the predictable cries of outrage, but the decision was correct. Canada simply could not pay the costs involved in developing a major weapons system on its own.

But Diefenbaker's problems had just begun. When he announced the cancellation of the Arrow in February 1959, the

prime minister indicated that Canada would acquire Bomarc surface-to-air missiles, which, he said, were effective only with nuclear
warheads. At about the same time, the government decided to
equip the Canadian brigade in Europe with Honest John rockets,
again to be nuclear-tipped, and rearm the air division in NATO
with CF-104 aircraft so that they could carry out a strike/recon-
naissance role that involved hitting Eastern European targets with
nuclear weapons. Those decisions were made by the cabinet without much discussion of the implications of adopting nuclear weapons since most ministers were more concerned about weapon costs
than about moral or political implications of the decision.

By the summer of 1959, however, Canada had a new secretary
of state for external affairs—Howard Green, a British Columbian
of long parliamentary service and great determination. Green believed that nuclear war was the great threat to humankind and
was bound to do all he could to reduce that danger. His zeal, his
friendship with Diefenbaker, and the support of his able officers
in external affairs helped to make him a formidable figure in the
disputes that wracked the cabinet and shaped Canadian–United
States relations over the next four years.

In the summer of 1959 there was one sign of what was to come.
An air defense exercise, "Sky Hawk," had been in preparation for
six months. Officials of both countries had arranged a full-fledged
test of NORAD, one that required a twenty-four–hour grounding
of civilian air traffic. When the cabinet learned of "Sky Hawk" in
August, it quickly fell prey to Green's concern that the exercise
was "totally inappropriate and provocative now," largely because
of Premier Khrushchev's impending visit to the United States.
The cabinet refused to agree to the exercise, and it held that position despite the appeals of President Eisenhower and Canada's
own ambassador in Washington. The ambassador, Arnold Heeney,
privately noted that the "Sky Hawk" affair had "come closer to
doing serious damage to the foundations of Canada–United States
relations in joint defence than any other event in my experience."
Certainly the Eisenhower administration never fully trusted Diefenbaker or Green again, and neither did the Kennedy administration.

The new administration arrived with fresh vigor and high
hopes in January 1961. President John F. Kennedy and Prime
Minister Diefenbaker met in Washington for one day in Febru-

ary and again in May in Ottawa. The initial meeting was a success, but the Ottawa talks were a disaster. Carrying briefing books from the Department of State that characterized the Canadian as indecisive, weak, and vain, Kennedy tried to move Diefenbaker too fast on a number of issues, notably nuclear weapons and Cuban relations; Diefenbaker bristled at the younger man's chutzpah. His impressions darkened further when he found, forgotten in a fold in a couch, a memorandum—"what we hope to achieve from this visit"—that urged the president to push the prime minister on these and other issues. To the growing strains between the two countries was now added a personal animus. But too much should not be made of the relations of the leaders as a determinant of policy. In May and June 1962, in the midst of and immediately following a Canadian general election that reduced Diefenbaker's government to a minority position, a speculative raid on the Canadian dollar led to a devaluation, a temporary import surcharge, and a rescue package that was worked out on an emergency basis by Canadian and American officials. Despite the chill between Washington and Ottawa, in a pinch the United States came to Canadian aid.

There was no reciprocity during the Cuban missile crisis of October 1962. Although a special emissary brought word of the crisis to Diefenbaker on the day Kennedy was to make his television address about the Soviet missiles, Diefenbaker delayed any Canadian action. He took a suggestion from the Department of External Affairs and proposed in Parliament that a United Nations mission go to Cuba to investigate the situation, a gesture that implicitly suggested that the American president and his photographs were not entirely honest. In the cabinet, Diefenbaker refused to agree to put the Canadian component of NORAD on alert. The defence minister, Douglas Harkness, explained to his colleagues on October 23 why an alert was needed. But to his surprise, as he later wrote, "the Prime Minister argued against it on the grounds that an alert would unduly alarm the people, that we should wait and see what happened, etc." The cabinet agreed, and Harkness, beside himself, returned to his department to give orders to institute an alert in everything but name. But it was a public announcement that Washington wanted, "to be reassure[d] . . . that we were prepared to fight."

The next day, as the American naval blockade of Cuba took

effect, the cabinet again refused to sanction a NORAD alert. During one meeting, Harkness shouted across the table at the prime minister that "we were failing in our responsibilities to the nation and *must* act, which produced an outburst . . . to the effect that he would not be forced into any such action." But when Harkness returned to his office, he learned that United States forces had been put on DEFCON 2, an alert status that suggested that war was imminent. "I at once went to see the Prime Minister . . . showed him the message and said we just could not delay any longer and, in an agitated way, he then said, 'all right, go ahead.'"

The prime minister's indecision had ended at last, but the Americans did not forget the political delays. The crisis, however, ended quickly when the Russians agreed to withdraw the missiles.

Quite clearly, the striking thing about the Cuban missile crisis in Canada was the unanimity of support for President Kennedy and condemnation for Prime Minister Diefenbaker. The press and the public believed that both men had been tested and that the Canadian had been found wanting. "The main lesson to be drawn from all this," one official in the Privy Council Office wrote, "is that when the U.S. President chooses to psychologically mobilize the American people on the occasion of a serious threat to them, the Canadian people will be drawn up in the process also."

Ironically, of course, Diefenbaker's delays in authorizing the alert did not have much impact. There were no nuclear warheads on any Canadian interceptor aircraft, and the Bomarc missiles, their installations now almost complete, were similarly unarmed. The Honest Johns and CF-104s overseas were also awaiting their nuclear components. What had happened was that the Canadian government had delayed the final decision to accept the nuclear warheads needed to make the weapons system it had purchased effective. Time after time from late 1959, the American ambassador had approached Diefenbaker to urge that the final protocols be signed. However, the prime minister had indicated, time after time, that the hour was not yet right, but that it soon would be. By November 1960, under the influence of Howard Green's pressure to have Canada lead the world to disarmament, Diefenbaker began to say that Canada would not make a decision on nuclear arms as long as progress toward disarmament continued. Kennedy's pressure increased the prime minister's resistance even more, and a growing public response against nuclear war added its substantial additional weight. By the time of the Cuban crisis, Diefenbaker and Green seemed firmly entrenched against taking the weapons they had ordered.

But Cuba changed the equation, and over the course of the next three months the cabinet spent much of its time debating the nuclear question. Cabinet subcommittees pored through the records, looking to determine just how and to what the country was committed. Ministers fought and argued around the cabinet table and schemed in their offices over drinks. Then, external events again interfered. In January 1963 General Lauris Norstad, retiring NATO supreme commander, told an Ottawa press conference that by not arming the CF-104s' weapons, Canada was failing to meet its commitments to the alliance. A few days later, with the Diefenbaker government seemingly on its deathbed and despite divided counsel in his own ranks, Liberal leader Lester B. Pearson reversed his party's opposition to nuclear weapons and told a Toronto audience that Canada had to honor its commitments. A Liberal government, he said, would end the evasion of responsibility that characterized Diefenbaker's policy, "by discharging the commitments [Canada] has already accepted. . . . It can only do this by accepting nuclear warheads for those defensive tactical weapons which cannot effectively be used without them but which we have agreed to use."

Pearson was on sound ground; opinion polls showed that Canadians wanted their forces to be armed with nuclear weapons. But Diefenbaker, usually sensitive to the trends of opinion, still refused to budge. And when he finally spoke on the subject in the House of Commons on January 25, 1963, his speech went in several different directions at once, simultaneously rejecting nuclear weapons while promising to accept them for the Canadian forces in NATO at least. The prime minister, however, had infuriated the Kennedy administration by including confused revelations of the secret negotiations between Ottawa and Washington and recent discussions between President Kennedy and Prime Minister Macmillan of Britain. The American response, delivered January 30 in the form of a State Department press release, was devastating. The release detailed the kinds of weapons Canada had acquired, noted the "inconclusive discussions" that had been held with Canada on arming them, corrected some of the prime minister's more egregious errors of January 25, and then noted with crushing finality that "the Canadian Government has not as yet proposed any arrangement sufficiently practical to contribute effectively to North American defense." As Secretary of State Dean Rusk commented in a later press briefing, "We regret it if our statement was phrased in any way to give offense. The need for this statement, however, arose not out of our making but because of statements which were made in the defense debate in Ottawa." Undoubtedly, as Theodore Sorenson later said, President Kennedy "did not like and did not respect Diefenbaker and had no desire to see him continue in office." What was so revealing was that the Kennedy administration, having reached that decision, was able to achieve its end with a mere press release. For the first time, the power of the United States was directed toward Canada; for the first time, the administration had become actively hostile to a Canadian government. The chill, as Canadian Ambassador Charles Ritchie noted, spread through every department and agency in Washington.

The Canadian government was now in a state of dissolution. Within days the defence minister resigned, the government was defeated in the House of Commons, and a clutch of additional ministers either resigned in protest or indicated that they would not run in the election of April 8, 1963.

In many ways, that election was just as much a referendum on Canadian-American relations as it was a judgment of the Diefenbaker government. The prime minister's desire, expressed to his ministers on several occasions, was to run against the Americans. As one of the ministers noted, "He was convinced he could win an election on an anti–U.S. appeal, and this, to him, was all that mattered." But his colleagues would not go along with this desire, and some threatened to resign if the campaign were overtly anti-American; Diefenbaker had to rein himself in. But material kept falling into his hands, and Diefenbaker was regularly able to focus his oratorical scorn on the Kennedy administration. *Newsweek* magazine did a vicious cover story on the prime minister, so malign in tone that the Conservative campaign sent thousands of copies across the land to rouse a sympathetic response. The Liberals ran a Kennedyesque campaign, sending a "truth squad" after Diefenbaker, issuing antigovernment coloring books, and practicing a gimmickry that, in the strained Canadian mood, left voters with the impression that the Liberals were both too hungry for power and too close to the Americans in style and policy. Diefenbaker also received a copy of a spurious letter from the American ambassador to Pearson, congratulating him on his nuclear policy and offering all possible help; that was useful in a whisper campaign. Most devastating of all, secret congressional testimony was released during the campaign that implied the Bomarcs were useful only because they would draw Soviet nuclear missiles to Canada. Diefenbaker, gleeful over this revelation, somehow managed to blame the Americans and the Liberals for the alleged deficiencies of a weapons system he himself had acquired for Canada.

The result of the election was a narrow Liberal win. Pearson's party elected 129 members of Parliament, compared to 95 Conservatives, and formed a minority government. By a slender margin, the Canadian people had voted to get rid of Diefenbaker, to honor their defense commitments, and for a policy of cooperation with the Americans. American Ambassador Walton Butterworth was pleased at a result that he saw as significant. The election had been about fundamentals, he wrote to journalist Walter Lippmann. "That is why facing up to them was so very serious and why the Pearson victory" was so important. There was no doubt in his mind that Canada's place in the world, and with the United States, was at stake, and that place now had been settled. "At any rate," he added, "the outcome holds salutary lessons which will not be overlooked by future aspirants to political office in Canada."

1963 to 1968: Mistrust

On July 12, 1965, a report prepared at the request of Prime Minister Pearson and President Lyndon Johnson by Arnold Heeney, twice ambassador to the United States, and Livingston Merchant, twice ambassador to Canada, was released simultaneously in Ottawa and Washington. "Canada and the United States—Principles for Partnership" was the product of a study the two men began in the wake of the nuclear arms controversy and the strains it caused. How could such a vicious and public fight be prevented in the future?

Their report suggested one important method. "The gut point

of this report," national security advisor McGeorge Bundy wrote in a White House memorandum, "is that it emphasizes the obligation of Canada to respect the political responsibilities of the United States in the world, and the obligation of the United States to respect the fact that its economic decisions have inevitable and heavy effects in Canada." To Bundy, "This is a very good trade from our point of view, especially as the press will take it as an implicit criticism of Pearson's Temple University speech" calling for an American bombing halt in North Vietnam. And so the Canadian press did take it—denouncing the Heeney-Merchant report in ringing terms for more or less implying that Canadians should keep quiet about American policy. Quiet diplomacy, it seemed, was no longer admired the way it once had been.

Bundy's memorandum neatly encapsulated the Canadian dilemma of the post-Diefenbaker period. As the United States came under increasing pressure caused by the Vietnam War, the competition from the resurgent economies of Japan and Western Europe, and the drain in gold and dollars, its defensive actions had important effects on Canada, its own economy suffering from some of the same problems and its people motivated by a new spirit of economic nationalism. But Canadians also were sometimes very critical of American policy, not least in Vietnam, and no Canadian prime minister could afford to say "ready, aye ready" to every policy and military initiative from Washington. The result was a tension in Canadian-American relations that took form very quickly after the brief euphoria produced by Pearson's victory. A new feeling of mistrust resulted on both sides of the border.

To Ottawa, President Johnson seemed to be so obsessed with the Vietnam War and so trapped in its escalating military effort as to be almost beyond reason. And in Washington, the Canadians were seen as yet another fair-weather friend, always free with advice and criticism but as slow or slower than others in assistance; all aid short of help was not enough.

Perhaps what is surprising is that despite this tension Canada managed to secure exemptions from three American measures designed to fight the balance-of-payments problem. In July 1963 the Interest Equalization Tax appeared to have been sprung on Ottawa without notice. But when a high-level delegation went to Washington, it won its case and an exemption. The same thing happened in December 1965 with the Voluntary Cooperation Program and in January 1968 with the Mandatory Direct Investment Guidelines. These results suggested that when Canadian concerns could be brought forcefully to American attention, they could be ameliorated. They also suggested that Canada, the largest American trading partner and the largest locale for foreign investment, was completely out of mind when policy was formed in Washington. The Canadian case was helped by the perennial balance-of-payments deficit that Canada ran with the United States, which indicated that Canada at least was not adding to the American deficits.

There was an obvious irony. Minister of Finance (1963–65) Walter Gordon was a nationalist who wanted to restrict American investment in Canada and encourage Canadianization of the economy. Nonetheless, Gordon had to send his officials to Washington in 1963 to seek an exemption and argue, as other Canadians would later, that if the United States interfered with the flow of investment capital to Canada, Canadian development would be slowed and Canada would have to cut back on imports from the United States for lack of American dollars. The very nature of the economic relationship was so interconnected, so much a web of interests and interest groups, that no one could pursue a dogmatic case for long.

The same pressures applied on foreign policy questions, especially on the Vietnam War. Canada had a connection with Vietnam through its membership since 1954 on the International Control Commission (ICC) set up by the Geneva Conference on Indochina. With the Poles and the Indians, Canadians served in miserable conditions trying to prevent two warring states and their great power allies from completely destroying a tenuous truce. There was no thanks for this role, particularly when the war intensified after 1963. To cite only one example, Dean Rusk told the Canadian ambassador that when the ICCs had been set up the idea was that the Indians would be neutral while the Poles and the Canadians were expected to be "somewhat partisan." What was the result? "In Rusk's view what we now had was a commission with only one partisan and two neutrals." The ambassador objected: "I did not think we were neutral." Nor was Canada; the Canadian officers on their tours of duty with the ICCs wrote reports of their observations in North Vietnam, and these found their way to the United States. They tried to overlook

American and South Vietnamese transgressions, and they reported the North's. And the Canadian diplomats on the ICC carried messages on behalf of the United States to Hanoi, trying to inform both sides of the intentions and attitudes of the other and, as a result, took blows from the Americans and, when details leaked in Canada, enormous abuse from the press and public for aiding and abetting the American war effort. The Vietnam War destroyed everything with which it came into contact—including trust.

Certainly this was true in April 1965 when Prime Minister Pearson accepted an invitation to speak at Temple University in Philadelphia. President Johnson's "rolling thunder" bombings of North Vietnam had been in progress for a month when the Canadian prime minister, greeted on arrival by a welcoming letter and an invitation from Johnson to visit Camp David, spoke to his audience:

> There are many factors which I am not in a position to weigh. But there does appear to be at least a possibility that a suspension of such air strikes against North Vietnam, at the right time, might provide the Hanoi authorities with an opportunity, if they wish to take it, to inject some flexibility into their policy without appearing to do so as the direct result of military pressure.
>
> If such a suspension took place for a limited time, then the rate of incidents in South Vietnam would provide a fairly accurate way of measuring its usefulness and the desirability of continuing it. I am not, of course, proposing any compromise on points of principle, nor any weakening of resistance to aggression in South Vietnam. . . .

Pearson knew what kind of reaction his speech would elicit. Secretary of State for External Affairs Paul Martin had threatened to resign if the speech were presented as drafted. Martin argued that the speech would destroy Canadian credibility in Hanoi by persuading the North Vietnamese leaders that Pearson had ended his usefulness in Washington. But Pearson's rejoinder was that he was a political leader, many Canadians were upset by American bombing attacks, and he had to say something. Martin stayed, unhappy. Meanwhile Pearson told the ambassador in Washington not to deliver a copy of the speech in advance to the White House. "It was quite deliberately held up," Charles Ritchie said. "It was Mike's own doing. He knew there would be a blow-up."

And there was. At Camp David the next day, Pearson was subjected to a patented LBJ scene. The speech had been "bad," "awful," one that lent support to the president's domestic critics. He was tired of advice from foreign visitors who should realize the efforts he, the president, was making to keep his hawks in line, the people who wanted to blast Hanoi back into the Stone Age. At one point in this monologue, Johnson apparently grabbed Pearson by the shirt front and pressed his harangue nose to nose. Pearson was shaken by the assault, as were all of the Canadian party. In his diary, the prime minister wrote only that "the President is tired, under great and continuous pressure, and . . . is beginning to show it."

What had most offended Johnson was not so much what Pearson had said, bad as that was from his point of view, but that he had chosen to say it in the United States. The Canadian had "pissed on my rug," Johnson said in his usual earthy way. For a year and a half, every Canadian visitor to the White House was given the same presidential message: "Give Lester my best. Tell him I enjoy working with him and tell him that if he's got any more speeches to make on Vietnam, please make them outside the United States." Of course, there was some justice in that reaction and in the advice of a presidential aide who told the Canadian ambassador "the circumstances surrounding the prime minister's speech at Temple were not the kind of enterprise that the president himself would have engaged in had he gone to Canada to receive an honorary degree."

The point of the Temple University speech and its aftermath was obvious. Canadian relations with the United States had improved since the dark Diefenbaker days, but relations were difficult at best, particularly if Canadians ventured to go offside on the great issues of the hour. Exactly as indicated in the Heeney-Merchant report, there were limits, beyond which Canadians could not go. Pearson was the most successful diplomat Canada ever produced, but he was also a politician, and political necessity—and the conviction that American policy was heading into a morass that might endanger the foundations of the Western alliance—had led him to speak out, albeit in a cautious and heavily qualified fashion. With any president other than Johnson, the reaction might not have been so full-throated or explosive. With Johnson, the reaction was such as to lead many Canadians to the view that the United States and the free world were being led by a man who was on the verge of being unhinged by the weight of his responsibilities. Despite the changes in the presidency, the concerns about the quality of American leadership were not to change in the next two decades: at the beginning of 1984 opinion polls showed that 51 percent of Canadians had no confidence in U.S. leadership in foreign affairs.

1968 to 1984: Suspicion

Pierre Trudeau, Pearson's successor, was an unknown quantity when he came into office in 1968. His charisma had been amply demonstrated during the leadership campaign that gave him his position and in the immediately following election; his intelligence had been proven by his academic writings. However, no one knew how Trudeau would survive in the rough-and-tumble of politics. As it turned out, of course, Trudeau proved to be remarkably skillful, a performer of amazing longevity who would retain power for the entire period to 1984, except for the minor accident of 1979. In the process, through administrative consolidation as much as through time in office, he centralized power in both his person and the prime minister's office to a greater extent than ever before. Trudeau had virtually unrivaled power in his own country.

But he was not unchallenged. Trudeau's whole raison d'être for being in politics was to oppose the rise of Quebec nationalism unchained by the quiet revolution of the early 1960s. Although he was ultimately successful in defeating the referendum on sovereignty-association in 1981, Trudeau presided over a quite astonishing devolution of power and tax dollars to the provinces. In effect, the Canadian federation was becoming more decentralized, and that diffusion of power to the provincial capitals made it more difficult for Canada and the United States to resolve bilateral problems. This was not a new phenomenon. There had been disputes between Ottawa and Toronto in the past that complicated hydroelectric power negotiations, and the long and arduous negotiations over the Columbia River had been disrupted by the demands of British Columbia's premier at the beginning of the 1960s. But the degree of tension was different by the mid–1970s, and the sudden emergence of active Quebec "consulates" throughout the United States and the representation of Ontario and Alberta, for example, in Washington were merely one indicator.

To Americans, Trudeau seemed to be both a socialist and a nationalist. To most Canadians, he was more difficult to label. If his National Energy Program, implemented after his return to power in the 1980 election, seemed radical to some in Alberta, it was just and necessary to others in Ontario and only a first step to economic nationalists. If the Foreign Investment Review Agency was an irritant to investors, it was a weak reed to those who worried about the increasing proportion of the economy that was controlled in the United States. And if Trudeau's government seemed to press the United States hard on environmental issues such as acid rain, to many Canadians he had failed to move with equal firmness against Canadian polluters. Trudeau's record, in other words, was not always as nationalist or as radical as it seemed to his critics in the United States or in Canada. What he was, in fact, was a leader whose primary interests were Canada's constitutional and linguistic problems. All other questions were secondary.

Even so, Trudeau spent more time worrying about Canadian-American relations than any president could. To a Canadian prime minister, the United States is always the major concern; to a president, Canada is only one of dozens of issues to be handled. What worried Canadians was how poorly the Canadian issues—and others, too—seemed to be treated.

Part of the problem was the crisis in the presidency. President Richard Nixon initially seemed powerful and shrewd in his exercise of strength, but Watergate brought him down. Gerald Ford, Jimmy Carter, and Ronald Reagan had some strengths in their very different ways, but in the post-Vietnam, post-Watergate era, they had to deal, with varying degrees of success, with an obstreperous Congress that stole much of their power. "Congress," Canadian ambassador to Washington Allan Gotlieb wrote, "has become much more jealous of its prerogatives, far less susceptible to White House pressures. No longer can a President work with only a few senior Congressional figures and expect to get his way with the Senate and House of Representatives." The breakdown in the congressional seniority system and the explosion in the number of committees and subcommittees also complicated the legislative process. The innumerable regulatory agencies in the capital changed almost out of all recognition, either by championing deregulation or by becoming a source of policy initiatives.

In other words, for a country like Canada, operating in Washington has become much more complicated. With a relatively less powerful president and administration, Canada no longer can look to the executive to press her interests with Congress as had been the case, for example, during the 1947–48 financial negotiations. The era of Roosevelt, Truman, and Eisenhower is long past, and even if not as antipathetic to Canadian leaders as Kennedy and Johnson were for part of their terms, a president cannot assist Canada much if to do so means a loss in the administration's bankable credit with Congress. As Gotlieb wrote:

> If the President is to get his way with Congress, he must marshall his forces carefully and, as we have seen with President Reagan, focus on only one or two issues over a given period. Of necessity, this means that the Administration cannot expend much effort on issues of relatively lower priority—or of priority only to a foreign power.

In practical terms, this means that Canada now cannot always get what she wants from Washington. Several times in recent years this has included the ratification of treaties, negotiated over long periods by Canadian and American officials: the East Coast Fisheries Agreement of 1979, the Tax Treaty of 1980, and the Pacific Salmon Treaty of 1983. All were either blocked or amended in the Senate or withheld from the Senate by an administration that feared the outcome. To some Canadians and those Americans who want to see the central power of the federal government remain strong, the failure to ratify demonstrated a grave weakness in the American system of government. John Holmes, the distinguished former Canadian diplomat, for example, wrote of a United States "burdened by a system of government designed for eighteenth-century gentlemen."

But another scholar, Donald Barry, suggested that the failure to secure Senate consent for the treaties was the product of bad preparation and sloppy tactics by the administration. In the case of the East Coast Fisheries Agreement, the Carter administration's special negotiator failed to consult New England fisheries' interests and their senators, and the result, despite combined Canadian and American lobbying, was the treaty's withdrawal. In the tax treaty case, Department of Treasury officials, who had negotiated the pact, were apparently unaware that one provision preempted an act of Congress, which forced a difficult renegotiation of the clauses in question. A similar collapse in the American consultative process also upset the Pacific Salmon Treaty and led to an administration decision not to send it to the Senate. "It is clear,"

Barry noted, "that Canada ought to be able to conduct treaty negotiations with the American government with the expectation that the U.S.A. will meet its commitments." So it is, but it is also clear that the United States is not going to alter its Constitution to meet the concerns of foreigners. It is, therefore, up to the administration to manage effectively its relations with Congress. Otherwise, carefully negotiated treaties, forged after each country's bargainers have made all their trade-offs, are subjected to attempts on the U.S. side to secure additional concessions as the price of Senate consent. This is frustrating and almost inexplicable to Canadians. Because it is not going to change, it does put the onus on Canada to collect its own information on American opinion and attitudes, lobby Congress more effectively, and rely less on administration assurances regarding the Senate. To be fair, however, Canadian frustrations are almost matched by American complaints about the division of powers between the federal and provincial governments, now entrenched in the new Canadian Constitution and unlikely to be altered. Both countries, in other words, must learn to work with the other in the world as it is.

In fact they do. Despite the shouting across the border, the usual course of relations is smooth. Difficulties make the press, but the hundreds of daily discussions on a multitude of subjects that produce agreement do not. Pragmatism, particularly on economic questions, is the order of the day.

It is less easy to be optimistic about questions of defense and foreign policy. To Americans (most noticeably during the Nixon and Reagan administrations) Canada has not always appeared to be a totally reliable ally. Trudeau was considered a virtual neutralist, the leader who cut Canada's NATO contribution in half, the friend of Castro, and the very reluctant supporter of new missile deployment in Europe and Cruise missile testing in Canada. In Trudeau's last days in office, his much publicized "peace initiative" and his visits to East Germany, China, and Moscow produced a frigid response in Washington, which clearly viewed the Canadian leader's actions as letting down the side. But Canadians are not Americans, and they do not look at the world in quite the same way. Opinion polls in Canada showed that, thanks to his peace efforts, Trudeau's party regained much of the public support that it had lost in the last two years of the prime minister's term.

If Canadians looked with favor on their country's peace initiatives, they have generally looked with dismay at American leadership since the early 1970s. Nixon was never popular in Canada, and Watergate seemed to confirm what many feared. Ford and Carter were seen as weak figures by Canadian leaders and the public. Reagan was not admired by Prime Minister Trudeau or by the media. The storm of protest over the American request to test the Cruise missile in Canada was as much an expression of fear over President Reagan's perceived bellicosity as it was a rejection of nuclear missiles. The difficulties faced by the United States, its nuclear superiority gone, have not received much sympathy from Canadians. Whether or not relations will be closer between the governments when Prime Minister Brian Mulroney and his Progressive Conservative government negotiate with President Reagan and his Republican administration remains unclear at this writing. Certainly there were clear signs of a good working relationship when Mulroney visited Washington before and after the September 1984 Canadian election that brought him to power. But there was also substantial criticism in Canada that the Conservative leader seemed to be tying his kite too closely to Reagan's.

Fears of nuclear war are probably central to the current Canadian concerns about the United States (and the Soviet Union), and the suspicions among many Canadians about the wisdom of American policy are the major result. Those fears probably are shared by politicians and officials, although certainly less strongly than by the public. What most concerns the Canadian leadership are the difficulties of operating in Washington as Canada tries to get the consideration and attention she requires. It seems there is no one to assist Canada in securing exemptions from American regulations and no one to work with the bureaucracy and Congress to smooth the path for measures beneficial to both nations.

Richard G. Lipsey

3

Canada
and the United States:
The Economic Dimension

Who Knows What about Whom?

One of the main themes of the Canadian–United States story is the importance of asymmetry, which is illustrated even this early in this chapter. Although it concerns both Canada *and* the United States, most of the introduction concerns Canada because, while most well-informed Canadians know a great deal about the United States, the reverse cannot be said about most well-informed Americans. Thus, background information is needed on Canada, while equivalent knowledge on the United States is common. Indeed, the asymmetry of knowledge that each country's citizens have about the other explains some of the problems that arise between them.

RICHARD G. LIPSEY *is the Sir Edward Peacock Professor of Economics at Queen's University at Kingston, Ontario, and senior research advisor at the C. D. Howe Institute, Toronto. Previously, he was the Irving Fisher Visiting Professor at Yale University. In addition to being an officer of several distinguished professional organizations, Dr. Lipsey served as president of the Canadian Economics Association. He is the author of five books including* An Introduction to Positive Economics *and* Economics: An Introductory Analysis (*with P. O. Steiner*), *both in their seventh editions. Dr. Lipsey is also the author of many articles for eminent journals.*

Canadians hardly can avoid knowing a lot about the United States. The majority of Canada's population is within easy receiving range of U.S. radio and television. Canadians listen to and watch them, read American periodicals, see U.S. films, or pop across the border for a quick weekend visit or just for an evening out. One of the dominant influences is that approximately 80 percent of the Canadian population lives within 100 miles of the Canadian–U.S. border, but only approximately 10 percent of the U.S. population does so. In most places in the United States, there is virtually no Canadian media penetration beyond the mostly sparsely populated border areas. Americans must make an effort to learn about Canada, and, not surprisingly, few of them do so. Indeed, it was only a slight tongue-in-cheek exaggeration that led Willis C. Armstrong of the U.S. embassy in Ottawa to write in 1976:

> The experience of the general public in the United States . . . with their Canadian opposite numbers . . . is very limited indeed. . . . The public is conscious of the fact that there are intergovernmental relations, but sometimes wonders why there is an American embassy in Ottawa, because it is not clear to them that Canada is a country, let alone a foreign country. (*Canada–United States Relations,* edited by H. E. English, 1976)

Armstrong put his finger on the key problem created by this asymmetry of information by later stating:

> This impression of Canada . . . that the "Canadians are like us"—and therefore good people—is one of ignorant friendliness and good will. . . . There is nothing seriously erroneous in the vague, well-intentioned set of perceptions about Canada . . . but it is essentially incomplete in one major respect. It does not recognize the disparity in size between the two countries. Not many Americans recognize that the United States has ten times the population of Canada and that such a disparity between neighbouring countries cannot avoid creating an attitudinal difference between them. Ignorance of this basic fact, coupled with American unawareness of the striving of Canadian elites for some identifiable set of qualities to distinguish Canada from the United States, can lead to misunderstanding. (English, 1976)

Some Fragments of Economic Geography

In terms of area, Canada is much larger than the United States. Indeed, it is the largest country in the world after the Soviet Union. Its climatic and other conditions are extremely varied.

Its extent runs 5,000 miles from the Atlantic seaboard to the Pacific coast. It extends from Windsor, Ontario, approximately the same latitude as northern California and Rome, to well inside the Arctic Circle. Much of the country is virtually uninhabitable. Although the southern portions have a population density comparable to that of the United States, the overall population is much smaller. Furthermore, not only does Canada have no area and no social equivalent of the U.S. South or the Sun Belt, but also she has no Midwest. Between what is sociologically the East in Ontario and the West, lies nearly 1,000 miles of the core of an eroded mountain chain called the Canadian Shield. There, but for the Canadian Shield, would have been the Canadian Midwest. The enormously strong influences exerted on American attitudes by the Midwest are absent from Canada.

Canada and the United States, along with Mexico, form the North American geographic unit. Many, but not all, of the natural geographic boundaries between the United States and Canada run north to south, at right angles to the east to west political boundary. This has an important implication. Canada and the United States have more potential for conflict on resource exploitation than do most other nations whose boundaries follow natural geographical division. A cost-benefit judgment is difficult enough within one country, but it is much more difficult when, as often happens with these two nations, the benefits are all in one while the costs are shared with the other that is "downstream," either literally or figuratively.

To quickly scan the two countries from east to west, the Canadian Maritime Provinces and New England form a natural unit. The narrow belt of heavy population running from Montreal through Toronto to include the peninsula that is southern Ontario is geographically a part of the American Midwest. Toronto, for example, is closer to the enormous population and industrial area bounded by Chicago, Cincinnati, Pittsburgh, and Detroit than are Minneapolis and St. Paul. In sociological terms, however, Toronto and Montreal are not Canada's Chicago; rather they are its New York (or any of several other eastern cities). Although geographically a part of the American Midwest, they are, in American terms, eastern rather than midwestern. Although Quebec and Ontario are known to themselves as the "Central Provinces," they are known to Canadians west of the Great Lakes as the "East." Moving west, past where but for the Canadian Shield the Canadian Midwest would have been, one next meets civilization at Winnipeg. One is now firmly in what Canadians call the West, an area that is the natural geographic extension of North Dakota, Montana, and Idaho. Finally, crossing the Rockies, we come to Canada's Pacific coast, a natural extension of the American Pacific Northwest, whose residents in some ways are closer to the southern neighbors in Washington and Oregon than they are to the often-hated "easterners" from Ontario and Quebec.

From the point of view of natural comparative advantage and realm of specialization, the Canadian Pacific coast province of British Columbia groups with the American Pacific Northwest; the Canadian western, or Prairie, provinces group with the American Wheat Belt states; the Canadian central provinces of Ontario and Quebec group with the U.S. midwestern states and, in some respects, particularly in finance, with New York City and, in other respects, particularly in rural Quebec, with upstate New York.

Some Fragments of Economic History

The development of the Canadian Maritime Provinces was not dissimilar to that of New England. Both regions had economies based largely on the exploitation of natural resources on the ground and in the sea and on related manufacturing industries such as timber products and shipbuilding. At the time of its annexation by England in 1763, New France was a thriving, mainly farming colony with a population of 85,000. After the conquest, that society was left largely untouched by a tolerant English administration. As a result, there was no positive response to two American invasions—the War of Independence and the War of 1812—when the invaders had expected the conquered French Canadians to rise up and throw off their English "oppressors."

English Canada in general, and the province of Ontario in particular, received a great population boost from the influx of refugees from the American Revolution—"Tories" to Americans and "United Empire Loyalists" to Canadians. For Canadians to have a United Empire Loyalist in their ancestry is as prestigious as it is for Americans to have a Mayflower passenger in theirs.

Throughout the nineteenth century, the eastern colonies grew steadily, and Canada was formed with the union of four eastern colonies in 1867. When British Columbia entered later in the decade, its terms of entry included an agreement to build a transcontinental railroad under private ownership, the Canadian Pacific Railroad (CPR). This was built with the aid of heavy government subsidies and government pressure to keep its route as close as possible to the U.S. border for political reasons. This set the tone for much that followed: close cooperation between state and private enterprise stemming from the feeling that Canada was too vast to be tamed by unaided private enterprise and a need to fend off "Yankee imperialism" that already had annexed part of Mexico and was soon to "gobble up" Spain's remaining colonies in the Caribbean and the Pacific.

Early commercial policy was set for the Canadian colonies by Britain and provided substantial tariff protection. Then, in 1846, Britain unilaterally adopted free trade. Alarmed by the loss of Imperial Preferences, the Canadian colonies entered into protracted negotiations with the United States, which culminated in 1854 with the Reciprocity Treaty that allowed free trade in a wide range of manufactured goods. This treaty was unilaterally abrogated by the United States in 1866. Some have argued that the abrogation was an attempt to punish the northern colony for Britain's clear preference for the South in the American Civil War. Others felt that it was an attempt to hurt the Canadian economy sufficiently enough to force her into union with the United States.

Attempts were made in 1869, 1871, and 1874 to get a new treaty, one that the Canadians were willing to extend to a wide range of manufactured goods. The U.S. Senate failed to ratify the draft treaty of 1874, and in the words of J. H. Young:

> an opportunity was missed . . . in 1874 which has not presented itself again. On a number of occasions attempts have been made to reach some kind of arrangement with the United States, but no Canadian government since 1874 has been prepared to include free trade on as wide a range of manufactured goods as that included in . . . [the 1874] draft treaty. (*Canadian Commercial Policy*, 1957)

After the failure of the Reciprocity Treaty of 1874, the new Canadian government of John A. MacDonald instituted the National Policy in 1879. In the words of Simon Reisman, this policy

> was a drastic change in the commercial policy under which the British North American colonies had developed and became a major focus affecting Cana-

dian economic development and industrial structure. . . . The main lines
of the protective system then introduced have never since been basically
altered. ("Canada–United States Free Trade," a paper delivered to the Conference on U.S.–Canadian Relations, The Brookings Institute, 1984)

For Canadians, the question "what if Canada had stayed with
free trade or at least with a relatively low, nondiscriminatory
tariff?" is one of the great issues of historical "might-have-beens."
Not surprisingly, disagreement on this question is rife.

Canadian economists W. A. Easterbrook and H. G. Aitken view
the effects of the National Policy as beneficial and state, "The protective tariff . . . rounded out a broad, consistent, and comprehensive programme of national planning." Where a tariff kept out
foreign products, they argue, it encouraged domestic manufacturing; where it did not, tariff revenue was generated to help finance railway construction. Either way, Canada was better off
than before. Canadian economist John Dales, on the other hand,
concludes that protectionism was a mistake since "we would have
been better off . . . if we had never tangled with the National
Policy." He argues that high tariffs prevented the economy from
fully realizing the gains from Canada's comparative advantage in
natural resource industries, that the fifteen-year period following
the introduction of the National Policy was one of slow growth,
and that substantial emigration of Canadians to the United States
occurred. Those who feel that the National Policy was a mistake
believe that prosperous resource-based industries would eventually have provided the risk capital to finance the growth of successful manufacturing industries able to stand on their own in
competition with American industry.

One unsolved issue concerns the merits of the model of static
comparative advantage to analyze this issue. Economists such as
Gunnar Myrdal and Francois Perroulx have emphasized the key
importance of "poles of attraction"—the tendency for an agglom-
eration of economic activity to grow spontaneously by pulling in
labor, capital, and entrepreneurs from elsewhere once it passes
critical size. This has some affinity with ideas of dynamic comparative advantage in vogue in the 1980s. According to both of these
views, small and peripheral areas, such as those then to be found
in Canada, tend to remain small and peripheral areas unless either
natural forces or public policy pull them past the critical size
where they become poles of attraction themselves. In this view,

the National Policy may have been critical in creating embryonic poles of attraction in Canada. Whatever else it did, the National Policy sowed the seeds of division between Ontario and Quebec, whose high-cost manufacturers received protection, and the resource-based western provinces, who were denied cheap manufactured goods that would otherwise have been available for import from the United States.

In 1911, the two countries succeeded in negotiating an agreement for a substantial lowering of tariffs on trade between themselves, this time at the Americans' initiative. But, before the agreement could receive legislative ratification in either country, a Canadian election intervened. The U.S. trade agreement was a major election issue, in which the Conservative opposition used the slogan "No Truck or Trade with the Yankees." The defeat of the Liberal government was taken as an expression of public opinion against freer U.S. trade.

In 1931 Britain abandoned the century-long policy of free trade and adopted the system of Imperial Preferences that kept tariffs low within the commonwealth and empire, but raised them elsewhere. Reinforcement of the National Policy was one motive for Canada's acceptance of this system. It raised tariffs against the United States and further encouraged the establishment of U.S. branch plants inside Canada to avoid the tariff not only on sales to Canada, but also to the entire British Empire, which included nearly one-quarter of the world's population at that time.

From the time of the National Policy until the end of World War II, both Canada and the United States prospered and grew along a rising secular trend while suffering similar bouts of alternating prosperity and slump over the business cycle. Both countries suffered severely during the Great Depression of the 1930s and both enjoyed prosperity during and immediately after World War II. Until the war, Britain had been Canada's most important trading partner. In 1938, for example, 40 percent of Canada's exports went to the United Kingdom while only 23 percent went to the United States. After World War II Canadians saw their increasing links with the United States as a symbol of their growing independence from the United Kingdom. Ironically, Canadian nationalists, who now fear the U.S. links, then welcomed them as a symbol of independence. More American investment meant less British investment, and a Canadian dollar tied to the U.S. dollar was a symbol of independence that took the Canadian dollar outside of the then far-flung Sterling Area.

Another important move in trade policy came in 1948 when a free trade arrangement was discussed at length and came as close as anything since the Reciprocity Treaty to producing free trade between the two countries. There seems, however, to be some disagreement on how much of the failure was due to the personal power of Prime Minister W. L. Mackenzie King or how much was due to an antagonism to the idea among the electorate to which that consummate politician was merely responding and on how much chance, in any case, the measure really had in the United States, once it was taken seriously there.

In the 1950s and 1960s both countries grew and prospered. Relations between them were reasonable, although major issues of concern and friction did exist. The tenor in Canada was internationalist, and Canadians tended to see imported capital as the vehicle to propel Canada to its manifest economic destiny. Public opinion polls showed no overriding hostility to American capital imports in the first twenty years following World War II.

Starting in the early 1950s, Canada for the first time admitted large numbers of immigrants from areas other than the British Isles. The Canadian social and economic fabric underwent changes that were in some ways similar to those that occurred in nineteenth century American society when waves of non-British immigrants transformed that society. Today, Canada is a multiracial society, although the ethnic origin of 45 percent of the population is British or Irish, as compared to 10 percent in the United States.

Canada's 1983 gross national product (GNP) of $385 Canadian was 9.4 percent of U.S. GNP, making her per capita GNP about 88 percent of U.S. per capita GNP. Because of her high degree of integration into the North American economy, Canada does a large amount of foreign trade. In 1983, 26 percent of Canadian GNP was exported, while only 9 percent of U.S. GNP was exported. In that year, 63 percent of Canadian exports were sent to the United States, while only 22 percent of U.S. exports went to Canada. Canadian exports to the United States are dominated by primary and energy products (plus automobiles due to the auto pact), while U.S. exports to Canada are dominated by nonprimary products.

Large Country, Small Country

The Canadian economy is only about 10 percent of the size of the U.S. economy. For trade with the United States to disappear would be an absolute disaster for Canada; for trade with Canada to disappear would be a very serious, but quite surmountable, problem for the United States. Similarly, the United States is the preponderant military power and diplomatic force in the Western world, while Canada is but a very small player in the world of international politics without even the strong moral position as an "honest broker" she enjoyed in the halcyon days when Nobel Peace Prize winner Lester Pearson represented Canada abroad. To the United States, Canada is just one of many trading partners and free-world allies. To Canada, however, the United States is an omnipresent colossus. It takes the bulk of Canadian exports and provides the bulk of Canadian imports and is an enormous presence in all dimensions. This size disparity has important impacts on policy.

IMPLICATIONS OF THE SIZE DIFFERENCES
FOR GENERAL POLICY

On one hand, for Canada, policies toward the outside world are largely policies toward the United States. Such policies are not determined just by generalized political and economic considerations but, instead, are policies toward a single, giant country whose presence always is obvious and with whom many Canadians have a love/hate/fear relationship. Of course, the proportions of love and hate and fear vary among individual Canadians, but the asymmetries of these relationships make Canadian attitudes—and, hence, Canadian policies—toward the United States much more complex than are U.S. attitudes—and, hence, policies—toward Canada. On the other hand, U.S. policy toward Canada is just a part of general U.S. policy toward its allies and trading partners. The United States is concerned mainly with maintaining normal relations with its best trading partner and the home of the largest slice by far of its foreign investment. As Willis C. Armstrong put it:

> The United States normally waits to see what Canada is going to do, decides whether the action or policy is likely to be injurious to some specific United States interest or policy, and acts accordingly. The reaction of the United

States is seldom sharp, but if it is, there is usually a good reason. In rare instances there is a United States initiative on a bilateral matter or on some global issue. . . . It takes a lot of patience for American officials to deal successfully and sympathetically with Canada. Canadian officials are tough, competent, well-organized, and briefed. . . . The United States suffers the disadvantage also of being ten times as big, and North America is always for the little guy. If the United States were to use its economic power to cow the Canadians, it would immediately suffer major psychological damage and not be able to carry through with its muscle. So American policy is normally reactive, nonaggressive, and patient. (English, 1976)

In the past there was something of a special relationship with Canada in U.S. policy according to which if the United States adopted some policy for global reasons, Canada could, if she were willing to make special representations, gain an exemption from that policy. There was also the tacit understanding that such representations would be low-profile, behind-the-scenes discussions that would not involve public political posturing. The special relationship was manifested in Canada's exemption—after some special pleading—from several measures the United States imposed in the 1960s in an attempt to help its deteriorating balance of payments. The relationship broke down in 1972 when the Canadians—for reasons they thought good at the time but which, in retrospect, they might have been wise to ignore—refused to take part in a series of bilateral talks proposed by the Nixon administration between the United States and various key trading countries. The talks were intended to outline a new payments system that might emerge from the wreckage of the fast-collapsing Bretton Woods system.

Today, Canada is just one of many foreign countries that concern U.S. policy makers. Proximity is important, and, as a result, Canada probably receives more attention than would a more distant country of similar size. The other reason for special attention is that Canada receives a large portion of U.S. foreign investment, and Americans worry about precedents set by Canadian policies that depart from the rules of the game with respect to foreign capital. This makes Canada's aberrant behavior, when it occurs, of particular concern to Americans.

IMPLICATIONS OF SIZE DIFFERENCES FOR MACROPOLICY

One important aspect of the big-country/small-country situation is seen in macroeconomic policy. On one hand, U.S. policy makers set their policies with their own objectives in view. Before the 1960s, American macropolicy could be understood largely in terms of a closed-economy model. With the breakdown of the Bretton Woods payments system in the early 1970s and the growth of world trade that followed on the rounds of the General Agreement on Tariffs and Trade (GATT) tariff reductions, international considerations began to matter more in the setting of U.S. macropolicies. Even then, however, Canada remained but a small thread in the overall foreign fabric that provided the backdrop to American domestic macropolicy.

Canadian macropolicy, on the other hand, has been conditioned by, and often totally dominated by, the U.S. stance at the time. Canada is close to the economist's model of a small open economy so that, in periods when the Canadian dollar was pegged to the U.S. dollar, Canada had little scope to operate an independent monetary policy. Indeed, many observers spoke of Canada as the "Thirteenth Federal Reserve District" and of the Bank of Canada as the "Thirteenth Federal Reserve Bank." Although this was merely a graphic way of describing what economic theory showed to be the situation of *any* small open economy, Canadian nationalists found it particularly galling to be described as an adjunct of the U.S. monetary system. When the Canadian dollar was pegged to the U.S. dollar, the Canadian rates of inflation and interest were tied very closely to those of the United States.

In the periods 1955–61 and from 1969 on, Canada maintained a regime of fluctuating exchange rates. This allowed Canada to obtain a certain amount of independence in its macroeconomic policy.

As was well established in economic theory by that time, floating rates gave Canadian monetary policy some freedom to take an independent line from that taken by its dominant trading partner. For example, the stagflation that accompanied the first Organization of Petroleum Exporting Countries (OPEC) price shock in 1974–75 was handled very differently in the two countries. The United States followed a contractionary fiscal and monetary policy that put the economy through a serious recession and halved the inflation rate quickly. Canadians avoided such a contractionary policy and experienced one of the mildest recessions of all of the Organization for Economic Cooperation and Development (OECD) countries but still left the inflation rate in the two-digit range.

Then, in the early 1980s, the Bank of Canada chose to follow the United States into the severe American monetary contraction that drove interest rates to the highest levels in modern history and precipitated the most severe recession since the 1930s. The positive result of this policy was the breaking of a seriously entrenched inflation. The exact motivation of the Bank of Canada is unclear, but, whatever its motivation, by hitching its monetary policy to that of the Federal Reserve, the Bank of Canada was able to break inflation in Canada, reducing it from the two-digit level to the 3.5 to 4.5 percent range within two years.

Canadians had two very strong worries about this policy. Many complained that the high interest rates were caused by U.S. policy. They called for much lower rates than ruled in the United States. Indeed, evidence shows that although Canadian rates are not determined totally by U.S. rates, and frequently diverge by two or occasionally three percentage points from U.S. rates, the realities of international capital markets require that Canadian rates cannot deviate further than that band of plus or minus two to three points on either side of the U.S. rate. But some Canadians, faced with interest rates that rose to the truly incredible height of over 20 percent in the early 1980s, called for a Canadian policy to set interest rates that totally diverged from U.S. rates. Thus, the call went out for "made-in-Canada interest rates." When international economists pointed out that, given modern capital market integration, such a major divergence of rates was impossible, many nationalists saw this as a sellout to American interest rather than as mere recognition of the facts of economic life.

The second Canadian worry was that the woes of her very serious recession were imposed on the economy by American policy makers. This view was aided and abetted by a Canadian administration that was content to let the Bank of Canada make antiinflationary policy for it and then avoid responsibility by claiming that the recession was not of its own making. In the end, the inflationary spiral was broken, although it took a year longer to do so in Canada than in the United States because Canadian inflationary inertias proved much stronger than those in the United States. Thus, the policy of restraint proved its worth by lowering an inflation rate of over 12 percent at the beginning of 1983 to below 4 percent by mid–1984. Nonetheless, ignorance of the complexities of cutting entrenched inflation caused general confusion, which, combined with the administration's pusillanimous refusal to admit that it had tacitly approved the Bank of Canada's antiinflationary policy, led many to blame the United States for imposing recession on Canada.

The generally poor level of economic sophistication on the part of both the Canadian public and media has two important results. First, it particularly causes the public to blame the United States for situations that really are the result of Canadian decisions to follow rather than resist U.S. policies, even when independent policy stances are possible. Second, it leads some Canadians to blame Canadian policy makers for following U.S. initiatives in cases where there is no choice but to do so (e.g., with interest rates where capital market integration holds Canadian interest rates within a narrow band around American rates).

BEHAVIORAL RULES SUGGESTED BY SIZE DIFFERENCES

In 1981 Canadian foreign policy expert Rodney Grey suggested two rules that should influence economic policies of large and small countries. The first states that "for a small country surrounded by larger countries and heavily dependent on trade with one of them, foreign policy should, in major part, be trade relations policy." Trade issues are survival issues to a small, open economy such as Canada, and foreign policy is concerned with survival issues. Other more intellectually attractive issues, such as nuclear disarmament, the "North-South issue," and the "Middle East question," often preoccupy Canadian policy makers. But, since Canada can have but marginal influence on these questions, to make them the *prime* concerns of foreign policy is little short of intellectual indulgence. Of course, when the opportunity arises to influence a big political issue, it should be grasped. Similarly, when a strong moral issue arises, the war in Vietnam for example, Canadian policy makers should sometimes take a stand, even when commercial interests may be hurt. According to Grey's dictum, however, all of Canada's bargaining capital should not be exhausted in taking strong political stands that hurt, rather than help, commercial interests.

Grey's second dictum indicates that for a large country carrying the lead in international diplomacy, trade relations policy will to some extent be used as an instrument of foreign policy. He supports this second point in the following words:

It is important to realize that, in the United States, trade relations policy (at least until the Trade Act of 1974) was used as an instrument of foreign policy. This was the case when President Roosevelt and Cordell Hull, his Secretary of State, launched the Reciprocal Trade Agreements Program; it was an element of Roosevelt's "good neighbor policy". . . . It was also the case [with] . . . the Kennedy Round of [GATT] negotiations. That negotiating round was to be a part of the "Grand Design" for strengthening Western Europe and the Atlantic Alliance. (*Trade Policy in the 1980's,* 1981)

Both dictums make good sense, but the one for the small country is often violated by Canada for two reasons at least. First, Canadian policy makers at times have found themselves out of sympathy with U.S. foreign policy and have felt it necessary to take independent stands irrespective of any harm it may do to their commercial relations with the United States. This has been true, for example, with Canada's early recognition of the communist government in China and Canadian policies on the sale of wheat to the Soviet Union, the building of the trans-Siberian pipeline in the 1980s, and toward Cuba and Central America. Second, and more important, because of the threat of the apparently overpowering presence of its giant neighbor, much of Canadian economic policy has been directed toward the presumed need to protect Canada's cultural and political identity rather than to maximize her economic well-being. This has led to a number of policies whose narrow economic values are debated in Canada and seem economically harmful to the United States, even though their underlying purpose is noneconomic.

To Grey's two normative dictums a third, more positive one, might be added: for a small country concerned with maintaining its political and cultural identity, trade relation policy, willy-nilly, becomes foreign policy. The tension between what Canadian trade relation policy should be by Grey's first dictum and what it is forced to be by the government's noneconomic objectives constitutes a major part of the explanation of how Canadian–U.S. relations have developed throughout history.

Different Institutions

If differences of size are the major theme of Canadian–U.S. relations, then different institutions are an important minor theme. Since most people are accustomed to thinking of nations as people,

British parliamentary procedures need little explanation even to those who do not understand their technical details. What is important about the British system, used in most of the English-speaking world outside of the United States, is that cabinet decisions are, with rare exception, passed by the legislature. Thus, agreements between negotiators or relevant ministers become laws in due course—provided only that the cabinet is willing to resist outside pressure to change its stance. However, this is not true in the United States. Many Canadians, including some politicians and senior civil servants who should know better, do not understand American procedures. Instead, they interpret outcomes as if they were produced by the British parliamentary system, causing incomprehension, at best, and destructive antagonism, at worst.

THE "NUISANCE-MAKING VALUE"

For example, after a long period of negotiation in 1979, the two countries signed a treaty that resolved their East Coast fishing disputes. Subsequently, key U.S. senators from the New England states objected to provisions of the treaty, and, fearing rejection, the Reagan administration withdrew the treaty from Senate ratification debate. Understandably not too well informed on the details, the Canadian public regarded this action as another example of the difficulty of negotiating with a country whose separation of powers made consistent behavior difficult to achieve. Indeed, for many Canadians, the failure of the East Coast Fisheries Agreement was a watershed in their reaction to the United States, and a sense of betrayal and futility about the normal bargaining process was expressed frequently by Canadians in all walks of life.

A more informed view, however, suggests that the failure was partly bureaucratic. It has been argued that American negotiators had failed to keep informed on the probably legitimate and certainly strong objections of local interests. A long time before the treaty was signed, informed people were saying that it would never pass in the Senate. Those few Canadians who knew this then blamed Americans for failing to foresee the objections. Americans who knew what was happening, however, say that any reasonably effective Canadian "ear-to-the-ground" in Washington would have detected the opposition, and, therefore, the surprise was as much a fault of the Canadian foreign service intelligence as of the American negotiators.

Another fact, apparently unknown in Canada, that suggests that

some Americans were aware of impending congressional resistance
was that the Canadians were offered a less hazardous route than
signing a treaty. According to the U.S. Constitution, negotiations
such as those concerning the East Coast fisheries can end in either
a *treaty* or an *executive agreement*. A treaty is reviewable by the
Senate in every detail, but an executive agreement comes to the
Senate for only a yes-or-no vote. In principle, the latter is less permanent—although it is doubtful how important this is in practice.
Presented with this choice, the Canadians elected to take the more
hazardous route of a treaty that, in any event, failed. To see the
internal memos on this decision would be of interest. Did the Canadians have any idea of the low chance of Senate acceptance? If
not, where was the failure of communication? If so, why did the
Canadians decide on such a hazardous route and then feel so bitter
when the hazards proved real?

Most Canadians only seem to know that the treaty failed and
blame some combination of American individuals and the American system. Not long ago, for example, a senior Canadian who had
negotiated with the United States on other matters was heard to
refer from the lecture platform to the "nuisance-making power of
the Senate," using this treaty failure as his example. To Americans, the power of the Senate to review treaties is a bulwark of
democracy; to Canadians such as this negotiator, it is a nuisance
that inhibits efficient management of international relations. As
long as Canadians persist in their smug view that their institutions
not only are superior but also the natural ones against which all
others should be judged, this sort of heat-generating confrontation
will persist.

But in the spectrum of Canadian opinion, "nuisance-making
value" is a mild view of the Senate's place in this sorry matter. A
typically extreme view was expressed in remarks to the Toronto
Canadian Club in 1984 by Michael Pitfield, one of the two or
three most influential powers-behind-the-throne in the administration of former Canadian Prime Minister Pierre Trudeau.

> Surely, we have had enough of situations like the autopact, the fisheries
> treaty, and the Alaska pipeline, where the vicissitudes of the American con-
> gressional system are used as justification for the American government
> backing out of its commitments or twisting our tail for further concessions.

Is it more frightening for a Canadian who wants reasonable relations with the United States to think that Pitfield is as ignorant

of the American system as the quote suggests, or to believe that he was playing to the crowd even this far after the event? Either way, these remarks reveal the mind set of those who guided Canadian economic policy through the 1970s. It would be interesting, for example, to learn what Pitfield meant by "the American government," because he apparently does not include the Senate since that body makes no commitment when U.S. negotiators sign a treaty.

The division of powers under the American Constitution has always meant that carefully negotiated compromises in treaty drafts may be "second guessed" and reopened by the Senate in ways not done by the Canadian Parliament. What is new in post-Watergate Washington is not only a shift of power from the administration to the Congress but also a more unruly atmosphere in Congress where committee leaders are not always as powerful as in the past. This is a fact of life, and Canadians have to learn, as the British did long ago, how to work tnrough Congress themselves rather than to expect the American administration to do their work for them. In this view, the failure of the East Coast Fisheries Treaty was the sort of transitional problem that could be expected to arise while the administrations of both countries learned to work with changing procedures. If so, it is a pity that so many Canadians see it otherwise—the outcome of a deep and enduring flaw in the American system.

Indeed many of the details on the list of grievances against the United States in commercial affairs are complaints against the operation of a system that Americans with some justice regard as a manifestation of real democracy. They have nothing to do with what should be the true focus of grievances—objectionable matters that are the result of real policy decisions that could be changed, not the result of the given underlying structure of the system.

One fixture common to both countries is the division of governmental powers between their central governments and the governments of the American states and the Canadian provinces. Although the individual states have less power under their Constitution than do Canadian provinces under theirs, both have sufficient power to exert substantial influence on international economic relations. The central government legislators and administrators of both countries have been surprised and upset on occasion when agreements made with their opposite numbers ran afoul of state or provincial opposition. Furthermore, states and provinces have recently been exerting substantial efforts to increase nontariff barriers to trade by such techniques as "buy-locally" laws.

The U.S. Policy Stance

Basically, the Reagan administration advocates, in principle, more freedom of movement of trade and capital. There can be no doubt that the United States has been a potent force in that direction since World War II and that decades of American administrations genuinely have believed in and been willing to urge more freedom of world trade. However, with respect to world trade in general and Canadian–U.S. trade in particular, there are several worries.

First, the changes in commercial policy tools following the Tokyo Round of the GATT negotiations led to a new burst of protectionism. In particular, countervailing duties aimed at other countries—often those of the European Economic Community (EEC)—have affected unintentionally, and sometimes severely, Canadian–U.S. trade. The perception of many in the American trade policy community that GATT rules are not being enforced properly and, therefore, that the present international trading order works to their disadvantage may or may not be correct. But, it was a viewpoint that began to shape U.S. trade policy in the mid–1980s along quite different lines from previous decades, a change that may bring about considerable turmoil in international trade. It could lead to a sequence of retaliatory actions between the United States and other countries that increases rather than decreases the degree of economic distortion in world trade. For example, in 1984 the EEC announced an increase in its export subsidy on wheat flour as a response to the export subsidy on wheat flour provided by the United States. The U.S. subsidy itself was introduced to offset the trade advantage in third markets obtained by the EEC because of its export subsidies, and thereby to induce the EEC to reduce its export subsidies on agricultural goods.

Second, the overvalued U.S. dollar has kept the exposed export- and import-competing industry sectors of the American economy under heavy pressure throughout the 1980s. This policy resulted in an upsurge of protectionist sentiment in the Congress and many state legislatures, which passed some "buy-American" legislation harmful to Canadian–U.S. trade.

Third, U.S. authorities are unhappy about many nationalist economy measures passed in Canada during the period of the Liberal government from the 1970s to the 1980s. While they recognized a sovereign country's right to control foreign investment, Americans argue that Canada's particular policies have violated seriously two of the major rules of the international investment game. Under the National Energy Program (NEP) Canadians changed the oil exploration and production rules retroactively to confiscate some profits of foreign oil companies, which reduced those companies' book values significantly and gave incentives for Canadian companies to purchase the foreign companies at what seemed to be bargain prices. The principle that foreign capital once in place should not be subject to discriminatory changes in applicable rules was violated. Another major culprit was the Foreign Investment Review Agency (FIRA). Established during the early 1970s to review all new foreign investments in Canada, in practice the FIRA often extracted enforceable commitments from many foreign firms admitted to Canada—commitments regarding employment, purchase plans, and exports—that were not required of Canadian firms. This violated a rule that foreign firms, once admitted, should be treated similarly to all other firms in the market, including domestic firms.

The United States is also concerned about Canada's agricultural safeguard system, which imposes a variable import levy when Canadian producers may be affected by relatively low domestic prices. There is further concern about Canadian quotas on egg imports and possible subsidies on egg exports. The United States is worried also about export credit subsidies offered by the Canadian governments. The extension of Canadian customs jurisdiction to the 200-mile limit, which involves levying tariffs on oil-drilling ships and equipment operating beyond the 12-mile limit, is a further source of friction between the two governments.

One further general concern, which would plague free trade area negotiations, is the Canadian need to aid poorer provinces. Equalization grants from the federal government to provincial governments with lower than average incomes are written into the Canadian Constitution. Beyond that, many subsidies and grants-in-aid are given to encourage industries that create jobs in poorer provinces. To Canadians these are an expression of an egalitarian ethic; to Americans they seem to be unfair subsidization of local industries that often compete with American imports and may also export to the United States.

By and large, however, in so far as its northern neighbor is noticed at all, American administrations can be seen to be trying to devise policies that will allow market transactions—which are normally assumed to be mutually beneficial—to take place in a relatively unimpeded fashion between the two countries.

If there is an American failure in working with Canadians, most likely it lies in the difficulty that even sophisticated Americans have in understanding the intensity of the Canadian desire both to be distinguished from and *seen* as distinguished from the United States. As a small example, Canadians who travel abroad find it galling that Europeans rarely are able to distinguish American from Canadian accents and, as a result, are inclined to regard all English-speaking North Americans as "Yanks." Americans who have traveled abroad never encountered this "national misallocation." Therefore, they find it hard to understand the sensitivities of Canadian leaders who, traveling during their formative years, fought an often-losing battle to establish themselves first as non-Yanks and later as Canadians.

Both countries sometimes have let their differences rise to confrontation. Harold Malgren discussed an example:

> A good example of bad management . . . on both sides of the border, has been the Canadian-American automotive agreement [which integrated the two countries' automobile industries and removed tariffs on the movement of cars and components across the border. . . .] The specific details are not so important as the fact that both sides then chose, and have continued to choose, to take polarized positions in public. The pressures consequently continue and periodically break out in congressional debate. It is a matter of time only until something unfortunate develops because of lack of management of the pressures. (English, 1976)

Canadians, and possibly Americans as well, often have the impression that the larger country has the superior bargaining position and, therefore, more often gets its way in confrontational situations. This is not always the case. Canadian political scientist David Leyton-Brown studied all the cases of conflict between the United States and Canada in commercial policy. He concluded that the outcomes are divided almost equally between the two countries' perceived interests. Even more interestingly, the Canadian government won more than it lost in those cases where the government chose to politicize and polarize the issue in question. (Of course it is easier to politicize Canadian–U.S. issues in Canada, since awareness of the United States is ubiquitous, than to do so in the United States where awareness of Canada is very low.) In spite of this favorable box score on politicized disputes, it does not follow that such a policy is in the long-run interests of Canada. In the long run, politicizing of issues that might have been handled quietly behind the scenes serves to erode the good will that many informed Americans feel toward Canada.

The Canadian Policy Stance

IMPORT SUBSTITUTION POLICY

The National Policy, introduced in the nineteenth century, provides across-the-board protection against imports of manufactured products. When the Tokyo Round of GATT negotiations led to a major reduction of the tariff protection for the local Canadian market, the Canadian government joined the ranks of countries seeking both covertly and overtly to erect nontariff barriers to imports to replace some of the lost tariff protection. The National Policy led foreign firms to establish branch plants in Canada to serve the local market and had a number of effects.

First, for many products the Canadian market is not large enough for plants to achieve complete cost efficiency. Thus, Canadian production is high-cost production with consequent reduction of living standards. Estimates of the cost of the tariff have put the loss in living standards between 5 and 10 percent of Canadian GNP.

Second, since the Canadian market is small, the typical industrial structure is oligopolistic. Not subject to foreign competition, these firms typically do not engage in active price competition among themselves; instead they compete by enlarging their range of differentiated products, which raises real costs of production yet further and leads to prices that are high in relation to the already high costs. Also, the high local costs make export difficult, although not impossible.

The National Policy has been one of import substitution, which uses import restrictions to protect the domestic market for domestic firms. Many developing countries long ago have become disillusioned with import substitution as a growth policy. It protects industries on too wide a front to reap available economies of scale and develop specialized production based on natural or acquired comparative advantage. From purely economic considerations, it is surprising that Canada clings to a policy that many economically less advanced countries already have seen to be counterproductive.

NATIONALISTS AND INTERNATIONALISTS

To understand Canadian trade policy, it is necessary to realize that it has always been pulled by two opposing forces: on the one side, a desire to shield the Canadian economy from various influences associated with the free flow of goods and factors between the United States and Canada; on the other side, a desire to reap a high proportion of the potential economic gains from trade between the two countries.

Two groups with opposing views on Canadian economic policy are the "Canadian nationalists" and the "Canadian internationalists." To understand the friction between these two groups and the influences their ideas have had on policy, it is necessary first to identify what the two groups are *not*. They are not distinguished by either their patriotism or political positions; strong patriots and members of all three of Canada's major political parties can be found in both groups. Most members of both groups value and wish to maintain Canada's political independence and its distinctive culture. They differ on the means to these ends.

Nationalists believe that American cultural penetration threatens Canadian culture, and they seek to preserve their culture by measures designed to restrict this influence. They also believe that Canada's political independence is constrained by activities of American-owned firms operating in Canada and that close economic ties with the United States would make likely Canada's absorption into the American union. Thus, they favor measures that protect the Canadian market for Canadian firms and restrictions on the import of foreign capital. Some also feel that American firms operate to the economic, as well as political, detriment of Canada and believe that protective measures will raise Canadian living standards. Others believe that protective measures lower Canadian living standards but accept this economic loss as a reasonable price for maintaining Canada's political and cultural independence.

Canadian internationalists hold opposing views on almost all these matters. Internationalists believe that Canada's culture and distinctive character are embedded too deeply to be threatened seriously by American cultural penetration. They are inclined to favor a free flow of ideas and free media access across the border in both directions. With rare exceptions, internationalists believe that foreign firms behave much the same as domestic firms and pose no serious threat to Canadian sovereignty or productive efficiency. They also believe that nationalist restrictions on trade seriously lower living standards and are not needed to protect political independence. The highest possible living standard is also, they argue, the best way to keep creative and productive Canadians at home rather than letting them join a "brain drain" to the United States. For all these reasons, internationalists tend to favor liberal trade policies.

THE HIGH TIDE OF CANADIAN NATIONALISM

There has always been a strong strain of nationalism among the Canadian elite. Such Canadians are willing to sacrifice some of the gains from trade and capital movements in pursuit of perceived national goals, although some argue that their restrictions would improve Canadians' prosperity as well as further social and political goals.

Many members of the Canadian elite feel threatened by the colossus to the south. They worry that American culture would so dominate Canada that Canadians would evolve into Americans and join politically with them as the last step in a natural evolutionary process. Many worry about U.S. foreign policy in such areas as Latin America and Vietnam and, wishing to distance themselves from American foreign policy, see commercial distancing as one means. Many worry that Canadian resources are increasingly owned and operated by Americans for their own profit. Many worry that when the chips are down, U.S. branch plants will become the instruments of U.S. foreign policy. Finally, many worry that American branch plants would retard Canadian development by doing research elsewhere, not encouraging exports, and regarding Canadian operations as marginal units of capital to be closed first during recessions and opened last during recoveries.

Nationalists have flirted often with the idea of reducing Canada's economic independence on the United States. For example, in the early 1960s Conservative Prime Minister John Diefenbaker announced a policy of shifting a substantial portion of Canada's trade from the United States to the United Kingdom. However, when the British government took him seriously and pointed out that the only way to do so was through a mutual reduction of tariffs, Diefenbaker reacted with horror, and the whole idea was forgotten quickly. More recently, in the early 1970s the Trudeau government invented the "third option." This option was described by Peyton Lyon as

> a comprehensive attempt to reduce Canada's dependence on its superpower neighbor through intensified relations with third countries, the rejection of further measures that would facilitate economic integration with the United States, and increased state intervention in the form, for example, of regulations to control foreign investment. (English, 1976)

The decade of the 1970s was the high watermark of Canadian nationalism with its accompanying willingness to sacrifice some gains from trade and capital in pursuit of perceived national goals. Then, in the 1980s a reaction set in and, frightened by an apparent loss of Canadian competitiveness in an increasingly competitive world, Canadian policy moved haltingly in a somewhat more internationalist direction.

In 1982 a Senate subcommittee supported a free trade area with the United States. This suggestion was, however, dismissed in a discussion paper issued by the Department of External Affairs. According to the department's document:

> The evidence to date of the need to proceed [with a free trade area] is not convincing nor does a call for free trade [with the United States] command broad support. Most assessments tend to highlight the economic advantages for Canada without taking full account of the costs or consequences both political and economic.

In the early 1980s Canadian initiatives were taken to move toward free trade arrangements in a number of individual sectors. Although American negotiators gave polite attention to this suggestion, as they do to most Canadian initiatives, few informed observers believed that the United States had sufficient interest to fight to reach real agreements to be signed by the negotiators and approved by the Senate. Nor did it seem that such sectoral agreements would be allowed under the rules of the GATT. For this reason, the idea of a free trade area continued to be mooted in spite of its earlier rejection by the Department of External Affairs. Canadians who were worried about Canada's lack of competitiveness in export markets and the failure of the import substitution policy continued to keep the idea of a free trade area with the United States in the arena of public debate.

Although the debate often confused a free trade area, a common market, and a customs union, it is important to note that these are three quite different arrangements. A *common market* is a complete integration of two or more economies not only allowing complete freedom of movement of goods and services, but also complete freedom of movement of all factors of production such as exists within a single, unified country. A *customs union* gives free trade in goods and services between two or more countries, without the necessity of freedom of factor movements, but with a complete harmonization of trade policy with respect to the outside world. A *free trade area* gives a completely free movement of goods and services between two or more countries but leaves each free to establish its own policies with respect to trade with third countries, and, hence, requires the continuation of customs points to control the movement of goods and services between the two countries to prevent goods from third countries entering the high-tariff country via the low-tariff country. The only one of these arrangements that was seriously advocated in Canada was a free trade area.

Arguments for Restricting Trade and Capital Movements

The reasons for Canadian restrictions on trade and capital movements have stayed the same since the National Policy was first promulgated in the 1870s; only the relative emphasis placed on each has changed. What are these reasons, and do they make sense?

NONECONOMIC REASONS

Preservation of Political Independence—In the course of a widely read, four-part article in May 1984, *Toronto Star* reporter Richard Gwyn stated that with free trade, "the mouse and the elephant would become a [single] economic unit, and so, almost inevitably, a single political one."

The originators of the European Common Market, such as France's Jean Monet and Belgium's Paul Henri Spaak, held this view and saw closer economic integration as a first step toward their real goal: political union of Western Europe. So did the Nobel Prize winning economist James Meade who argued that the pressures generated by an attempt at economic union would push the participating countries willy-nilly to more and more political cooperation and eventually toward political union. The Meade view is also stated in the Department of External Affairs discussion paper and is attributed to "many Canadians, including a number of those who would accept the validity of the economic case for free trade. . . ." The present state of national divergences among the countries of the EEC surely shows that economic union does not force political union. If ever an idea was refuted, insofar as any theory about human affairs can be, this one has been. Yet, in spite of strong evidence to the contrary, many Canadian decision makers continue to believe that free trade between Canada and the United States would lead "almost inevitably" to political integration.

Preservation of Cultural Independence—Common among Canadian nationalists is the view that trade restrictions are needed to preserve Canada's culture. However, this stance shows not only a lack of appreciation of the evidence from other parts of the world but also a surprising lack of understanding that a separate Canadian culture exists and that it is more than skin-deep.

First, look at the evidence from other countries. Separate existence in the United States of social customs and values of the South, New England, Texas, and the Midwest, to name but a few, shows that substantial divergences persist even within the common market of a single country. The more relevant sort of integration would be that existing, for example, between the Republic of Ireland and the United Kingdom. In spite of a high degree of economic integration between these two countries, which until the mid–1970s included a monetary union, first outside of, and then within, the EEC, no visitor to Dublin or Cork ever could think it was London or Manchester, or vice versa.

Second, there are deep cultural differences between Canadians and Americans that are rooted in hundreds of years of different national experiences. It is characteristic of Canadian economic *nationalists* to think that Canadian culture is so fragile that it will be destroyed by excessive reading of American periodicals or excessive listening to American radio stations. Of course, the universalization of the media has led to some reduction of many surface cultural differences. This is inevitable in all countries. But these reductions do not come near to threatening basic cultural differences. It is characteristic of Canadian economic *internationalists* that they have sufficient confidence in the depths of Canadian culture to believe it will withstand—as do the British and French cultures—a surfeit of Coca-Cola, "M*A*S*H," *The Empire Strikes Back,* The Grateful Dead, and McDonald's hamburgers.

Preservation of Cultural and Intellectual Activities—The Canadian market is too small to support many activities that can be supported by a nation of over 200 million. If 1 percent of American households want to buy something, that is a market of about a million purchasers. If 1 percent of Canadian households want to buy the same item, that is a market of only about 100,000 purchasers. This means that all sorts of cultural activities will find difficulty flourishing if their appeal is solely to Canadian consumers.

In order to support Canadian culture as a way to establish and preserve the Canadian identity, successive Canadian governments have thought protection necessary. A host of schemes have been used. For example, radio and television stations are forced to allocate a proportion of their broadcast time to "Canadian content," which, in music for example, means Canadian orchestras, Canadian soloists, or Canadian composers. The content rules are quite stringent and can cause problems. In 1984, for example, Canadian cable television companies complained that their inability to compete with other forms of entertainment media was caused partly by Canadian content rules that made them broadcast too much material that had too little audience appeal. Outlets forced to follow this policy had to be protected from loss because consumers clearly preferred more American content. Because of these consumer preferences, a long-standing rear guard action was fought against U.S. penetration. In 1977, Canadian companies advertising on American radio and television were no longer allowed to deduct the expenses for tax purposes. This hit American border radio and television stations very hard, and a great deal of friction was generated. Later, the federal government made television satellite dishes illegal. But this time, consumer resistance was too strong. In the face of a consumer revolt, satellite receivers had to be made legal. Consumers are now permitted unlimited choice between content-regulated Canadian stations and unregulated American ones.

The persistence of such policies in Canada indicates a significant difference in transborder attitudes. Americans usually are willing to trust the market to determine the product. The British more commonly mistrust the market and rely on a degree of paternalism by leading rather than following; the subsidized media are expected to influence standards of taste for the better. In this respect as in so many others, Canadians are somewhere between the British and the American attitudes. Many Canadians are attracted to the British view but feel some substantial unease in its application. No doubt they are aware that the quality of the Canadian Broadcasting Corporation (CBC) is substantially higher than that of American radio, yet they also know that the CBC is a subsidized perquisite for its mainly middle-class listeners. When they collect this perquisite, are they right in saying that the policy is justified as a way of leading style and taste? Or are they merely easing their consciences over collecting a subsidy paid by general taxpayers, many of whom could care less about the CBC's high-level programing?

In another policy move in 1965, advertising placed in foreign-controlled periodicals ceased to be a tax deductible Canadian business expense. (At first, the Canadian editions of *Time* and *Reader's Digest* were exempted; then, after years of acrimonious debate, the exemption was allowed to stand for *Reader's Digest* but removed from *Time*.) This policy argues that Canadian editions of foreign periodicals, such as *Time,* "enfeeble" domestic publications by taking from them a large proportion of the relatively small total of advertising revenue that is available to support Canadian magazines. It also argues that these editions constitute unfair competition because much of their editorial content is high-cost material imported at low cost since expenses have already been covered in the U.S. market. According to Davidson Dunton:

> Canadian concerns and disagreements about magazine editions are probably not understood easily by many in the United States. To many Americans, brought up in the tradition of the First Amendment, any attempt to tamper in any way with activities of any periodical is abhorrent. . . . Most Cana-

dians adhere in general to the same principle, but many also want a reasonable chance for a Canadian periodical press to exist. . . . It is important to recognize that in Canada no voice is calling for restrictions or penalties on American publications entering Canada. . . . (English, 1976)

The U.S. edition of *Time* is still available and widely sold in Canada. Once again it is a matter of behavior required to achieve goals of social policy where, from an economic viewpoint, the market is too small.

There can be no question that the market for Canadian cultural activities would be much less than at present and often too small to support many activities were it not for these policy restrictions. Given the policy goals, many Canadian cultural policies make sense. Nonetheless, there is a thin line between protectionism that helps Canada produce world-standard material and protectionism that merely perpetuates the mediocre.

Consider two examples. For many years Stratford, Ontario, has had a very successful summer Shakespeare festival. In the early years, many stars and directors came from abroad, particularly from Britain. Later, Canadian policy made it more and more difficult for non-Canadians to fill these jobs. Insofar as the policy was fighting an irrational prejudice against Canadians, it made sense. Insofar as it was preventing the employment of the best people, the policy was threatening the future of a highly successful venture. Internationalists argue that the import of foreign talent will help to educate local Canadian talent by setting world standards. They worry that a prohibition on foreign hiring will, in the long run, work to the disadvantage of Canadian performers, since they will not be forced to rise to world standards.

A similar case occurred at universities. Until the 1960s, many of the best Canadian intellectuals were drained to the United States and Britain, particularly in fields outside of the natural sciences. In the 1960s and 1970s, many Canadian departments rose to world standards. Canadians, particularly in the humanities and the social sciences, no longer felt they had to study abroad, and stay there afterward, if they were to compete in the world league. Many Canadian expatriates returned to Canadian universities. The universities were also extremely lucky to be able to cash in on the brain drain from Britain when, in the mid–1970s, a determined attack was mounted by the British government on the living standards of British academics. Then, in the early 1980s, the same nationalist policy that affected Stratford made it nearly impossible to hire foreigners to Canadian academic posts. The danger posed is that removed from the need to compete against world standards, Canadian university standards will fall. How many Canadian university departments have reached a self-sustaining critical mass, even when the stimulus of foreign competition is removed, remains to be seen. Undoubtedly, however, some will fall by the wayside. A policy is hard to regard as successful when it protects the cultural and intellectual activity of a country at the cost of making it second rate.

Preservation of Diversified Economy—Although mainly social, the necessity of restrictions that are needed to preserve a diversified economy also has economic dimensions. There is debate about the long-term effects of the National Policy. Although not everyone agrees, it possibly was needed to establish firmly the infant secondary and tertiary industries. Be that as it may, there is persistent fear among modern Canadians that the only thing that keeps them from reverting en masse to a nation of "drawers of water and hewers of wood" is trade restriction. That view, however, seems to be unfounded. The Toronto-to-Windsor corridor is a geographic part of the U.S. Midwest and is closer to many of the centers of midwestern population than are the twin cities of Minneapolis and St. Paul, which, nonetheless have carved a reasonable economic niche for themselves. Furthermore, Toronto, now one of the great English-speaking cities of the world, is well beyond the critical size needed to create a pole of attraction. As with the East, so with the rest of Canada. Why should British Columbia's strategic location and great beauty of Vancouver, unique charm of Victoria, and natural resources of the hinterland suddenly become different in economic balance from Washington and Oregon—resource-based economies with large superstructures of secondary and tertiary industries erected on the primary bases?

ECONOMIC REASONS

Key Industry Protection—Some feel that barriers are needed to protect employment in key areas, such as textiles, where the entire population of specialized towns could be thrown out of work. It is no doubt correct that textile and shoe industries would be different, possibly smaller, industries were it not for trade barriers in

Canada and the United States. The extent to which the policy of shoring up such declining industries has long-run viability is debatable. In the short term, there is no doubt that such policies are firmly entrenched. However, there is no reason why such embattled industries would not succeed in carving specialized niches for themselves if they were forced into a free trade area with the United States. Many observers would agree with Professor H. E. English of Carleton University when he wrote in 1983 that "the textile and clothing sector concentrated in Quebec would . . . specialize on the basis of access to the [large] U.S. market."

Local Employment Protection—Municipal and provincial governments see local-content legislation as a means to preserve local employment. These forces can be seen on both sides of the border, but they may be stronger in Canada since Canadian provinces have a greater share of total political power than do American states. In Canada, these measures are concerned partly with Canadian versus *foreign* content, but, increasingly, they impose "local-provincial" versus "rest-of-Canada" content. Apparently uninhibited by any knowledge of these policies' eventually self-defeating nature, the moves by Canadian provinces toward local protectionism are ominous. Robert B. Logan of IBM Canada Limited has ironically pointed out that provincial initiatives sometimes force IBM to behave in ways not only contrary to IBM's established practices, but also in the same ways that nationalists accuse foreign subsidiaries of doing voluntarily. He stated:

> Recently I have witnessed several occurrences of both the federal and provincial governments promoting Canadian content in certain procurement situations. This consideration of product content runs directly contrary to specialized missions (e.g., world product mandating that encourages exports but necessitates imports) and indeed discourages them in favor of inefficient branch plant operations. (Working Paper No. 8322C, University of Western Ontario)

Foreign Branch Plants—Some Canadians subscribe to the view that capital must be kept out because foreign firms are not as effective as domestic firms. A series of charges are common. For example, in 1982, Gordon Dewhirst alleged:

> the operations of many foreign-controlled branch plants have been characterized by low levels of research and development, export limitations, and short, inefficient production runs. Moreover, such companies often rely to

large extent on imported technology, resulting in a lack of capacity to develop and undertake the kind of innovation needed to develop products capable of meeting intense competition from other countries in both domestic and international markets.

Many of the costs associated with foreign ownership stem from the "truncated" nature of many of these enterprises; that is, key activities are often performed abroad by the parent or some other affiliated firm. One result is that Canadians have been denied the opportunity to develop the skills or capacities that are needed to support and develop internationally competitive businesses. Foreign-controlled subsidiaries also tend to import components and subassemblies rather than utilize competitive Canadian supplier industries, thus inhibiting the development of those industries in Canada. (*Proceedings of the First Annual Workshop on U.S.–Canadian Relations,* Institute of Public Policy Studies, University of Michigan)

The research and development (R&D) evidence has been studied extensively in Canada. First, according to crude data, Canada indeed does have a lower R&D/GNP ratio than any other OECD country. Some products, however, require less R&D than others, and, normalizing for product mix, Canada appears about average when compared to other OECD countries. Allowing for R&D information that is imported through multinational corporations, Canada surfaces near the top.

Evidence on cost and other measures of performance seems strongly against Dewhirst's view. Although foreign branch plants that operate in Canada seem, in some cases, less efficient than their parent companies operating abroad, this is usually because of the small size of the Canadian market, which prevents full realization of potential economies of scale. The critical factor is that Canadian branch plants are neither more nor less efficient than comparable Canadian firms operating in Canada.

The "truncation hypothesis" referred to by Dewhirst is typical of the peculiar ideas in this field. Of course, any multinational company practices division of labor by doing some work in one country and other work elsewhere. From the point of view of any *single* country, the local branches of all of its multinationals—whether the company is owned locally or abroad—will be engaged in "truncated" activities.

Beliefs of the sort that are restated by Dewhirst were influential in preparing the way for the establishment of the Foreign Investment Review Agency (FIRA) in 1973. Throughout the 1970s, the

FIRA was alleged to have reduced significantly the foreign influx of capital. The FIRA's rejection rate of 20 percent represented a formidable barrier to possible investors, and certainly it was high compared to rates of approximately 1 percent for other countries that used analogous screening processes. Also, the length and cost of the application process no doubt discouraged some firms from even applying.

Evidence is hard to compile, but investment consultants assert that the FIRA had a major effect in discouraging foreign investment, particularly among small firms who felt that the cost and hassle just were not worthwhile. Judging from Ottawa's own behavior, this must have been perceived since, when attitudes changed with respect to foreign investment, it was deemed necessary to send a delegation around the world with the message that Canada now welcomed foreign investment.

Under a new minister in the early 1980s, the review process was streamlined, and the rejection rate reduced to less than 5 percent. If the FIRA becomes an easy hurdle for most firms, it may remain in place both as a screening device to stop a few cases where some generally perceived national interest is at stake and as a symbolic institution to assure Canadians that some watch is being kept at the door. However, given its past reputation, a name change was deemed desirable. The Conservative government that was elected in September of 1984 changed the name to Investment Canada and pledged to reform its practices.

Foreign Ownership—There is concern that capital controls are needed to stop too much industry from being owned abroad. The profusion of foreign branch plants in Canada is itself the result of the National Policy, which created the tariff incentive to build branch plants to serve the protected Canadian market. Nonetheless, foreign ownership is an important issue in Canada. A significant portion of the Canadian public always has worried that too much of Canadian industry was foreign—particularly American—owned, and toward the end of the 1960s there was a dramatic rise in the number of persons holding this view. A poll that asked if recent purchases of Canadian firms by American corporations was bad for the Canadian economy found 34 percent answering "yes" in 1969, 41 percent in 1970, 44 percent in 1971, 46 percent in 1972, and 55 percent in 1973.

Concern about excessive foreign ownership was one of the incentives behind the most nationalistic of the policies of the 1970s
and early 1980s—the NEP. The unfortunate timing of the NEP
(from the Canadian viewpoint) made the policy a very unprofit-
able business. Foreign equity was bought out at peak prices, just
before the break in oil prices reduced greatly the value of equity,
and the funds for purchases were raised by debt just as interest
rates soared. This was a matter of bad luck for Canadians and good
luck for Americans, but it illustrates the risks of a policy of buying
foreign capital to bring economic benefits to the home country.

The merits to Canada of using scarce investment funds to buy
back its oil and gas industry, rather than using the funds to create
new capital, are debatable. This author's observation of 1981 still
stands today:

> A significant part of our current scarce investment funds is used to transfer
> ownership of existing capital in the oil industry to Canadian hands. This
> policy had a consequence that seems to have gone unnoticed so far. Buying
> out American oil firms provides no real capital for Canada; it merely trans-
> fers ownership of existing capital and leaves the former owners with the
> funds needed to create new capital. There are then two possibilities. First,
> the former owners may invest their funds in other Canadian industries—
> call them the "widget industries." In this case we do get new real capital
> but the proportion of all capital that is owned by Canadians is not increased.
> Canadians merely own more of the oil industry's capital and less of the
> widget industry's capital. Second, and this seems much more likely to me,
> after the foreign investors get the message that they are unwelcome in
> Canada and that the proceeds of their investment may be subject to partial
> confiscation once the investment is made, they may invest some of their
> repatriated funds in countries other than Canada. In this case when all the
> dust has settled, scarce Canadian investment funds have gone to create
> American-owned capital outside Canada. ("Supply Side Economics: A Sur-
> vey," in *Policies for Stagflation: Focus on Supply,* edited by L. Tarshis)

Whatever the merits of the NEP from the Canadian viewpoint,
American and other foreign owners could not object if the "buy
backs" were made at fair market value. The major international
objection, however, was to schemes such as the federal government's "back in" provisions that changed the rules on foreign investment after the investment was made and substantially reduced
the market value of foreign investment before repurchase. This is
an unfortunate practice for a nation that is as dependent on for-

eign capital as is Canada. If the federal government is unwilling to compensate foreign firms in this case, it is important that this case be established as a special one, never to be repeated, rather than as a precedent. The difficulty lies in making this assurance believable.

The Assessment of the Nationalist Debate

The latter part of this chapter has reviewed the professed motives that have driven Canadian economic policy with respect to the United States over the last couple of decades. However, there may be real forces that lie below the ones that have been allowed to surface. In the world of policy discussion, there are two types of debate: debates that are amenable to rational argument and evidence because what is at issue is what is being debated and those not amenable to arguments and evidence because what is at issue is not actually what is being debated. Canadian nationalists' arguments regarding economic issues may sometimes belong to the latter. No amount of study and research has diminished debates on any of these issues, and people often seem impervious to evidence. It may be that the nationalist position is to be understood in sociological and psychological terms, and arguments about the economic effects of American investment are mere rationalizations; if one argument is proved wrong, two more will be invented to fill the gap. This view of the nationalist is not meant to be condescending. It only indicates that the nationalist position goes deeper than economics. It would persist even if every nationalist were satisfied that foreign investment in Canada had no undesirable economic consequences.

Most, but not all, Canadian economists are internationalists. Critics such as the members of the Canadian Science Council explain this as "conservatism," which prevents internationalists from accepting new ideas. One of the most influential monographs by the Science Council, *The Weakest Link,* states that "orthodox Canadian economists . . . jump to the conclusion that the origins of Canada's productivity problems lie in the tariff protection of Canadian industry" and "the belief of Canadian economists in the free trade doctrine is a theoretical position, not a practical proposition, because it does not depend on the pragmatic appraisal of Canada's present industrial system."

Those on the other side of this debate explain the interna-

tionalism of so many economists as the consequence of economists'
dedication to hard research and their unwillingness to be stam-
peded by fads and slogans with no intellectual substance. In an assessment of the Science Council's research paper that argued
against the "orthodox" internationalist position, A. E. Safarian
wrote:

> the authors seem strangely unaware both of the scope of the "orthodox"
> argument and of the number and quality of studies which have tested it. . . .
> What is not cited [by the Science Council authors] . . . are the studies for
> Canada and other developed countries which attempt to quantify most
> directly and fully the hypotheses advanced. . . . Despite the wealth of
> data . . . no statistical tests of any kind are used to attempt to separate
> the effects in which the Science Council is interested from other influ-
> ences. . . . Their reporting of other studies is extraordinarily careless.
> (*Canadian Public Policy,* Summer 1979)

Probably the most famous Canadian internationalist economist
was Professor Harry Johnson who, during his illustrious career,
held chairs of economics at Manchester, the London School of Economics, Chicago, and Geneva but who still maintained strong interest in, and ties with, Canada. In 1963, outspoken as always,
Johnson said about Canadian nationalism:

> As a Canadian I am disturbed because nationalism in its recent form seems
> to me to appeal to, and to reinforce, the most undesirable features of the
> Canadian national character. In these I include . . . the mean and under-
> handed anti-Americanism which serves many Canadians as an excuse for
> their failure to accomplish anything worthy of genuine national pride. . . .
> As an economist, I have been even more disturbed by the protectionist and
> anti-foreign investment proposals which have been associated with national-
> ist sentiment. . . . These proposals seem to be attempting to enlist, by
> specious reasoning, the support of a confused nationalist sentiment for mea-
> sures whose chief effect will be to increase the profits and power of particular
> interests at the expense of the community. . . . What is also serious, the
> emphasis that has been placed on foreign competition and American in-
> vestment in Canada as causes of Canada's recent economic difficulties has
> served to attract the attention of the general public . . . from the fact that
> these difficulties are in large part attributable to an inept and perhaps will-
> ful . . . failure of those in charge of Canadian economic policy to take
> appropriate remedial measures. Thus, far from contributing to the growth
> of a stronger, more independent, and identity-conscious nation, Canadian
> nationalism as it has developed in recent years has been diverting Canada
> into a narrow and garbage-cluttered cul-de-sac. (*The Canadian Quandary*)

This comment's strength reveals the force of the debate. Both sides are concerned with the same ends, and both seem convinced that the other is utterly misguided in the choice of tools to do the job. Although surprising perhaps, the tone of this quotation captures the tone of the debate—nationalists sometimes attack internationalists as living in a theoretical vacuum and being behind the times; internationalists sometimes attack nationalists as political populists with no dedication to dispassionate research whose studies are designed to prove preconceived positions rather than to find real answers to honest questions.

RECENT CHANGES IN THE CANADIAN POLICY STANCE

The high watermark of Canadian nationalist programs occurred with the promulgation of the NEP. Since that time, policy has evolved toward a more internationalist position. The rules of the FIRA have been slackened and their administration streamlined to make them less restrictive. Initiatives have been developed toward increased U.S. trade liberalization. The Canadian initiative in the mid–1980s was toward sectoral free trade analogous to the auto pact, but there was also much talk about moves toward across-the-board, bilateral reductions of U.S. trade barriers.

The driving forces in this retreat from Canadian nationalism are partly cyclical. Traditionally, Canadians have looked outward whenever serious recessions have threatened their economy. In 1984 Simon Reisman observed that Americans tend to look outward toward freer trade when times are good and inward toward protectionism when times are bad; Canadians, on the other hand, tend to do the reverse.

When resource rents are high, Canadians feel secure enough to invest some of them in nationalist economic policies. For example, in the mid–1950s Prime Minister Louis St. Laurent tried to force foreign countries to change their financing in an effort to secure more of the rents for Canadians; the thrust that led to FIRA gathered most force during the 1960s when, once again, resource rents were high; the enormous oil rents in the 1970s led to the NEP; and so on.

These forces are also in part a secular change in the "fear component." Canadians have realized the increasing force with which the chill winds of foreign competition are blowing. Just as an invasion from Mars would put USSR–U.S. differences into a wonderful new perspective, so does the increasing intensity of competition from the developing countries put Canadian-American differences into a new perspective—at least for Canadian economic nationalists.

In part, too, this retreat is influenced by secular changes in the "confidence component." There is new confidence, particularly among younger Canadian business leaders, that they can "hold their own" in tough international competition. They know they cannot compete across the board, but they believe that they can carve out niches for specific, made-in-Canada products. This is just what should be expected of a small, open economy. The ability to compete everywhere would be a denial of the concept of comparative advantage, but the ability to compete in niches that seem from a global viewpoint, but nonetheless, account for the entire exposed sector of the Canadian economy, is consistent with economic reasoning.

On the American side, the secular commitment of the administration to freer trade remains in place. There is, however, a cyclical movement, largely centered in Congress and state governments, for increased trade restrictions. The overvalued dollar with its accompanying massive trade deficit has influenced Americans to look inward to protect their large home economy from foreign competition.

RECENT CANADIAN POLICY CONCERNS

Canadians worry that while they are innocent bystanders they still may be hurt by U.S. action directed at third parties. University of Michigan professor R. M. Stern has explained that "for example, U.S. actions to restrict imports of specialty steel during 1983 were aimed primarily against government steel subsidies in certain EEC countries. Yet Canada may be adversely affected even though its exports are not subsidized."

Canadians are anxious that the asymmetries between the two countries may cause some new economic instruments to affect Canada disproportionately. For example, R. J. Wonnacott wrote in 1984:

The risk that U.S. countervail may be invoked in the future may effectively prevent a company wishing to service the North American market from establishing in Canada—because by so doing, it would run the risk of a future U.S. countervail that would damage its sales in more than 90 percent of the North American market. (Here we use North Americans loosely, to represent only Canada and the U.S.) Accordingly, the firm establishes in the U.S., where the threat of exactly the same Canadian countervail would involve little risk: less than 10 percent of its market would be affected. (Working Paper No. 8323C, University of Western Ontario)

Another worry concerns the currently evolving U.S. concept of reciprocity. In Canadian-American relations, reciprocity used to refer to a bilateral reduction of barriers to trade. The American reciprocity concept, sometimes called "aggressive reciprocity," refers to policies whereby the United States may increase barriers to trade against countries whose existing barriers are judged to be higher than corresponding American barriers. In his previously cited work, Professor Wonnacott described the policy as follows:

> Aggressive reciprocity is based on a very special and controversial concept of equal treatment. In trade negotiations in the past, the attempt, by and large, has been to equalize *changes* in protection; but this new concept of reciprocity attempts to equalize *existing levels* of protection. In other words, the U.S. would be raising trade barriers against trading partners whose levels of protection may not have changed at all; their only offense may be that their *existing* barriers are judged by *Americans* to be higher than those of the U.S.

Although Japan appears to be a major target for aggressive reciprocity, Canada's level of tariffs is higher than corresponding American tariffs on many commodities and is clearly vulnerable to this policy tool.

Conclusion

These nations exist side by side, sharing an undefended frontier of nearly 5,000 miles. One is a physical giant, the other, a population heavyweight; one is almost pathologically aware of its neighbor, the other, almost criminally unaware; one is a star actor in international affairs, the other, a minor supporting player. Both are the other's most important trading partner and each other's most important location for foreign investment; both flirt with restrictions on trade with each other, but they deeply understand the need for a relatively free flow of goods and services across their common border; one toys with restrictions on capital movements but, when the chips are down, puts the nation's money on a relatively free movement of capital, the other remains largely unaware of capital imports from its neighbor so that political issues concerning such movements never have a chance of arising; both were battered in the 1980s by strong forces of foreign competition, have a mutual interest in fostering more trade between themselves, and have their futures inextricably tied to the other. Both carry some real grievances against the other's political and economic policies, but these grievances seem small when viewed against each nation's underlying self-interest in mutual economic cooperation.

Concerned citizens in both countries can only hope that a spirit of rational self-interest will guide the relations between the two countries in the 1980s and the 1990s and take them toward closer economic cooperation that will enhance the economic security and living standards of each, while leaving each to remain the strong, independent, and individual society that it undoubtedly is.

Seymour Martin Lipset

Canada and the United States:

The Cultural Dimension

Twenty years ago I published a lengthy paper seeking to specify and analyze the similarities and differences between Canada and the United States. As I noted then, "Although these two peoples probably resemble each other more than any other two nations on earth, there are consistent patterns of difference between

SEYMOUR MARTIN LIPSET *is the Caroline S.G. Munro Professor of Political Science and Sociology, and a senior fellow of the Hoover Institution, at Stanford University. Previously, he was the George Markham Professor of Government and Sociology at Harvard University. His first faculty post was at the University of Toronto. Dr. Lipset is the recipient of many honorary degrees and awards. He has served as president of a number of professional groups, including the American Political Science Association. Dr. Lipset is the author or coauthor of twenty volumes. This chapter continues a thesis first presented in his 1963 book,* The First New Nation: The United States in Historical and Comparative Perspective. *The logic and evidence are developed more fully in "Revolution and Counterrevolution: The United States and Canada," in Thomas R. Ford (ed.),* The Revolutionary Theme in Contemporary America *(1965) and "Values, Education and Entrepreneurship," in Lipset and Aldo Solari (eds.), Elites in Latin America (1967). The analysis is modified in "Radicalism in North America: A Comparative View of the Party Systems in Canada and the United States,"* Transactions of the Royal Society of Canada, Volume 14 *(1976) and "Revolution and Counterrevolution—Some Concluding Comments. . .," in R. A. Preston (ed.),* Perspectives on Revolution and Evolution *(1979).*

them." In emphasizing the variations, I was reiterating the impressions of earlier foreign visitors, such as Friedrich Engels in the 1880s and James Bryce a few decades later. Engels once remarked that in coming to Canada from the United States he imagined he was "in Europe again." And Bryce emphasized that in spite of "the external resemblances to the United States . . . in character and in political habits there are marked differences."

Over the last two decades the amount of literature and research bearing on the North American societies has grown considerably. In part, this is simply the product of time, for much has happened and more has been written. But I have to confess that I have become more sensitive to relevant work in a broader variety of fields, including religion, law, and literature. Comparative analysis is not a monopoly of the social scientist.

The most widely cited and discussed sociological analyses of the two North American democracies, those of S.D. Clark, Gad Horowitz, Kaspar Naegele, John Porter, and Dennis Wrong, were written in the sixties or earlier. For the most part they emphasized the idea, also developed in my earlier work, that Canada has been a more conservative, traditional, law-abiding, statist, and elitist society than the United States.

Although both differ from the postfeudal European nations, Canada has remained more like traditional Britain and France. As Kaspar Naegele put it in "Canadian Society: Some Reflections" in *Canadian Society* (1968), edited by B. R. Blishin et al., "The same values are valued in Canada as the United States—but with more hesitancy. There seems to be less optimism, less faith in the future, less willingness to risk capital or reputation. In contrast to America, Canada is a country of greater caution, reserve and restraint."

The Historical Background

The variations between Canada and the United States stem from the founding event which gave birth to both, the American Revolution. This initial source has been reinforced by differences in their religious traditions, variations in their political and legal institutions, and in their socioeconomic structures and ecologies.

Both major Canadian linguistic groups sought to preserve their values and culture by reacting against liberal revolutions. English-speaking Canada exists because she opposed the Declaration of

Independence; French-speaking Canada, largely under the leadership of Catholic clerics, also sought to isolate herself from the anticlerical democratic values of the French Revolution. The leaders of both cultures, after 1783 and 1789, consciously attempted to create a conservative, monarchical, and ecclesiastical society in North America. Canadian elites saw the need to use the state to protect minority cultures, English Canadians against Yankees, French Canadians against Anglophones. In the United States, by contrast, the Atlantic Ocean provided an effective barrier which helped sustain the American commitment to a weak state that did not have to maintain extensive military forces.

Much of the writing on comparative aspects of culture, politics, economy, religion, law, and literature in North America has emphasized the causal importance of the varying origins of the two nations. Canadian historians have noted that the democratic or populist elements lost their battle on many occasions. Frank Underhill summed up that history:

> Our forefathers made the great refusal in 1776 when they declined to join the revolting American colonies. They made it again in 1812 when they repelled American invasion. They made it again in 1837 when they rejected a revolution motivated by the ideals of Jacksonian democracy, and opted for a staid moderate respectable British Whiggism which they called "Responsible Government." They made it once more in 1867 when the separate British colonies joined to set up a new nationality in order to preempt expansionism. . . . It would be hard to overestimate the amount of energy we have devoted to this cause. (*In Search of Canadian Liberalism*, 1960)

The United States remained through the nineteenth and early twentieth centuries as the extreme example of a classically liberal or Lockean society which rejected the assumptions of the alliance of throne and altar, of ascriptive elitism, of mercantilism, of noblesse oblige, of communitarianism. Friedrich Engels, among other foreign visitors, noted that as compared to Europe, the United States was "purely bourgeois, so entirely without a feudal past." Canada, on the other hand, maintained a European-type society which lacked the economic dynamism of the United States. "Here one sees how necessary the *feverish speculative* spirit of the Americans is for the rapid development of a new country," and Engels looked forward to the abolition of "this ridiculous boundary line" (Karl Marx and Friedrich Engels, *Letters to Americans*). Engels was of course wrong. Canada, while maintaining her independence, became a successful, highly industrialized, bourgeois nation, albeit lagging somewhat behind the United States in per capita wealth. It was able to do this, as many writers have suggested, while retaining important elements derivative from the British and prerevolutionary French models. These involved approval by the dominant sectors of the communitarian practices of state responsibility for assorted social and economic needs.

Ironically, some of the same modern scholars who see Canada as a more British- or European-type conservative society stress that the values inherent in a monarchically rooted conservatism give rise in the modern world to support for social democratic redistributive and welfare policies. Conversely, a dominant laissez-faire Lockean tradition is antithetical to such programs. Northrop Frye, Canada's leading literary critic, called attention to this alliance of opposites when he stated in "Letters in Canada" in 1952: "The Canadian point of view is at once more conservative and more radical than Whiggery [the liberal ideology of the American Revolution], closer both to aristocracy and to democracy [equality]."

These political differences have been reinforced by religious institutions, which have consistently differed in the two societies. The American tradition and law have placed much more emphasis on separation of church and state than has the Canadian. A large majority of Americans have adhered to Protestant sects, which had opposed the established state church in England. These have a congregational structure, and foster the idea of an individual relationship to God. Most Canadians have belonged to either the Roman Catholic or the Anglican churches, both of which have been hierarchically organized state religions in Britain and Europe. While efforts to sustain church establishment ultimately failed in Canada, state support of religious institutions, particularly schools, has continued into the present. Hence religion contributed to antielitist and individualist beliefs in the United States and countered them in Canada.

The two nations vary considerably in their ecology, demography, and economy. Canada controls an area which, while larger than her southern neighbor's, is much less hospitable to human habitation in terms of climate and resources. Her geographical extent and weaker population base have induced direct government involvement in the economy to provide various services, for which sufficient private capital or a profitable market has not been available. South of the border, the antistatist emphasis subsumed in the revolutionary ideology was not challenged by the need to call upon the state to intervene economically to protect the nation's independence against a powerful neighbor.

Self-Definitions

Given these differences, it is not surprising that the peoples of the two countries formulated their self-conceptions in sharply different ways. The United States was organized around what Lincoln called a "political religion." This set of beliefs was formulated in the egalitarian and populist principles of the Declaration of Independence, and subsequently elaborated in internal political struggles. Canada, by contrast, was experiencing the repeated defeat of her populist forces. As W. L. Morton emphasized in 1961 in *The Canadian Identity,* Canada "arrived at freedom through evolution in allegiance and not by revolutionary compact." Hence, her "final governing force . . . is tradition and convention."

As an ideological nation whose left and right *both* take sustenance from the American Creed, the United States is quite different from Canada, which lacks any founding myth, and whose intellectuals frequently question whether the country has a national identity. Sacvan Bercovitch has well described America's impact on a Canadian during the conflict-ridden sixties.

> My first encounter with American consensus was in the late sixties, when I crossed the border into the United States and found myself inside the myth of America . . . of a country that despite its arbitrary frontiers, despite its bewildering mix of race and creed, could believe in something called the True America, and could invest that patent fiction with all the moral and emotional appeal of a religious symbol. . . . Here was the Jewish anarchist Paul Goodman berating the Midwest for abandoning the promise; here the descendant of American slaves, Martin Luther King, denouncing injustice as a violation of the American Way; here, an endless debate about national destiny, . . . conservatives scavenging for un-Americans, New Left historians recalling the country to its sacred mission. . . .
>
> Nothing in my Canadian background had prepared me for that spectacle. . . . It gave me something of an anthropologist's sense of wonder at the symbols of the tribe. . . . To a Canadian skeptic, . . . it made for a breathtaking scene: a pluralistic pragmatic people openly living in a dream, bound together by an ideological consensus unmatched by any other modern society.

Let me repeat that mundane phrase: *ideological consensus.* . . . It was a hundred sects and factions, each apparently different from the others, yet all celebrating the same mission. . . . ("The Rites of Assent: Rhetoric, Ritual and the Ideology of American Consensus," in *The American Self: Myth, Ideology and Popular Culture,* edited by S. B. Girgus, 1981)

Bercovitch noted that the American myth originated in New England long before the Revolution which transformed it into a political ideology. He cites Max Weber concerning the significance of the absence of feudal precapitalist institutions and values, and the importance of the Protestant Ethic founded by the Calvinists and reinforced in America by the Revolutionary ideology.

Bercovitch argued that Canada, alternatively, could not offer her citizens "the prospect of a fresh start, . . . because (as the Canadian poet Douglas Le Pan put it) Canada is 'a country without a mythology.' " To justify her separate existence, both linguistic cultures deprecated American values and institutions. Basically, as Frank Underhill noted in *In Search of Canadian Liberalism,* Canadians are the world's oldest and most continuing anti-Americans. Until relatively recently, the predominant form which that negation took was conservative, monarchical, and ecclesiastical. A good summary of these views during the nineteenth century may be found in *Canada Views the United States: Nineteenth-Century Political Attitudes,* a collection of articles by two historians, one a Canadian, S. F. Wise, and the other an American, R. C. Brown. Their detailed analyses were summed up by David Potter's chapter in that book:

The diversity of the two countries arises from the difference in their experience. . . . The United States had a revolution which gave ascendancy to democrats and impaired the prestige of the elite; Canada received a migration of Loyalists, many of whom clung to the concept of an elite on the British model as a means of preserving social order. . . .

Canadians felt the distinctiveness of their own values and character. Often they were at a loss to define with clarity this distinctiveness which they felt. . . .

Canadians believed that the state, through some authority, should provide moral direction for the society it governed. Moral direction meant discipline, order, responsibility, obedience, even inhibition. America, too, has believed in discipline, order, responsibility, and the rest, but it has believed in them as self-imposed, through the acceptance of a Protestant ethic, not imposed by public authority. . . . Therefore, Americans have countenanced not only extremes of freedom and permissiveness, but even violence, corruption, license, and social deviancy in preference to a public authority strong enough to control them. Perhaps there can be no more basic difference in social philosophy than the one illustrated by these diverse attitudes.

The formative national events and images continued to affect the way the two countries regarded themselves into the pre–World War II era. A student of Canadian literature on America, John Charles Weaver, in his Duke University doctoral dissertation, called attention to various writings in the 1920s by Canadian observers who "discern and condemn an excessive egalitarian quality derived from notions of independence and democracy which have been set free during the Revolution."

James Bryce, in *Modern Democracies* (1921), viewed most of the differences between the two North American democracies as reflecting credit on Canada, which did not exhibit the "spirit of license, the contempt of authority, the negligence in enforcing the laws" found in the United States and other populist countries. These Canadian virtues could be credited to habits "formed under governments that were in those days monarchical in fact as well as in name, and it has persisted. . . ." He also stressed the Francophones' continued adherence to prerevolutionary values, noting: "So far as they belong to France, it is to a France of the eighteenth, not of the twentieth, century. . . . They have been but slightly affected by [modern] French political institutions or ideas. . . ."

The 1930s witnessed the first efforts at a systematic sociological investigation of opinions in Canada concerning themselves and Americans. Canadian political scientist H. F. Angus coordinated a series of studies, *Canada and Her Great Neighbor: Sociological Surveys of Opinions and Attitudes in Canada Concerning the United States,* which was published in 1938. One of the most important and prolific contributors to the research was S. D. Clark, then starting his scholarly career. In the Angus volume, Clark summarized the findings in the following terms:

> Canadian national life can almost be said to take its rise in the negative will to resist absorption in the American Republic. It is largely about the United States as an object that the consciousness of Canadian national unity has grown up. . . .
>
> Constantly in the course of this study we shall come across the idea that Canadian life is simpler, more honest, more moral and more religious than life in the United States, that it lies closer to the rural virtues and has

achieved urbanization without giving the same scope to corrupting influence which has been afforded them in the United States.

Canadian attitudes during the 1920s varied along political lines. Conservatives stressed the linkage to Britain, the superiority of British institutions, and were especially deprecating about egalitarianism and democracy in the United States. On the other hand, many Liberals were continentalists, adhering to a classically liberal tradition that was closer to that of Americans. At the same time, leftists worried about an American takeover of Canada. The radicals tended to be the most nationalistic.

The Continued Discussion

The past two decades have witnessed a considerable growth in books and articles seeking to evaluate Canada and the United States in comparative perspective. As might be expected, this literature has been quite controversial. Analysts of North American societies have disputed the facts and, where they agreed on the existence of significant differences, as they generally have, they have disagreed on the sources of the variations.

The argument essentially has been between those like myself, who emphasize the distinctiveness of the *values* of the two countries, and the ways these in turn affect behavior, beliefs, and institutional arrangements, and those who place primary importance on various *structural* differences, particularly geographic, economic, and political factors.

Structural and cultural differences between Canada and the United States are declining. Both countries have experienced a high level of urban and economic growth, a sharply improved standard of living, an explosion in the numbers in higher education, greater leisure, and a shift in the composition of the economy. These have been accompanied by a greater acceptance of communitarian welfare and egalitarian values, a decline in religious commitment, a move toward smaller nuclear families, increasing sexual freedom, and more equality for minorities and women. Yet many traditional national differences continue to exist, while others emerge, for example, a much higher union membership rate in Canada than in the United States. The debate as to the sources and nature of the differences continues. Before turning to an evaluation of the comparative empirical materials, some indication of the content of the conceptual arguments concerning the impact of cultural and structural factors in North America may be in order.

The most "idealistic" interpretation of American and Canadian societies, that of Louis Hartz and his followers, contends that there is little real variation between the two North American democracies. Both are perceived as "fragment societies" which left behind in the Old World those classes and values which were to sustain postfeudal class relations and institutions. English Canada is seen as almost as liberal, or as Lockean, as America. British North America simply manifests the liberal Whiggish values of the settlers in a slightly slower, but essentially similar, fashion. But Hartz also noted in *The Founding of New Societies* that English Canada is "etched with a tory streak coming out of the American Revolution."

The Marxist sociologist Arthur K. Davis contended that what variations exist are a result of structural differences, cultural gaps derivative from the fact that Canada has been less developed, more of an exploited hinterland than a center. But toward the end of his article, Davis himself noted various differences between Canada and the United States, much like those I described, and suggested that they result from the fact that

> American colonies broke their ties with England, and the philosophy of *laissez faire* Manchesterism could run wild until the rise of new internal oppositions late in the nineteenth century. . . . In England, on the other hand, elements of pre-industrial classes and values survived industrialization. The first reforms in the nineteenth century were sparked . . . by Tories from the old landed classes motivated by feudal norms like *noblesse oblige*. Something of these restraining values seems to have carried over into English Canada. ("Canadian Society and History as Hinterland versus Metropolis," in *Canadian Society: Pluralism, Change and Conflict,* edited by R. J. Ossenberg, 1971)

Other structural explanations for the greater emphasis on Tory values and policies in Canada are subsumed under the heading of the Laurentian thesis advanced by scholars like Harold Innis and Donald Creighton. Canada, as Innis has noted, had a less populous so-called "hard" frontier based on fur trapping and mining. Without state intervention and economic links with Europe, she could not have survived as a separate country. The Laurentian thesis assumes the need for a strong central authority, heavy state intervention in the economy, and an emphasis on law and order linked to the national government.

Cultural (values) and structural approaches are not mutually exclusive frameworks. As noted earlier, the cofounder of the most influential structural approach of all, Friedrich Engels, was one of the first writers to contend that Canada's economic backwardness relative to the United States is primarily a function of her value system. More recently, Harold Innis, in *Essays in Canadian Economic History,* though clearly emphasizing structural factors, noted the importance of "the essentially counter-revolutionary traditions, represented by the United Empire Loyalists and by the Church in French Canada, which escaped the influences of the French Revolution." On the other hand, in his 1968 work, *The Developing Canadian Community,* S. D. Clark, the doyen of the cultural interpretation of North American comparative sociology, has called attention to the fact that "geography, which favoured individual enterprise and limited political interference in the conduct of economic, social and religious affairs over a large part of the continent [America], favoured on this part of the continent [Canada] . . . widespread intervention by the state." He emphasized that ecological factors weakened "the development within Canadian society of capitalist, urban, middle-class social values and forms of social structure."

There is a continuing literature concerned with the impact of cultural differences. Five books published in the last decade can be mentioned as examples of this work: one is an analysis of Canadian society by an American sociologist, Edgar Friedenberg; a second is a discussion of "national character" by a Canadian writer, Pierre Berton; a third is a political analysis by William Christian and Colin Campbell; a fourth is a comparative analysis of policy elites by Robert Presthus, an American political scientist working in Canada; and the fifth is a study of Canada's economic culture by Herschel Hardin. All strongly emphasize the ways historically conditioned value differences continue to affect variations in the behavior and attitudes of Canadians and Americans in similar terms to the sociological writings of two decades earlier.

The differences between the two North American nations show up in a variety of institutional variations, as well as in the attitudes and values of the peoples. I now turn to a discussion of some of these—literature, religion, economy, law and crime, stratification, and national unity.

Literature and Myths

Of all artifacts, the art and literature of a nation should most reflect as well as establish her basic myths and values. As one of Canada's most important novelists, Margaret Atwood, noted in *Survival:* "Every country or culture has a single unifying and informing symbol at its core. . . . The symbol, then—be it word, phrase, idea, image, or all of these—functions like a system of beliefs . . . which holds the country together and helps the people in it for common ends." Many students of North American literature have emphasized the continuing effects of the "myths and the psychic consequences of founding a country on revolution or the rejection of revolution." (See Russell M. Brown's unpublished paper, "Telemachus and Oedipus: Images and Authority in Canadian and American Fiction.")

Canadian literary critics tend to see their country and their literature as reflecting defeat, difficult physical circumstances, and an uninteresting history, while America is perceived in more optimistic terms. Thus Robert McDougal, in the autumn 1963 *Canadian Literature,* reiterated R. W. B. Lewis's emphasis on the innocent Adam who has vast "potentialities" as the authentic symbol of the American. But there is no equivalent "simple myth or ideology . . . available" for Canadians. In distinction to the optimistic Adamite American writing, a variety of Canadians, Grove, Callahan, MacLennan, and many others, have been pessimistic. The representative Canadian "images are those of denial and defeat rather than fulfillment and victory."

Russell Brown argued that a revolt against tradition and authority, against king and ancestral fatherland, is at some deepest level an Oedipal act. He noted that the writings of various American authors such as Hawthorne, Melville, Crane, Tarkington, Twain, Dreiser, Penn Warren, O'Neill, Salinger, and Mailer have been identified by critics as reflecting Oedipal themes.

Brown suggested there is an alternative to Oedipus in Greek literature and myth, Telemachus, whose story is reflected in a great deal of Canadian writing. Telemachus's problem is that "the king, his father, has departed, has left him to grow up fatherless in his mother's home for reasons he cannot fully grasp, or at any rate experientially comprehend." Hence he sets out at the beginning of the Odyssey to find his father, trying to discover the events which took him away from his son.

Brown concluded his analysis by saying: "The American desire to free oneself from the father is also a desire to escape the past with its tradition and authority. It is no surprise that the American hero par excellence is that man without father, Adam. . . . The American flight from history is the root of the American dream, the Horatio Alger myth, the self made man." In Canadian writing, on the other hand, it is Noah,

> the *nth* Adam, the modern man recapitulating a process handed down across untold generations stretching back to the ultimate Father, the first-namer. There are Canadian books which emphasize Noah, such as J. MacPherson's book of poems, *The Boatman,* or Robinson Crusoe, as in Leo Simpson's novel, *Arkwright.* Noah, the man who carries all pre-existent history with him, the Biblical archetype that informs Leo Simpson's novel, *Arkwright*— recast in more modern terms he becomes Robinson Crusoe, the man capable through the activity of his mind of reconstructing his civilization even in a wilderness.

Mary Jean Green, an American student of Quebec literature, though agreeing with the importance of the counterrevolutionary emphasis in forming Canada's culture, suggested that the family tension myth north of the border is reflected more in the mother-daughter relationship than in the father-son one. According to the Freudian scenario, the son rejects the father, but the daughter "though . . . initially overcome by hostility . . . can never fully abandon her very strong feelings of attachment and continuity with the mother." Hence, "the importance accorded mother-daughter interaction in the ideological context of Quebec" and Anglophone Canada as well. The theme of many recent novels in both parts of the country has been the feminine one "of rejection and reconciliation," not the more masculine sharp break.

The assumption that Canadian experience can be more fruitfully explored in feminine rather than in masculine terms suggests an answer to the puzzle of why "women writers occupy . . . [more] central positions in Canadian literature in both English and French" than in the United States. "Perhaps it is because female voices have a special resonance for the culture as a whole that, in Canada, women writers have assumed such an important role in defining a reality that is not uniquely feminine but, rather, profoundly Canadian" ("Writing in a Motherland," unpublished paper, 1984).

The revolutionary-counterrevolutionary theme has also been explicated by Claude Bissell, Northrop Frye, Norman Newton, A. J. M. Smith, and Ronald Sutherland. In *The New Hero* Sutherland noted that national traits of Canadians and Americans which sprouted at the time of the Revolution "became powerful conditioning forces in American and Canadian culture and literature."

Canada's leading literary critic, Northrop Frye, makes similar points, noting in *Divisions on a Ground* that "a culture founded on a revolutionary tradition, like that of the United States, is bound to show very different assumptions and imaginative patterns from those of a culture that rejects or distrusts revolution." In *The Bush Garden* Frye asserted that American literature has been more populist, much more likely to emphasize violence than Canadian. "The strong romantic tradition in Canadian literature has much to do with its original conservatism." When radicalism has emerged in Canada, it has been much less likely to assume "that freedom and national independence are the same thing. . . . [but rather] has something in common with the Toryism it opposes." Claude Bissell has contended in various essays that Canadian writers have repeatedly rejected American egalitarian models and populist writers in favor of European ones. He argues that Canadian novels fit in more as part "of European than American literature."

A similar emphasis may be found in the analyses of A. J. M. Smith, who notes that Canadian literature until recently reflected the spirit of colonialism. This engendered "the feeling of an inescapable inferiority." In the United States, on the other hand, the emphasis on national ideals made American literature "critical and profoundly subversive," while that in Canada remained conservative until the past decade. (See "Evolution and Revolution as Aspects of English-Canadian and American Literature," in *Perspectives on Revolution and Evolution,* edited by R. A. Preston.)

In *Survival* Atwood suggested that the symbol for America is "The Frontier," which implies "a place that is *new,* where the old order can be discarded" and which "holds out a hope, never fulfilled but always promised, of Utopia, the perfect human society." And, like Smith, she noted that most twentieth century American literature is about the "gap between the promise and the actuality, between the imagined ideal . . . and the actual squalid materialistic dotty small town, nasty city, or redneck-filled outback."

The central symbol for Canada, based on numerous examples of its appearance in French and English Canadian literature, is

"Survival, *la Survivance*." The main meaning of survival in Canadian literature is the most basic one, "hanging on, staying alive." Atwood noted the continued Canadian concern with Canada: does it exist, will it exist, what is Canadian identity, do we have an identity, etc.? As she put it: "Canadians are forever taking the national pulse like doctors at a sickbed; the aim is not to see whether the patient will live well but simply whether he will live at all."

Like others, Atwood stressed the difference in the way the two societies look at authority. She argued that Canadians, unlike Americans, do not see authority or government as an enemy. "Canada must be the only country in the world where a policeman [the Mountie] is used as a national symbol." Rebels or revolutionists are not heroes in Canadian literature.

Atwood illustrated her general theme by looking at the different ways in which the family is treated in the literature of the two countries. Like Brown, she stressed that "in American literature the family is something the hero must repudiate and leave; it is a structure he rebels against, thereby defining his own freedom, his own frontier. The family . . . is something you come from and get rid of." Canadian novels, however, treat the family quite differently, for "if in America it's a skin you shed, then in Canada it's a trap in which you're caught."

The varying political traditions have also been used to account for the differences in the way poetry has developed across the border. In *The Bush Garden* Frye suggested these variations are related to "a more distinctive attitude in Canadian poetry and in Canadian life, a more withdrawn and detached view of life which may go back to the central factor of Canadian history, the rejection of the American revolution." In the winter 1972 issue of *Canadian Literature,* Norman Newton pointed to a much more conservative emphasis in Canadian poetry which "is closely bound up with the Canadian character as it expressed itself in our formative years," resultant from opposition to the American and French Revolutions.

Nineteenth century Canadian poets wrote "public poetry," which explicitly spoke to the values and needs of the country and identified with the government. American "poets who have consciously identified themselves with the political establishment . . . have found their poetic stock plummeting as a result." Moreover, Newton cites Tocqueville, as well as other visitors to the United

States, as stressing that "United States society is anti-poetic because it is anti-aristocratic and anti-monarchical." Canada, on the other hand, tended to glorify archaic preindustrial values; "many of the social ideals upheld by the 'Establishment' up to the end of the Second World War were aristocratic ones."

The differences in themes in the two national literatures have declined in the past two decades. Smith, in "Evolution and Revolution," and Sutherland, in *The New Hero,* called attention to the effects of a new nationalism north of the border, one which has produced a more radical literature. But ironically, as Sutherland pointed out, these changes are making Canada and her fiction more American, involving, as they do, a greater emphasis on values such as pride in country, self-reliance, individualism, independence, and self-confidence.

It may be argued, however, that these changes, while reducing some traditional differences, have enhanced others. The new nationalism, often linked among intellectuals to socialism and Toryism, seeks to resist takeover of Canada's economy and increased cultural and media influence by Americans, and its weapon in so doing is the remedy of state action. As Christian and Campbell observed in this context in *Political Parties and Ideologies in Canada:* "Toryism, socialism, and nationalism all share a common collectivist orientation in various forms."

The study of a nation's arts and literature is important to any effort to *understand* her values. But as Sutherland has suggested, literature also helps *form* national values: "The greatest writers of a nation . . . respond to the forces that condition a nation's philosophy of life, and they in turn condition that philosophy." Literature is, of course, not alone or even predominant in these respects. Religion, which will be considered in the next section, plays a similar role.

Religion and Values

Harold Innis may have said it all when he wrote that a "counter-revolutionary tradition implies an emphasis on ecclesiasticism." As noted earlier, the majority of Canadians adhere to the Roman Catholic or Anglican churches, both of which are hierarchically organized and continued until recently to have a strong relationship to the state. On the other hand, most Americans have belonged to the more individualist "nonconformist" Protestant sects. As Edmund Burke noted in his speech to Parliament trying to explain the motives and behavior of the American colonists at the time of the Revolution, their religious beliefs made them the Protestants of Protestantism, the dissenters of dissent, the individualists par excellence. In *The New Hero*, Sutherland summed up the differences as follows:

> American puritanism, developing as it did from the peculiar notions of a small and persecuted sect, underlined self-reliance and the responsibility of the individual. . . . Canada, by contrast, had relatively sophisticated church systems among both Catholics and Protestants. New England Puritanism and subsequent evangelical movements called for personal seeking of God, working out one's salvation in "fear and trembling." Canadians, on the other hand, had the security of reliance upon a church establishment, detailed codes of behaviour, a controlling system; and in general, *until very recently,* Canadians have tended to depend upon and to trust systems which control their lives.

Tocqueville pointed to the importance of volunteerism as a factor strengthening religion in the United States. Voluntary competitive institutions which rely on membership for funds and support are likely to be stronger than institutions supported by the state. Sociologists of religion have also noted that variations in theology (the fostering of individualism by the sects compared to an organic collectivity relationship nurtured by the churches) and organizational structure (congregationalism contrasted to hierarchy) have affected the values and institutions of the two countries.

As John Webster Grant pointed out in *Studies in Religion,* spring 1973, Canadians have "never succeeded in drawing with any precision a line between areas in which the state has a legitimate interest and those that ought to be left to the voluntary activities of the churches. . . . Few Canadians find 'the separation of Church and State' an acceptable description either of their situation or of their ideal for it."

Comparing French and English Canada, Roger O'Toole, in the 1982 *Annual Review of the Social Sciences of Religion,* emphasized that in Quebec, the Roman Catholic church has until recently retained the informal role of the state church of French Canada. Though the Anglican church failed in its effort to become a "national" church in English Canada, it helped establish the founding ethos of the country and to legitimate "monarchy, aristocracy, and British constitutionalism . . . [as] part of a sacred scenario." Its condemnation of mass democracy, egalitarianism, republicanism, and revolution as the work of the devil left an indelible mark on English-Canadian political life.

In "Mainline Protestantism in Canada and the United States of America: An Overview" (*Canadian Journal of Sociology,* spring 1978), Harold Fallding noted that the close linkage of sectarian Protestantism to the national identity in the United States led to the emergence of what Robert Bellah has described as America's "civil religion." As Fallding paraphrased Bellah: "This civil religion expressed the conviction that in public and cultural affairs men and women are pursuing the will of God." He contended, however, that Canada's civil religion is quite different. "It consists in the religious legitimation of sovereignty, a practice which it inherited from Britain. The American civil religion sanctifies the future to be built whereas the Canadian civil religion upholds the authority already established."

Evangelical Protestant moralism has led to a greater propensity toward crusades, both domestic and foreign, south of the border, as well as powerful antiwar movements. The American religious tradition has also encouraged many new denominations, while the Canadian has been much less theologically fecund.

In the spring 1978 *Canadian Journal of Sociology,* Kenneth Westhues noted the differences between the American and Canadian Catholic church. He suggested there has been an "acceptance by the American . . . of the role of voluntary association . . . as the most it could hope for." Thus, as the French Dominican R. L. Bruckberger has noted, the American church has taken over many of the characteristics of Protestantism, including a strong emphasis on individual moralism. Westhues asserted that, as a result, the Vatican has frowned on the American church and has, in fact, not treated it as well as the Canadian affiliate. The conflict between the Catholic church and the United States is a result of the difference

> between that world-view, espoused by the American state which takes the individual as the basic reality of social life, and the church's world-view, which defines the group as primary. American non-recognition of the church is thus not merely a political matter. . . . It is instead a genuinely sociological issue, resting as it does on a fundamental conflict of values.

And Westhues argued the "major question always before the Catholic church in the United States has been how far to assimilate to the American way of life." This question "has never arisen in Canada, basically for the lack of a national ideology for defining what the Canadian way of life is or ought to be."

Religion in both countries has become more secularized in tandem with increased urbanization and education. Still, religion in the United States, particularly among evangelical Protestants, has shown less tendency to do this than elsewhere in the developed world, including Canada. Americans, according to data from sample surveys presented below, are much more likely to attend church regularly than Canadians and to adhere to fundamentalist and moralistic beliefs.

Canadian Catholicism, particularly in Quebec, has modified its corporatist commitment from a link to agrarian and elitist anti-industrial values to a tie to leftist socialist beliefs. These variations, of course, parallel the changes in French Canadian nationalism. Public opinion research suggests that Francophone Catholics have given up much of their commitment to Jansenist puritanical values particularly as they affect sexual behavior and family size. The continued strength of Protestant evangelical, sectarian, and fundamentalist religion in the United States has meant that traditional values related to sex, family, and morality in general are stronger in the United States than in Canada.

A large body of public opinion data gathered in the two countries bears on these issues. Unfortunately, most findings are not precisely comparable because of variations in question wording. But a research organization linked to the Catholic church, the Center for Applied Research in the Apostolate (CARA), undertook a systematically comparative study of values in twenty-two countries, including Canada and the United States. The data were collected by the Gallup Poll at the start of the eighties. The preliminary report on Canada and the U.S. differentiates the responses of English and French Canadians. Given the sponsorship of the study, it is not surprising that many of the questions bear on religious values. (The results for the U.S. are based on 1,729 respondents; for Canada, 1,251 respondents; for French-speaking Canadians, 338 respondents; and for English-speaking Canadians, 913 respondents.) The following are some of the relevant CARA findings.

Americans are more religious and more moralistic than either

English or French Canadians. In response to the question "how important is God in your life?" answered on a ten-point scale from 1 meaning not at all to 10 very important, 59 percent of the Americans placed themselves on scale point 9 or 10, as opposed to 44 percent of the English Canadians and 47 percent of the French Canadians. Close to two-thirds of the Americans, 65 percent, said they believe "there is a personal God," compared to 49 percent of the English Canadians and 56 percent of the French Canadians. Respondents were asked to react to the Ten Commandments, as to whether each was accepted by the respondent fully or to a limited extent, and whether each should apply to others. Averaging answers to all of the Commandments shows that 83 percent of the Americans said that the Ten Commandments apply fully to themselves. The comparable mean response by English Canadians was 76 percent and by French Canadians, 67 percent. The same pattern held with respect as to whether the Ten Commandments apply fully to others, presumably whether others should obey them. Thirty-six percent of Americans said they are meant to apply fully to other people as, on the average, did 28 percent of English Canadians and 23 percent of French Canadians.

The questions designed to measure the degree of fundamentalism in the population showed Americans far outnumber Canadians generally in giving expression to Protestant fundamentalist beliefs, with Anglophones in Canada more likely to hold them than Francophones. Thus, when asked whether they believed in "the devil," 66 percent of Americans said yes as did 46 percent of English Canadians and only 25 percent of French Canadians. The response to questions about belief in "hell" was similar, 67 percent for the Americans, 45 percent for the English Canadians, and 22 percent for the French Canadians. The overwhelming majority of Americans, 84 percent, said they believed in the existence of heaven, as did 73 percent of the English Canadians and 58 percent of the French Canadians. Almost three quarters, 71 percent, of Americans expressed belief in life after death, compared to 61 percent of the English and 63 percent of the French Canadians. A question on belief in a soul produced 88 percent of Americans saying yes as compared to 80 percent of both Canadian linguistic groups.

Congruent with the variation in religious practice and belief, the CARA data indicate that Americans are more puritanical than Canadians, with Francophones the most tolerant with respect to sexual behavior. In reaction to the statement "marriage is an outdated institution," 19 percent of the French Canadians agreed, as did 11 percent of the English Canadians and 7 percent of the Americans. Francophone Canadians (24 percent) were also more likely than Anglophone Canadians and Americans (18 percent) to believe that "individuals should have a chance to enjoy complete sexual freedom without being restricted." When asked "if a woman wants to have a child as a single parent but she doesn't want to have a stable relationship with a man, do you approve or disapprove?" Americans voiced the highest rate of disapproval, 58 percent, compared to 53 percent for the Anglophones and 34 percent for the Francophones.

A similar pattern was reflected in replies to the question "if someone says that sexual activity cannot entirely be left up to individual choice, there have to be moral rules to which everyone adheres, do you tend to agree or disagree?" A small majority, 51 percent, of the Americans agreed, as did 49 percent of the English Canadians but only 34 percent of the French Canadians.

Earlier survey data largely from the files of the Gallup Polls in the two countries, presented by Alex Michalos in his comprehensive five-volume *North American Social Report: A Comparative Study of the Quality of Life in Canada and the USA from 1964 to 1974,* yielded similar national differences. He reported:

> In 1969, 73% of a national sample of Americans and 49% of a similar sample of Canadians said they would "find pictures of nudes in magazines objectionable." Seventy-six percent of the former and 67% of the latter said they would "find topless night club waitresses objectionable." These responses are consistent with those concerning objectionable sex on television.

Americans were also more likely in the sixties and early seventies to say that they thought "it is wrong for people to have sex relations before marriage." In 1969, 68 percent of Americans said so, whereas the percentage for Canadians for 1970 was 57 percent. By 1973 the American figure had dropped to 48 percent while the Canadian had fallen to 36 percent.

Institutionally, national values should be clearly expressed in a nation's system of laws and the way individuals are treated under and react to them, as the next section details.

Law and Deviance

The difference in the role of law in the two societies is linked to the historical emphases on the rights and obligations of the community as compared to those of the individual. The concern of Canada's Founding Fathers with "Peace, Order, and Good Government" implies control and protection. The American stress on "Life, Liberty, and the Pursuit of Happiness" suggests upholding the rights of the individual. This concern for rights, including those of people accused of crime and of political dissidents, is inherent in the "due process" model, involving various legal inhibitions on the power of the police and prosecutors. The crime control model, more evident in Canada, as well as Europe, emphasizes the maintenance of law and order, and is less protective of the rights of the accused and of individuals generally. As John Hagen and Jeffrey Leon noted:

> The due-process model is much concerned with exclusionary rules of evidence, the right to counsel, and other procedural safeguards thought useful in protecting accused persons from unjust applications of criminal sanctions.
>
> . . . The crime-control model places heavy emphasis on the repression of criminal conduct, arguing that only by insuring order can individuals in a society be guaranteed personal freedom. It is for this reason that advocates of crime control are less anxious to presume the innocence of accused persons and to protect such persons against sometimes dubious findings of guilt. ("Philosophy and Sociology of Crime Control," in *Social System and Legal Process,* edited by H. M. Johnson, 1978)

Property rights and civil liberties are also under less constitutional protection in Canada than in the United States. John Mercer and Michael Goldberg noted:

> In Canada . . . property rights are not vested with the individual but rather with the Crown, just the opposite of the U.S. where the Fifth and Fourteenth Amendments to the U.S. Constitution guarantee property rights. Interestingly, in the . . . [recently enacted] Canadian Charter of Rights and Freedoms property rights (as distinct from human rights) were explicitly not protected. . . . There is no appeal to a higher authority, even the new Charter of Rights and Freedoms. Such a state of affairs would be unacceptable in the United States where individual rights and particularly those related to personal and real property are sacrosanct. ("Value Differences and Their Meaning," University of British Columbia Working Paper No. 12, UBC Research in Land Economics, 1982)

The Canadian government has greater legal power to restrict freedom of speech and to invade personal privacy. Acting through an order-in-council, it may limit public discussion of particular issues and, as in 1970 during the Quebec crisis, impose a form of military control. Comparing American and Canadian public reactions to violations of privacy by the government, Alan F. Westin wrote:

> It is important to note that in Canada there have been some incidents which, had they happened in the United States, would probably have led to great *causes célèbres*. Most Canadians seem to have accepted Royal Canadian Mounted Police break-ins without warrants between 1970 and 1978, and also the RCMP's secret access to income tax information, and to personal health information from the Ontario Health Insurance Plan. If I read the Canadian scene correctly, these did not shock and outrage most Canadians. ("The United States Bill of Rights and the Canadian Charter: A Socio-Political Analysis," in *The U.S. Bill of Rights and the Canadian Charter of Rights and Freedoms*, edited by W. R. McKercher, 1983)

That Canadians and Americans differ in the way they react to the law is demonstrated strikingly in the aggregate differences between the two with respect to crime rates for major offenses. Americans are much more prone than Canadians to commit violent offenses like murder, robbery, and rape and to be arrested for the use of serious illegal drugs such as opiates and cocaine. There is, however, much less difference between the two with respect to crimes involving property, e.g., theft and burglary.

The variations reported in Table 1 contradict the assumptions of those like I. L. Horowitz, who, in "The Hemispheric Connection" (*Queen's Quarterly*, autumn 1973), challenged the cultural interpretations by reference to a supposed decline in differential crime statistics in tandem with structural changes. However, as criminologists Hagen and Leon pointed out: "The results reveal

TABLE 1.   ROBBERY AND MURDER IN THE UNITED STATES AND CANADA (PER 100,000 POPULATION)

| | United States | | Canada | |
	Robbery	Murder	Robbery	Murder
1970	172.0	7.9	54.6	2.0
1974	209.0	9.8	75.5	2.4
1977	187.0	8.8	83.6	2.9
1981	251.0	9.8	108.6	2.5

Sources: Statistics Canada, Justice Statistics Division, *Crime and Traffic Enforcement Statistics* (Ottawa: Statistics Canada, 1970–82); U.S. Bureau of the Census, *Statistical Abstract of the United States: 1984* (Washington, DC: Department of Commerce, 104th edition), p. 176.

conclusions opposite to those of Horowitz. . . . In short, the national difference in reported crime in 1970 is substantial, and more so than in 1960."

Comparable variations were reported in *Assassination and Political Violence* by J. F. Kirkham, S. G. Levy, and W. J. Crotty. Their work is a comprehensive analysis of differences in rates of violence across many countries. The United States not only has a much higher rate of homicide than Canada (and most other western countries), it also is considerably higher than Canada with respect to an index of political violence. Data reported in the *World Handbook of Political and Social Indicators* also demonstrate that Canadians have been much less likely than Americans to engage in protest demonstrations, riots, or political violence between 1948 and 1977 (Table 2). Although the United States population outnumbers the Canadian by about ten to one, the ratios for political protest activities have been from two to four times as large, i.e., from twenty to one to forty to one.

The lower rates of crime and violence in Canada are accompanied by greater respect for police, public support for stronger punishment of criminals, and a higher level of support for gun control legislation. Various studies of the attitudes of American police indicate a common complaint that they are looked down on by the public. However, members of the Royal Canadian Mounted Police in British Columbia and the Calgary Police Service were more likely to feel that the public appreciated them. (See *Criminal Justice in Canada* by Curt Griffith et al., 1980.)

TABLE 2.   POLITICAL PROTEST AND VIOLENCE IN CANADA AND THE UNITED STATES

	Canada		*United States*	
	1948–67	*1968–77*	*1948–67*	*1968–77*
1. Number of protest demonstrations	27	33	1,179	1,005
2. Number of riots	29	5	683	149
3. Deaths from political violence	8	4	320	114

Source: Calculated from data in Charles Lewis Taylor and David A. Jodice, *World Handbook of Political and Social Indicators,* Vol. 2, (New Haven: Yale University Press, 1983, 3rd edition), pp. 19–25, 33–36, and 47–51.

These impressions are reinforced by national opinion findings in both countries. When asked by the Canadian Gallup Poll in 1978 to rate the local, provincial, and Royal Canadian Mounted Police, a large majority said "excellent or good" for each, 64 percent, 64 percent, and 61 percent. The corresponding percentages reported by the Harris survey for local, state and federal law enforcement officials in 1981 were 62, 57, and 48. In the early eighties, the CARA surveys conducted by Gallup found more Canadians (86 percent) than Americans (76 percent) voicing a great deal or quite a lot of confidence in the police. There was no significant difference between the two Canadian linguistic groups on this item. The cross-national variations in attitudes toward "the legal system" were similar, 63 percent of Canadians were positive, compared to 51 percent of Americans. On this question, however, French speakers revealed more confidence (72 percent) than English ones (59 percent).

Although Canada has lower crime rates than the United States, her citizens are more disposed to favor severe treatment of criminals than are their southern neighbors. As Michalos summed up his report on North American attitudes toward crime: "Although Canadians had less crime to contend with, they tended to take a tougher line than Americans on the death penalty" and favored "stiffer prison sentences." When asked by the Canadian and American Gallup Polls in 1969 "in your opinion what should be the penalty or prison sentence for the following crimes: dope peddling, armed robbery, arson, passing bad checks," for dope peddling those who answered over ten years in prison constituted 85 percent in Canada and 41 percent in the U.S.; for armed robbery, 60 percent in Canada and 33 percent in the U.S.; for arson, 53 percent in Canada and 23 percent in the U.S.; for passing bad checks, 16 percent in Canada and 7 percent in the U.S.

In "The Gun Control Issue: A Sociological Analysis of United States and Canadian Attitudes and Policies" (unpublished 1983), Ted E. Thomas points out that in the United States, gun ownership has been regarded as a "right," one linked to a constitutional guarantee established to protect the citizen. Canada's policy is based on the belief that "ownership of 'offensive weapons' or 'guns' is a privilege, not a right."

Canadians have consistently been much more supportive of gun control legislation than Americans and have been much less likely to own guns, although the level of handgun ownership in Canada has been "about one-fifth that of the United States." Thus when asked by the Gallup Poll "would you favor or oppose a law which would require a person to obtain a police permit before he or she could buy a gun?" in 1968, 86 percent of all Canadians favored such a law compared to 68 percent of the Americans. In 1975, 83 percent of Canadians voiced support compared to 67 percent of Americans. Analysis of the 1975 Canadian data at the Roper Center revealed no difference in the attitudes of the two Canadian linguistic groups on this issue.

The American emphasis on due process is accompanied by a greater litigiousness and formal efforts to enforce the law. As a more elitist society, Canada relies more heavily on mechanisms of social control rather than on officers of the court. Consequently the United States has many more lawyers per capita than Canada. Michalos noted, "In the 1967–74 period there were always more practicing lawyers per 100,000 inhabitants in the United States than in Canada. By 1974 the American rate was about 180 compared to 100 for Canada. . . . The growth rates beyond 1967 for both countries in this period were about 35%." America also spends more per capita on police, courts, and correctional institutions.

Although the cross-national behavioral and attitudinal variations with respect to law and crime have continued down to the present, Canada has been involved since 1960 in a process of changing her fundamental rules in what has been described as American and due process directions. The adoption of a Bill of Rights in 1960, replaced by the more comprehensive Charter of Rights and Freedoms in 1982, was designed to create a basis, absent from the British North American Act, for judicial intervention to protect individual rights and civil liberties.

While these changes are important, it is doubtful that they will come close to eliminating the differences in legal cultures. Canadian courts have been more respectful than American ones of the rest of the political system. As Kenneth McNaught concluded in 1975:

> Our judges and lawyers, supported by the press and public opinion, reject any concept of the courts as positive instruments in the political process. . . . Political action outside the party-parliamentary structure tends automatically to be suspect—and not least because it smacks of Americanism. This

deep-grained Canadian attitude of distinguishing amongst proper and improper methods of dealing with societal organization and problems reveals us as being, to some extent, what Walter Bagehot called a "deferential society." ("Political Trials and the Canadian Political Tradition," in *Courts and Trials: A Multidisciplinary Approach,* edited by M. L. Friedland, 1975)

Other continuing differences have been noted by Edgar Friedenberg:

The Crown in Canada can appeal against an acquittal in a criminal procedure and demand that the accused be tried again. . . . The American Bill of Rights provides no person shall "for the same offense be twice put in jeopardy of life or limb." A similar provision under Section 10 (h) of the Canadian Charter of Rights and Freedoms is made ineffective in preventing what an American court would call "double jeopardy" by the inclusion of the word "finally"—"finally acquitted," "finally found guilty"—since the process is not considered final till the Crown has exhausted its rights to appeal [an acquittal] which under American law, it wouldn't have in the first place. ("Culture in Canadian Context," in *An Introduction to Sociology,* edited by M. M. Rosenberg, 1983)

The Charter of Rights and Freedoms is not the American Bill of Rights. Instead of an insistence on "due process of law," the Charter refers to "principles of fundamental justice" as the basis under which basic individual rights are assured. Given the continuation of parliamentary supremacy, the Canadian Constitution provides that Parliament or a provincial legislature may "opt out" of the constitutional restrictions by inserting into any law a provision that it shall operate regardless of any part of the Charter. The new rights do not include assurance that an accused person shall have a lawyer, nor that he has the right to remain silent, nor that he need not answer questions which may tend to incriminate him in civil cases or investigatory proceedings.

The next area to be explored in this effort to detail the relationships among values, structure, and behavior in the two North American nations is economic activity.

The Economy: The Private Sector

The United States, born modern, without a feudal elitist corporatist tradition, could create, outside of the agrarian South, what Engels described as the purest example of a bourgeois society. Canada, as we have seen, was somewhat different, and that difference affected the way her citizens have done business. As Herschel Hardin put it in *A Nation Unaware:*

> What makes for a dynamic free enterprise culture, or a private enterprise culture, is an habitual commitment to the rules and the game—an indefatigable zest of a compulsive kind—rooted deep in the popular consciousness, which at the same time creates an appropriate institutional pattern that will feed the compulsion instead of choking it. Greed and hard work and ambition are not enough. . . . It was . . . rough egalitarianism, practical education . . . and the relentless psychic push to keep up in the "Lockean race" that made the exceptional United States go.
>
> To expect that on this side of the border, out of a French Canada tied to its clerical, feudal past, and out of an English-speaking Canada, which, although it inherited much of the spirit of liberal capitalism, was nevertheless an elitist, conservative, defensive colony—to expect it *without an intense, ideological revolution*—was to dream a derivative impossibility.

And as a result, according to Hardin, Canadian entrepreneurs have been less aggressive, less innovating, less risk taking than American. Drawing in large part on works by J. J. Brown and Pierre Bourgault, Hardin sought to demonstrate that private enterprise in Canada "has been a monumental failure" in developing new technology and industry, to the extent that Canadian business has rarely been involved in creating industries to process many significant inventions by Canadians, who have had to go abroad to get their discoveries marketed. Charles McMillan, now advisor to Prime Minister Mulroney, concluded, while still a professor of business, that "the Canadian record of diffusion of existing technology in various areas of secondary manufacture remains relatively poor, and the traditional management values and organizational processes act as deterrents to making product innovation a major corporate strategy" (*Journal of Canadian Studies,* spring 1978).

Compared to Americans, Canadian investors and financial institutions are less disposed to provide venture capital. According to the Science Council of Canada, they "tend consistently to avoid offering encouragement to the entrepreneur with a new technology-based product . . . [or to] innovative industries."

The thesis has been elaborated by economists. As summarized in Harry H. Hiller's *Canadian Society,* Jenny Podoluk found "investment is a much more significant source of personal income in the United States than in Canada. . . . When Canadians have invested, the risky new Canadian enterprise has not been as attractive as the established American corporation." Kenneth Glazier also reported that Canadians invest heavily in the United States and are unwilling to take risks in Canada. In explaining the Canadian pattern, he said:

> One reason is that Canadians traditionally have been conservative, exhibiting an inferiority complex about their own destiny as a nation and about the potential of their country . . . President A. H. Ross of Western Decalta Petroleum, Ltd., Calgary, in a recent annual report said that most of Western Decalta's exploration funds are "from foreign sources because the company has not been able to find enough risk capital in Canada."

> Thus, with Canadians investing in the "sure" companies of the United States, Canada has for generations suffered not only from a labor drain and a brain drain to the United States, but also from a considerably larger capital drain. (*Journal of Contemporary Business,* autumn 1972)

Controlling for the varying sizes of the two populations (ten to one) and per capita GNPs (twelve to one), Canadians invest much more money south of the border than Americans send north. According to Murray Smith, the research director of the Canadian-American Committee, as of the end of 1981, the value of the stock of United States direct investment in Canada amounted to about 60 billion Canadian dollars, while the equivalent Canadian input into the American economy was 21.6 billion Canadian dollars. In an effort to counteract these tendencies, the Canadian government has instituted regulations which permit Canadians to deduct 20 percent of the dividends of Canadian-owned companies for income tax purposes and require pension funds to invest in Canadian stocks.

This phenomenon is not new. In *The History of Canadian Business*, R. T. Taylor noted of the pre–World War I period, "Financial capital moved from Canada to the U.S., industrial capital back to Canada. Canadian funds went to support American stock exchanges or into corporate bonds. . . . Canada in effect ended up 'borrowing' back its money in the form of direct investments by American firms." The large Canadian insurance company, Sun Life, "generally preferred American investments to Canadian ones. . . . Canadian brokers dealt more heavily in American than in Canadian stocks."

The Science Council of Canada has noted that while Canadians tend to be savers, a "great part of these savings go into bank deposits, pensions, and life insurance," that Canadians proportionately have "much more life insurance in force" than Americans. At the end of 1982, in per capita terms, the average Canadian had $22,060 life insurance coverage compared to $19,291 for the American. As of 1982, the personal savings rate in Canada was 13.7 percent, while the American was 6.5 percent. Americans, however, have been more disposed to invest in stocks. As of 1981, stock investment amounted to 0.9 percent of the Gross Domestic Product in the United States and 0.2 percent in Canada.

Data drawn from opinion polls reinforce the comparative generalizations about the greater economic prudence of Canadians. Studies of English- and French-speaking Canadians indicate that on most items, Anglophones fall between Americans and Francophones. When asked by the American and Canadian Gallup Polls in 1979 (U.S.) and 1980 (Canada) about usage of credit cards, 51 percent of Canadians said they never used one, as compared to 35 percent of Americans. The latter were more likely than Canadians to report "regular" usage, 32 percent to 16 percent. Francophones made less use of credit cards (64 percent, never) than Anglophones (44 percent, never). English speakers were also more likely to be regular users than French speakers. The CARA surveys which asked respondents to choose five items which they "consider to be especially important" among a list of seventeen "qualities which children can be encouraged to learn at home" found 21 percent of Francophone Canadians most disposed to include "thrift, sparing money and things" in their list, with Anglophones second, 12 percent, and Americans third, 9 percent. While most people on both sides of the border did not put thrift high, the rank order corresponds to that found for use of credit cards.

Comparable results were obtained in a secondary analysis of two surveys, one conducted in the United States in the fall of 1968 and the other of an English Canadian sample in the spring of 1970. The findings were in harmony with the assumptions that Americans are more likely than Canadians to take economic risks, to use credit, and to try new things in the economic arena (see Table 3).

In discussing these results, Stephen Arnold and James Barnes emphasized that Canadians exhibit much more "financial conservatism" than Americans, as is evident in their varying attitudes toward use of credit. They quote a marketing executive in the automobile industry as reporting that the advertising used in his

TABLE 3.   ATTITUDES TOWARD RISK AND USE OF CREDIT (PERCENT)

Items	Mean Level of Agreement	
	Canada	U.S.
I like to try new and different things	71	74
I often try new brands before my friends and neighbors do	39	48
When I see a new brand on the shelf, I often buy it just to see what it's like[F]	43	52
I like to wait and see how other people like new brands before I try them	31	29
I keep away from brands I never heard of	48	54
I buy many things with a credit or charge card	29	43
In the past year we have borrowed money from a bank or a finance company	39	46
I like to pay cash for everything I buy	80	72
To buy anything, other than a house, on credit is unwise	61	50
I probably need more insurance[M]	35	57
I like to shop where I feel at home[F]	83	89

Source: S. J. Arnold and D. J. Tigert, "Canadians and Americans: A Comparative Analysis," *International Journal of Comparative Sociology,* 15 (March–June 1974), pp. 75, 76.

[F] Females only
[M] Males only

industry varies from that across the border since the "Canadian buyer is much more cost conscious . . . than the American" ("Canadians and Americans: Implications for Marketing," in *Problems in Canadian Marketing,* edited by D. N. Thompson, 1977).

Americans are more disposed than Canadians to express attitudes that reflect greater absorption of the values of the business-industrial system. The CARA surveys posed a number of questions dealing with feelings about work, including (a) pride in "work that you do"; (b) feelings about "being taken advantage of or exploited" on the job; (c) whether employees should unquestionably "follow their superior's instructions on a job"; and (d) how satisfied respondents were with their jobs.

On the first three questions, Americans were more disposed to give the "business" answer, English Canadians were second, and French Canadians third. The percentages expressing "a great deal" of pride in work ran 84, 77, 38; those saying they never felt exploited, 37, 44, 56; and reporting following superior's instructions, 68, 57, 45. But Americans were least likely to be high (top three categories) on a ten-point scale with regard to job satisfaction, 63 percent, with English Canadians in the middle, 69 percent, and French Canadians most satisfied, 74 percent. This response pattern, the inverse of those reported for pride in the job and feelings of exploitation, may reflect a greater interest by Americans in changing to a better job.

The question mentioned earlier which asked respondents to choose from among a list of "qualities which children can be encouraged to learn at home" produced results which on the whole reflect these distinctions. Americans led English Canadians who in turn led French Canadians in the percentage choosing "independence," 32, 27, 15, and "hard work," 26, 21, 17. (I have reported only items in which there is a consistent difference of 5 percent or more. Other items for which there were no large differences included: good manners and politeness, honesty, patience, tolerance of others, self-control, and obedience.)

If Canadians have been more conservative than Americans in their behavior in the private sector, they have been much more prone to rely on the state to handle economic and other matters, as the next section indicates.

The Economy: The Public Sector

In "Revolution and Counterrevolution" I emphasized that Canada "has clearly been much more collectivity-oriented than the United States," while the latter has placed a greater emphasis on "self-orientation." A related thesis has been elaborated in *A Nation Unaware* by Herschel Hardin, who contended that "Canada, in its essentials, is a public enterprise country, always has been, and probably always will be," while the United States has a "private enterprise culture."

The proportion of the Canadian GNP in government hands as of the mid-seventies was 41 percent, compared to 34 percent in the United States; as of 1982 the ratio was 44 to 38 percent. Subtracting defense spending, roughly 2 percent for Canada and 5 to 6 percent for the U.S., widens the gap between the two countries considerably. Taxes as a share of total domestic product were 35 percent in Canada as compared to 30 percent in the United States in 1982. In "The Free Enterprise Dodo Is No Phoenix" (*The Canadian Forum,* August 1976), Canadian political scientist A. J. T. McLeod noted "the pervasiveness of state intervention, regulation, and the frequent appearance of public ownership in Canada," where "the State has always dominated and shaped the economy." Unlike "the United States, [Canada] has never experienced a period of pure unadulterated laissez-faire market capitalism." The period since 1960 has witnessed a particularly rapid expansion in the number of crown corporations: fully 70 percent of them were created in the past quarter of a century. In their previously cited work, Mercer and Goldberg summed up the magnitude of government involvement in the Canadian economy as of 1982:

> Of 400 top industrial firms, 25 were controlled by the federal or provincial governments. Of the top 50 industrials, all ranked by sales, 7 were either wholly owned or controlled by the federal or provincial governments. For financial institutions, 9 of the top 25 were federally or provincially owned or controlled. . . . Canadian governments at all levels exhibit little reticence about involvement in such diverse enterprises as railroads, airlines, aircraft manufacture, financial institutions, steel companies, oil companies, and selling and producing atomic reactors for energy generation.

Research based on opinion poll interviews indicates that Canadians, at both elite and mass levels, are more supportive than Americans of state intervention. Summarizing surveys of high-level civil servants and federal, state, and provincial legislators, Robert Presthus, in *Elites in the Policy Process,* reported

> the sharp difference between the two [national] elites on "economic liberalism," defined as a preference for "big government." . . . Only 17 percent of the American legislative elite ranks high on this disposition, compared with fully 44 percent of their Canadian peers. . . . The direction is the same among bureaucrats, only 17 of whom rank high among the American sample, compared with almost 30 percent among Canadians.

In *Cross-National Perspectives: United States and Canada,* Presthus noted that differences related to party affiliation in both countries emphasize the cross-national variations. Canadian Liberal legislators score much higher than American Democrats on economic liberalism and Canadian Conservatives score much higher than Republicans. Conservatives and Republicans in each country are lower on economic liberalism than Liberals and Democrats, but *Canadian Conservatives are higher than American Democrats.*

Mass attitudinal data reinforce the thesis that Canadians are more collectivity oriented than Americans and therefore are more likely to support government intervention. In the 1968–70 studies of American and English Canadian attitudes discussed earlier, Arnold and Tigert found that, compared to Canadians, Americans were more opposed to big government and less likely to believe that government should guarantee everyone an income (see Table 4A). They, however, emphasized other results, which showed that Americans were more likely than Canadians to take part in voluntary communitarian activities (see Table 4B), as challenging the assumptions that the latter were more collectivity oriented. In a subsequent article, Arnold, writing with James Barnes, concluded: "Americans were found to be individualistic, whereas Canadians were more collectivity oriented," more supportive of state provision of medical care or a guaranteed minimum income. Craig Crawford and James Curtis, in reporting on surveys of two comparable communities on both sides of the border, also initially concluded that their research did not support the assumption that Canadians were more "collectivity oriented" than Americans. But the Crawford-Curtis questions, as Curtis acknowledged in a subsequent discussion, deal with the role of individuals in helping others through voluntary activities, not beliefs about the role of government. What these studies demonstrate is that Americans are more likely to take part in voluntary efforts to achieve particular goals, while Canadians are more disposed to rely on the state. As the CARA studies document, Americans are much more likely to belong to voluntary associations than Canadians.

The existence of an electorally viable social democratic party,

TABLE 4–A. ATTITUDES TOWARD GOVERNMENT (PERCENT)

Items	Mean Level of Agreement	
	Canada	U.S.
The government in Ottawa (Washington) is too big and powerful	40	54
The government should guarantee everyone at least $3,000 per year whether he works or not	36	14

TABLE 4–B. COMMUNITY ACTIVISM (PERCENT)

Items	Mean Level of Agreement	
	Canada	U.S.
I am or have been active in the PTA	24	39
I have helped to collect money for the Red Cross, United Fund, or Miles for Millions (March of Dimes)	41	51
I like to work on community projects	39	44
I do volunteer work for a hospital or service organization on a fairly regular basis	20	20
I am an active member of more than one service organization	16	23
I would be willing to pay higher taxes to get better schools	38	58

Source: S. J. Arnold and D. J. Tigert, "Canadians and Americans: A Comparative Analysis," *International Journal of Comparative Sociology,* 15 (March–June 1974), pp. 80–81.

the New Democrats (NDP), in Canada has been taken by various writers as an outgrowth of the greater influence of the Tory-statist tradition and the stronger collectivity orientation north of the border. Conversely, the absence of a significant socialist movement to the south is explained in part by the vitality of the antistatist and individualist values in the United States. There is, of course, good reason to believe, as Louis Hartz, Gad Horowitz, and I, among others, have argued, that social democratic movements are the other side of statist conservatism, that Tories and socialists are likely to be found in the same polity, while a dominant Lockean liberal tradition inhibits the emergence of socialism as a political force. But other plausible explanations for the difference in the political party systems of Canada and the United States suggest that the contrast in socialist strength should not be relied on as evidence of varying predispositions among the two populations. As I noted in a 1976 article on "Radicalism in North America," one of the main factors differentiating the United States from Canada and most other democratic countries has been its political system, the direct election of the president so that the nation is effectively one constituency and the American electorate is led to see votes for anyone other than the two major candidates as effectively wasted. Seemingly, the American constitutional system serves to inhibit, if not to prevent, electorally viable third parties, and has produced a concealed multiparty or multifactional system, working within the two major parties. And many, such as Michael Harrington, former national chairman of the Socialist party of the U.S., have argued that there is a social democratic faction in America that largely operates within the Democratic party.

The thesis that a Tory-statist tradition is conducive to the emergence of socialist movements, moreover, has been criticized by Robert J. Brym on the grounds that socialist parties have been weakest in the most traditional parts of Canada, Quebec and the Maritimes. However, two Canadian political scientists, William Christian and Colin Campbell, see the recent rise to power in Quebec of a social democratic movement, the Parti Québécois, as reflecting the propensity for a leftist collectivism inherent in Canadian elitist values, that can appear only after the bulwarks of the traditional system break down. In their 1983 work, *Political Parties and Ideologies in Canada*, they concluded that the emergence of socialism

> in Quebec in reaction to the incursions of liberalism and capitalism is hardly surprising from a Hartzean viewpoint, for . . . Quebec's stock of political ideas includes a strong collectivist element. This collectivism is deeply embedded in Quebec's institutions: from the earliest days of New France, the government actively intervened on a broad scale in economic affairs. . . .
> The Church, by its nature a collectivist institution, has long encouraged community enterprise. . . . Quebec's collectivist past provided receptive and fruitful soil for socialist ideas once the invasion of liberal capitalism had broken the monopoly of the old conservative ideology.

Evidence, independent of the effect of diverse electoral systems, that the forces making for class consciousness and organization, linked to collectivity orientations, are more powerful in Canada than the United States may be found in the trade-union membership statistics. Canada not only has had much stronger socialist parties than America since the 1930s, but workers in the northern country are now much more heavily involved in unions than those in the south. By 1983, only one-fifth of the nonagricultural labor force in the United States belonged to labor organizations compared to 40 percent in Canada. In the U.S., the percentage organized in unions has fallen steadily from a high point of 32.5 in 1954, while in Canada, the figure has moved up from 22. Organized labor in Canada surpassed that in the United States for the first time in 1973, a continuing difference which may also reflect variations in labor legislation. In harmony with the evidence that Francophones are more collectivity oriented than Anglophones, a larger proportion of workers in Quebec belong to unions.

To explain these changes and variations would go beyond the scope of this chapter. It may be suggested, however, that the long postwar prosperity refurbished the antistatist and individualistic values of the United States, while in Canada, economic growth in the context of the silent revolution reinforced class and collectivity orientations. Certainly, the successful campaign conducted by Brian Mulroney and the Progressive Conservatives in 1984 continued to emphasize the Tory welfare tradition, while antistatist conservativism (Lockean liberalism) has been strengthened in America.

From a consideration of the role of the state with respect to economic policies, it seems appropriate to turn to aspects of stratification.

Elitism and Equalitarianism

In "Revolution and Counterrevolution" I suggested that Canada and the United States vary with respect to the values of equalitarianism-elitism and achievement-ascription. Achievement, of course, refers to an emphasis on the goal of equality of opportunity, elitism is presumed to be reflected in diffuse respect for authority. Equalitarianism, which I originally perceived as the polar contrast to elitism, was not well elaborated, except to define it in Tocquevillean terms as generalized respect "for all persons . . . because they are human beings."

Equalitarianism, however, has many meanings, not all of which are incompatible with elitism. Conceptualized as "equality of result," it enters into the political arena in efforts to reduce inequality on a group level. And following up on the assumptions of Northrop Frye, Louis Hartz, and Gad Horowitz, it may again be suggested that Tory stimuli, elitist in origin, produce social democratic responses, efforts to protect and upgrade the position of less privileged strata.

Conceptualizing equalitarianism in this fashion leads to the expectation that nations which rank high with respect to the value of achievement, "equality of opportunity," will be less concerned with reducing inequality of condition. If the United States is more achievement oriented and less elitist than Canada, then the U.S. should place more emphasis on educational equality as the primary mechanism for moving into the higher socioeconomic positions. Canada, on the other hand, should be more favorable to redistributive proposals, thus upgrading the lower strata, as, in fact, she is.

In "The Development of Welfare States in North America," in *The Development of Welfare States in Europe and America,* edited by P. Flora and A. J. Heidenheimer (1981), Robert T. Kudrle and Theodore R. Marmor noted that "the ideological difference—slight by international standards—between Canada and the United States appears to have made a considerable difference in welfare state developments." Canadian programs were adopted earlier, "exhibited a steadier development," are financed more progressively, and/or are more income redistributive in the areas of old age security, unemployment insurance, family allowances (nonexistent in the U.S.), and medical care. Similarly, a recent unpublished study by Geoffrey R. Weller of health care practices noted that "the equity objective in health has had a much higher priority in Canada than in the United States."

The main evidence bearing on the relationship between elitism and equality of opportunity in my earlier essay concerned education. As of 1960, the proportion of Canadians aged twenty to twenty-four in higher education (16 percent) was much lower than that of Americans (32 percent). The educational literature of the time also called attention to the more elitist character of the Canadian system, the fact that education in the north was more humanistic and less vocational and professional in orientation.

The number of people attending higher education has increased greatly in both North American societies during the past two decades, although there is still a considerable gap. As of 1979, the percentage of the Canadian age cohort in higher education had risen to 36, but the comparable American figure had increased to 55. The proportion of Canadians enrolled in tertiary education jumped by 125 percent; that of Americans by 72 percent. The Americans, however, moved up more in absolute terms, 23 percent, to 20 percent for Canadians.

Some analysts of recent changes in Canadian universities have referred to them as "Americanizations." Canada not only sharply increased the number of universities and places for students, but her higher education institutions, following public policy, have changed. They have incorporated practical and vocationally relevant subjects, expanded the social sciences and graduate programs, and placed greater emphasis on faculty scholarship. As Claude Bissell, former president of the University of Toronto, emphasized, his country has been moving away from an elitist conception of higher education.

> By endorsing a policy of open accessibility and the concept of the social value of new knowledge, Canada was, one might say, at long last accepting in its educational practices some of the concepts implicit in the American Revolution. . . .
>
> [It was giving up] the conservative, antirevolutionary concepts that had dominated higher education in Canada—the bias to languages and philosophy, the emphasis on thoroughness in the undergraduate degree, and the untroubled merger of the religious and the secular. ("The Place of Learning and the Arts in Canadian Life," in *Perspectives on Revolution and Evolution,* edited by R. A. Preston, 1979)

The changes in the size and content of higher education in Canada should lead to a reduction in the proportion of persons without professional training who hold top jobs. Comparative data indicate that Canada has differed from America, and resembled Britain, in disproportionately recruiting her business and political administrative elites from those without a professional or technical education. As Charles McMillan reported in his previously cited article, "Canadian managers tend to be less well educated than their counterparts in any other industrialized country with the possible exception of Britain."

This conclusion is documented by Wallace Clement's studies of the business elites which reveal that the Canadians not only have less specialized education than the Americans, but also that the former are much more likely to have an elitist social background. As Clement reported in *Continental Corporate Power,* "Entrance to the economic elite is easier for persons from outside the upper class in the United States than in Canada. . . . The U.S. elite is more open, recruiting from a much broader class base than is the case in Canada." Sixty-one percent of the Canadian top executives are of upper-class origin compared to 36 percent of the Americans. Similar cross-national differences among top civil servants were reported in *Cross-National Perspectives* by Robert Presthus and William Monopoli from studies done during the late sixties and early seventies. These revealed a much higher proportion of Canadian than of American bureaucrats were of upper-class origin. In *Elite Accommodation in Canadian Politics,* Presthus explained the phenomena "both in industry and government" as reflecting

> strong traces of the "generalist," amateur approach to administration. The Canadian higher civil service is patterned rather closely after the British administrative class, which even today tends to symbolize traditional and charismatic bases of authority. Technical aspects of government programmes tend to be de-emphasized, while policy-making and the amateur-classicist syndrome are magnified.

As with many other Canadian institutions, the civil service has been changing. A more recent survey of bureaucrats in central government agencies by Colin Campbell and George Szablowski, *The Superbureaucrats: Structure and Behavior in Central Agencies,* found that in "the past decade Canada has seen a remarkable influx of bureaucrats representing segments of the population traditionally excluded from senior positions in the public service," that many of those interviewed had "experienced rapid upward mobility." These developments may reflect the documented decrease in educational inheritance in Canada as the higher education system has grown.

The changes in Canada have been particularly evident in recent years in the central agencies of the federal government. According to Campbell and Szablowski, those in charge, particularly in Finance and the Treasury Board Secretariat, now look for well-trained, specialized people. Conversely, the more politically involved units such as the Prime Minister's Office, the Privy Council Office, and the Federal-Provincial Office are still more willing to hire generalists, often with a legal training. Thus, as Campbell and Szablowski note, "a very sizeable proportion of our officials are generalists."

High-level Canadian bureaucrats, therefore, still differ from those in the United States in that "in the public service generally, [they] enter government much later in life," and, reflecting a generalist rather than a bureaucratic specialist background, they "rarely view their career choice as a vocation," receiving promotion as they "move from ministry to ministry."

Four academic studies based on survey data, one concerned

with national variations in value orientations, two dealing with occupational prestige, and a fourth looking at child-rearing practices, support the conclusion that Canada is more elitist than America. Thus in a study of two communities situated on different sides of the border, discussed earlier, Craig Crawford and James Curtis reported that Americans scored lower than Canadians on an elite orientation scale, and higher on achievement orientation. The variations held up among age groups. Peter Pineo and John Porter found to their surprise that Canadian rankings of occupational prestige on the average were higher than those in the United States. As one possible explanation for the variation, they note: "It occurs to us that there may be a deferential element in the Canadian rankings derived from the elitist pattern suggested by Lipset as being important in Canadian society. The tendency in Canada to rank jobs higher is greatest for the professional and semi-professional categories of jobs where on the average the jobs are ranked about four points higher than in the U.S." (in *Social Stratification in Canada,* edited by J. E. Curtis and W. G. Scott, 1973). Another Canadian sociologist, Neil Guppy, after studying the degree of consensus across the social hierarchy with respect to the prestige rankings given to different occupations by cross-national samples, concluded in *The Canadian Journal of Sociology* (winter 1983–4) that the comparison provides "support, albeit of a serendipitous nature, for Lipset's . . . argument that in the United States less emphasis is placed on hierarchical patterns of deference." The findings are congruent with the assumption that there is "stronger class hegemony in Canada," since her privileged classes appear to have more influence over others with respect to evaluations of the worth of occupations. Wallace E. Lambert, Josiane F. Hamers, and Nancy Frasure-Smith also reported that their findings in *Child Rearing Values: A Cross-National Study* (1979) "are consistent with Lipset's . . . argument that Canadians may be more 'elitist' than Americans," since they found that variations related to class position were more pronounced among Canadians of both language groups than among Americans.

If some researchers report agreement with my hypotheses, an American social psychologist, Milton Rokeach, has noted the discrepancy between the expectations concerning egalitarianism implicit in my earlier work and his findings, although on other issues, such as achievement orientation, his results are supportive. Reporting on a survey of attitudes of students in colleges in both countries, in his chapter in *Perspectives on the Social Sciences in Canada,* edited by T. N. Guinsberg and G. L. Reuber (1974), he indicates that Canadian undergraduates were "less achievement and competence-oriented," but cared "somewhat more for equality . . . than their American counterparts." The latter finding is, however, congruent with my restatement of the issues here, i.e., Canada is more equalitarian, if the term refers to redistributive goals.

Cross-national surveys conducted in recent years have explicitly sought to estimate support for meritocracy when contrasted with equality of result. Their findings point to strong differences between Americans and Canadians on these issues. In the fall of 1979, national samples in the two countries were asked by a Japanese research group to choose between the two in fairly direct fashion:

Here are two opinions about conditions existing in our country. Which do you happen to agree with?

A. There is too much emphasis upon the principle of equality. People should be given the opportunity to choose their own economic and social life according to their individual abilities.

B. Too much liberalism has been producing increasingly wide differences in people's economic and social life. People should live more equally.

In *Index to International Public Opinion, 1980–81,* Elizabeth H. Hastings and Philip K. Hastings reported 41 percent of the Canadians chose the more egalitarian and collectivity oriented option B. The proportion of Americans responding this way was 32 percent. Clearly the pattern of responses suggests that Canadians value equality of result more than Americans, while the latter are more achievement oriented.

CARA put the same issue in the following way:

I'd like to relate an incident to you and ask your opinion of it. There are two secretaries, of the same age, doing practically the same job.

One of the secretaries finds out that the other one earns $20 per week more than she does. She complains to her boss. He says, quite rightly, that the other secretary is quicker, more efficient, and more reliable at her job. In your opinion, is it fair or not fair that one secretary is paid more than the other?

The way this question is formulated is clearly biased in favor of saying that the more productive secretary should be paid more, and large majorities on both sides of the border responded this way. Close to twice the proportion of Francophone Canadians as Americans, 32 percent to 17 percent, said it is unfair to pay the more efficient worker a higher rate, while the Anglophones fell in the middle, 23 percent.

The CARA study also found that the different North American groups adhered to expectation when choosing between classic statements of the conflict between liberty and equality. They were asked:

> Which of these two statements comes closest to your own opinion?
>
> (A) I find that both freedom and equality are important but if I were to make up my mind for one or the other, I would consider personal freedom more important, that is, everyone can live in freedom and develop without hindrance.
>
> (B) Certainly both freedom and equality are important, but if I were to make up my mind for one of the two, I would consider equality more important, that is, that nobody is underprivileged and that social class differences are not so strong.

Most respondents chose freedom over equality, but not surprisingly, Americans led in this preference. Seventy-two percent of them agreed with the first statement as compared to 64 percent of the English Canadians and 57 percent of the French Canadians. Conversely, 38 percent of the Francophones, 29 percent of the Anglophones, and only 20 percent of the Americans agreed that an emphasis on the reduction of class differences is more important than freedom.

If greater commitment to equality of result leads Canadians to voice a higher preference for equality over freedom or liberty, the assumption that Canada is more elitist than the United States implies, as I noted in my original comparison of the two societies, that Canadians should be less intolerant toward deviants or dissidents than Americans. And the CARA data bear this anticipation out. When asked about various kinds of unpopular people, which of them you *"would not* like to have as neighbors," Canadians, the Francophones particularly, were more accepting than Americans. The latter were more likely (49 percent) than English Canadians (40 percent) or French Canadians (30 percent) to say that they were opposed to having "people with a criminal record as neighbors." Americans also were more disposed to find "emotionally unstable people" offensive as neighbors (47 percent) than

English Canadians (33 percent) or French Canadians (13 percent). Not surprisingly, Americans exhibited less tolerance for people described as "extremists." Thus, "left-wing extremists" were rejected as neighbors by 34 percent of the Americans, 31 percent of the English Canadians, and only 20 percent of the French Canadians; while "right-wing extremists" were turned down by 26 percent of the Americans, 24 percent of the Anglophone Canadians, and 14 percent of the Francophones.

As a final subject, this analysis turns to national unity, to the ways that subgroups, ethnic and regional, behave in the two societies.

Mosaic and Melting Pot: Center and Periphery

In "Revolution and Counterrevolution" I asserted that "Canada is more particularistic (group-attribute conscious) than the seemingly more universalistic United States." These differences are reflected a) in the Canadian concept of the "mosaic," applied to the right to cultural survival of ethnic groups, as compared to the American notion of the "melting pot"; b) in the more frequent recurrence and survival of strong regionally based third parties in Canada than in the United States; and c) in the greater strength of provinces within the Canadian union, compared to the relative weakness of the states and the nationalization of politics, i.e., the decline of regionalism, in America.

The origin of these cross-national differences can also be traced to the impact of the Revolution. American universalism, the desire to incorporate diverse groups into one culturally unified whole, is inherent in the founding ideology, the American Creed. Canadian particularism, the preservation of subnational group loyalties, an outgrowth of the commitment to the maintenance of two linguistic subcultures, is derivative from the decision of the Francophone clerical elite to remain loyal to the British monarchy, as a protection against the threat posed by Puritanism and democratic populism from the revolutionary south. Given the importance of the French-speaking areas to British North America, the subsequent Canadian federal state incorporated protections for the linguistic minority, and the provinces assumed considerable power.

These differences, however, should have declined with modern-

ization. Most analysts have assumed that industrialization, urbanization, and the spread of education would reduce ethnic and
regional consciousness, that universalism would supplant particularism. As Nathan Glazer and Daniel P. Moynihan noted in
Beyond the Melting Pot, it was generally believed that "divisions
of culture, religion, language [and race] . . . would inevitably
lose their weight and sharpness in modern and modernizing societies, . . . that common systems of education and communication would level differences." In the February 1973 issue of
Publius: The Journal of Federalism, Samuel Beer emphasized that
modernization inherently led to a growth in authority at the center and a decline in state and provincial power as the different
parts of federal countries became more differentiated and interdependent. As he put it: "In the United States, as in other modernizing societies, the general historical record has spelled centralization. . . . The main reasons for this change are . . . to
be found . . . in the new forces produced by an advanced
modernity."

The validity of the assumptions that structural modernization
would sharply reduce ethnic and regional diversity and the power
of federal subunits has been challenged by developments, generally for ethnicity, and in Canada particularly, for subnational
territorial areas. From the sixties on the world has witnessed an
ethnic revival in many countries. In Canada, even prior to the
revival, the values underlying the concept of the "mosaic" meant
that various minorities, in addition to the Francophones, would
be able to sustain a stronger group life than comparable ones in
the United States. As Arthur Davis pointed out in his previously
cited work:

> Ethnic and regional differences . . . have been more generally accepted,
> more legitimatized [in Canada] than they have been in our southern neigh-
> bor. There has not been as much pressure in Canada for "assimilation" as
> there has been in the United States. . . . Hutterite communities unques-
> tionably are granted more autonomy in Canada than in the United States.
> Likewise, the Indians of Canada, however rudely they were shunted into
> reservations . . . were seldom treated with such overt coercion as were the
> American Indians.

A comparison of the Mennonites in the two countries points up
the way in which the varying national values and structures have
affected group behavior. In the spring 1978 *Canadian Journal of
Sociology,* Rodney Sawatsky noted: "In America, the Mennonites

with their ethnic and non-conformist heritage experience many difficulties with their dual American and Mennonite loyalties." He contends that north of the border they "tend to feel more at home in their adopted homeland. . . . Canadian Mennonites have not needed to deny their past or reorient their religion to embrace denominationalism to verify their acceptability as Canadians. . . . Canadian Mennonites appear to have shared less of the strain of identity experienced by their American brethren."

In the same publication, Stuart Schoenfeld noted that the differing organization of Jews in Canada and the United States also shows how the structure and behavior of an ethnic-religious group may vary with national environments. Canadian Jewry is much better organized as a community than its American counterpart. A single national organization, the Canadian Jewish Congress, represents all Jews in Canada, while there is no comparable group in the United States. A much higher proportion of Jewish youth is enrolled in day schools in Canada than in the United States, while the intermarriage rate is lower north of the border in spite of the fact that the Canadian Jewish community is much smaller than the American. The size factor should have led to greater assimilation in Canada, but the emphasis on particularistic group organization subsumed in the mosaic character of Canada seemingly helps to perpetuate a more solidaristic Canadian Jewish community.

Canadian ethno-cultural groups continue in a more protective environment than American ones, because of the official acceptance of "multiculturalism," stemming from the need to conciliate the French Canadians. Ironically, Anglophone Canadians have become more committed to this concept than Francophones who prefer a two-cultures model. The former may see in multiculturalism a way of denying the French equal status, according to David J. Elkins and Richard Simeon in *Small Worlds: Provinces and Parties in Canadian Political Life.* Ever since the publication in 1969 of the fourth volume of the *Report of the Royal Commission on Bilingualism and Biculturalism: The Cultural Contribution of the Other Ethnic Groups,* the country has been committed to helping all ethnic groups. A cabinet ministry was established in 1973, whose exclusive responsibility is multiculturalism. The government now gives grants to the assorted ethnic minorities for projects designed to celebrate and extend their cultures.

During the past two decades Blacks have assumed a role within

the American polity somewhat similar to that which the Québécois play in Canada. The call for "Black Power," in the context
of demands for group, as distinct from individual, rights through
affirmative action quotas and other forms of aid, has led the
United States to explicitly accept particularistic standards for
dealing with racial and ethnic groups. Blacks, like French Canadians, are "unmeltable ethnics," and much as Francophones have
legitimated cultural autonomy for other non–Anglo-Saxon Canadians, the changing position of the Blacks has enabled other
American ethnic groups and women to claim similar particularistic rights. In effect, the United States has moved toward replacing
the ideal of the "melting pot" with that of the "mosaic."

In evaluating the variations in the position of ethnic groups in
North America at the end of the seventies, John Porter in *The
Measure of Canadian Society* argued that a "melting pot course
towards the development of a universalistic modern character and
culture emphasizing common human qualities . . . and shedding
the particularisms of history . . . [is] the revolutionary option,"
and he concluded his analysis with the "judgement that despite
the current revival of ethnicity the United States veers more towards the revolution than does Canada."

But if the two North American countries have reduced some of
the variation in the ways they define the position of minorities,
they are more disparate than before with respect to the importance of the center and the periphery—the national government
versus the regions, states, and provinces. Regional differences have
steadily declined in the United States. They have remained important or have even increased in Canada.

Canadian provinces have become more disposed than American
states to challenge the power of the federal government. Movements advocating secession have recurred in this century, not only
in Quebec, but in part of the Maritimes, the Prairies, and British
Columbia as well. The tensions between Ottawa and the provinces and regions are not simply conflicts among politicians over
the distribution of power. Public sentiment in Canada remains
much more territorial than in the United States, reflecting more
distinct regional and provincial interests and values. Roger Gibbins in *Regionalism: Territorial Politics in Canada and the
United States* reported that in a comparative analysis of "voting
between 1945 and 1970 in seventeen western nations, Canada

ranked among the least nationalized, the most diversified regionally, while the United States was the most nationalized. Over the
time span of the study, voting in the United States was progressively nationalized whereas Canada experienced no change."
Three other studies, two dealing with the elections in English
Canada through this century, and the third for all of Canada from
1878 to 1974, each concluded that provincial differences had not
declined or had actually increased over time.

The sharp discrepancy between Canadian and American developments, on the one hand a weakening of the power of the national government, on the other a strengthening of it, has led
political scientists to ask "what has accounted for these contra-
dictory developments?" The answers suggested are manifold. Few
Canadian scholars are ready to agree, as John Porter was, that the
difference represents the continued influence in Canada of counterrevolutionary traditions and institutions, or that, as Thomas
O. Hueglin noted in an as yet unpublished paper, the variations
represent a "choice of different sets of values, as the choice between a preference for the maintenance of group identities or for
the diffusion of individual universalism." Rather, as Milton J.
Esman pointed out, they discuss a variety of relevant factors:
"*societal* (economic, demographic, and international forces) and
institutional (the formal or constitutional structures of the state)"
("Federalism and Modernization," *Publius: The Journal of Federalism,* winter 1984).

Two variables, both of which may be linked to the outcome of
the American Revolution, appear to be most important. One is
the role of the French Canadians discussed earlier. The other is
the effect of the variation between the presidential-congressional
divided powers American system and the British parliamentary
model. As Roger Gibbins emphasized, "the Québécois . . . have
used the Quebec provincial government as an instrument of cultural survival and, because the stakes are so high, provincial rights
have been guarded with a vigor unknown in the United States."
Smaller provinces, seeking to protect their autonomy, have been
able to do so because Quebec has always been in the forefront of
the struggle.

The much greater propensity of Canadian provinces as compared to American states to engage in recurrent struggles with the
federal government and to support a variety of particularistic

"third parties" may be explained by the fact that regional interests are much less well protected in Parliament than in Congress. As I argued three decades ago in *The Canadian Forum:* "Given the tight national party discipline imposed by a parliamentary as compared with a presidential system, Canadians are forced to find a way of expressing their special regional or other group needs. . . . The Canadian solution has been to frequently support different parties on a provincial level than those which they back nationally," so that provincial governments may carry out the representation tasks which in the United States are fulfilled by congressional interest blocs. Or, as Donald Smiley put it in the winter 1984 *Publius: The Journal of Federalism:* "Congressionalism appears to inhibit the direct confrontation of federal and state governments, while the parliamentary forms in their contemporary Canadian variant sharpen the conflict between federal and provincial jurisdictions."

Conclusion

Without succumbing further to the temptation of discussing other Canadian-American differences, there can be little doubt that regardless of how much emphasis is placed on structural or cultural (value) factors in accounting for variations, that Canada and the United States continue to differ considerably along most of the dimensions suggested in my previous work. My main modification of prior formulations is the recognition that an emphasis on elitism in a democratic industrialized society is accompanied by concern for redistributive equalitarianism. And much as Canadians are more supportive of this orientation than Americans, Francophones are now more favorable than Anglophones.

As noted earlier, some critics of the cultural approach, such as Arthur Davis and I. L. Horowitz, have contended that the differences between the two nations have largely been a function of "cultural lag," that Canada, traditionally somewhat less developed economically than the United States, has been slower to give up the values and life styles characteristic of a less industrialized, more agrarian society. Presumably then, as the structural gap declines, Canada should become more like the United States. A similar thesis, on a broader scale, has been enunciated by various proponents of world system or convergence theories, who see national cultural differences diminishing, if not vanishing, as the industrial systems of the developed countries come to approximate each other. In the specific case of Canada and the United States, the two should become even more similar since the "American Connection" has resulted in increased domination by American companies over broad sections of Canadian economic life, while Canada has also become more culturally dependent on its southern neighbor through the spread of the American mass media, particularly television, as well as various forms of journalism. Ironically, this argument, that Canada must inevitably become American culturally, finds greatest support among Canadian leftist scholars, who also most disparage the culture to the south of them.

Since World War II, substantial changes, in economic productivity, education (quantitatively and qualitatively), and in rates of upward social mobility, that have been described in French Canada as the "quiet revolution" and in the United States and English Canada as "the post-industrial revolution" have clearly reduced the structural gap. But there has been no consistent decline in the patterns of differences in behavior and values.

The United States has grown more centralized politically, while Canada has moved in the opposite direction. The same inverse relationship has occurred with respect to nationalization of politics; similar lines of cleavage increasingly cut across all sections south of the border, while in the north, regional diversity has increased. Behavioral indicators of Canadian and American economic cultures, for example, with respect to savings or use of credit, suggest greater, not less, variation across borders. The difference in class organizational behavior in the two countries, as reflected in rates of trade-union membership, has also grown greatly.

The cross-national variations have narrowed in other respects. The due process rights of the accused are now much stronger in Canada than previously, as a result of constitutional changes, but the distinction between greater Canadian adherence to a crime control model and American to a due process one still holds. Canada's increased concern with extending equality of opportunity, however, has also helped to make the two societies more comparable with respect to the scope of their educational systems and opportunities to enter the elites. Both countries have witnessed an ethnic revival, an increase in particularistic demands by minorities, which has led to a greater acceptance of multiculturalism. The United States, however, continues to be more universalistic in this respect than its neighbor.

Cross-national variations in religious behavior and attitudes continue, although their content has changed. The adherents of the ecclesiastical churches, Catholic and Anglican, which predominate in Canada, have become more secular and liberal in their attitudes and lower in their level of religious participation; the adherents of the evangelical and fundamentalist Protestant sects, more characteristic of the United States, have become more committed and activist. Related to these changes is the further fact that Canadians are now more liberal than Americans with respect to sexual morality, and that national variations in birth rates and divorces have declined greatly. (The latter also reflects modifications in the law).

Survey data and impressionistic literature continue to support the thesis that Canada is a more elitist or deferential society than the United States, although less so than two decades ago. But at the same time the evidence and logic of analysis suggest that Canadians have grown more supportive than Americans of redistributive equalitarianism. Canadian political parties, including the recently victorious Tories, remain committed to an activist welfare state and state ownership of industry. American parties, particularly, but not exclusively, the Republicans, have returned to advocacy of a weaker state, one which is less involved in redistributive welfare programs.

I have paid more attention here than in my earlier writings to variations between the two Canadian linguistic cultures. The evidence indicates that Francophone Canadians vary more from their Anglophone conationals than the latter do from Americans. Quebec, once the most conservative part of Canada, has become the most liberal on social issues and has a quasi-socialist provincial government. Clearly, as John Porter and others have emphasized, there are Canadian styles and values that differentiate both linguistic cultures from the American one.

The cultural and political differences between the two North American nations suggest why they occasionally have some difficulty understanding each other in the international arena. There are the obvious effects of variations in size, power, and awareness of the other. Canadians object to being taken for granted, and to being ignored by their neighbor. As citizens of a less populous power, they sympathize with other small or weak countries who are pressed by the United States. But beyond the consequences of variations in national power and interests, Canadians and Americans, as I have tried to spell out here, have a somewhat different *Weltanschauung*, world view, ideology. Derivative from their revolutionary ideological and sectarian Protestant heritages, Americans, more than other Western peoples, tend to view international politics in nonnegotiable moralistic and ideological terms. Canadians, like Europeans, with whom they share a church rather than a sectarian religious tradition, and a national self-conception drawn from a common history rather than a revolutionary ideology, are more disposed to perceive foreign policy conflicts as reflections of interest differences, and therefore subject to negotiation and compromise.

In trying in the early fifties to answer the question what is "distinctively Canadian," Frye noted in "Letters in Canada" that "historically, a Canadian is an American who rejects the Revolution." By the mid-sixties, I suggested that the national self-images were changing as a result of varying perceptions of international events, that "many Canadians now view their country as more 'leftist' or liberal in its institutions and international objectives than the United States." Since then, many Canadians, including Conservatives, have supported the "Revolution" in various places, such as Vietnam, Nicaragua, and El Salvador, while the United States has backed the "Counterrevolution," the "contras." (Americans, it should be noted, often take this position in the context of a belief that they are backing democracy, the people, against actual or potential tyrants.)

Some Canadian literary critics, such as Ronald Sutherland and A. J. M. Smith, contend that Canadian literature has changed greatly in the past decade or two, coming to resemble American fiction, in line with the presumed shift in national political identifications and the postwar "modernization" of Canadian society. As Sutherland noted, during the 1970s

a new hero, as it were, suddenly exploded from the pages of Canadian fiction. In many respects he is an exponent of traditional American rather than Canadian values—self-reliance, individualism, independence, self-confidence. . . . Clear examples of the new hero are found in novels from both French and English Canada, indicating that Canadians of each major language group are simultaneously and at long last creating a new image of themselves. ("A Literary Perspective: The Development of a National Consciousness," in *Understanding Canada,* edited by William Metcalfe, 1982)

And if there is a new image, a new hero, the expression of new national attitudes and behavior cannot be far behind.

The United States and Canada remain two nations formed around sharply different organizing principles. As various novelists and literary critics have emphasized, their basic myths vary considerably, and national ethoses and structures too are determined in large part by such myths. One nation's institutions reflect the effort to apply the universalistic principles emphasizing competitive individualism and egalitarianism, while the other's are an outgrowth of a particularistic compact to preserve linguistic and provincial cultures and rights and elitism.

Although some will disagree, there can be no argument. As Margaret Atwood has well put it in *Second Words:* "Americans and Canadians are not the same, they are the products of two very different histories, two very different situations."

Albert Legault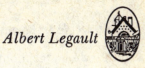

5

Canada
and the United States:
The Defense Dimension

Canada's strategic importance is mostly an accident of geography. Canada, in a sense, is a country without a "region." The importance of her territory may vary as it is seen through American or Canadian eyes. It may also depend on a critical dimension: the evolution of technology. Developments in outer space or the Arctic or the North Atlantic may affect the relative decline or strengthening of Canada's strategic importance. Hence, even the geographical factor is, in a sense, relative.

Before considering the major policy issues that Canada and the United States may confront in the next fifteen years or so, discussion of Canada's strategic importance seems warranted. In a classic article in *International Journal* (Summer 1962) on the strategic importance of Canada, Dr. Robert Sutherland considered three

ALBERT LEGAULT *is a professor of political science at Laval University and a member of the board of the Canadian Institute for International Peace and Security. From 1973 to 1980 he was director-general of the Centre Québécois de Relations Internationales and associate executive director of the Canadian Institute for International Affairs. Dr. Legault also served as the Canadian expert for the United Nations Study Group on Nuclear Weapons. He is an international lecturer, has written many articles for distinguished scientific journals and newspapers, and is the coauthor of* The Dynamics of Nuclear Balance.

constant elements of Canada's strategic posture: geography, economic potential, and broad national interests.

The Strategic Importance of Canada's Geography

On the whole, technological evolution is likely to strengthen, as much as reshape, the strategic importance of Canada's geography for North American defense. Several factors can be invoked in support of this thesis. First, there is the technological factor, which has two opposing influences. On one hand, the role of the North American Aerospace Defense (NORAD) system has declined in importance over the years because of the balance of nuclear deterrence afforded by the second-strike capability of the superpowers' ballistic missiles. On the other hand, during this same period the requirements for early detection of an enemy's aerial movements have become more stringent and critical to the security of the North American continent. Adequate warning time, together with the ability of systems to provide detailed analysis of the extent and nature of hostile aerial movements, is needed in order to reduce the vulnerability of U.S. retaliatory forces, to facilitate the coordination of means for countering the threat, and to provide greater flexibility in the choice of appropriate response.

Second, there is every indication that the bomber threat will reappear with heightened intensity toward the end of the 1980s. In recent years the bomber has emerged as a natural platform eminently suited to the role of stand-off launcher for Cruise missiles equipped with conventional or nuclear warheads. A new Soviet bomber, as well as a new Cruise missile carrier, is under development. Currently considerable progress is being made in the Cruise missile area. Given their accuracy, the supersonic capability they may acquire, and their low radar signature, Cruise missiles can reasonably be expected to become an important element in the strategic strike forces of either superpower toward the end of the 1990s. Such an important structural change in composition of their strategic strike forces would undoubtedly impose new demands on air defense.

Third, these developments, coupled with the evolution of U.S. strategic doctrine toward greater flexibility in nuclear response, probably make it imperative that protection of the main command, control, and communication centers of the U.S. strategic forces be a matter of first priority. For both sides the bomber is likely to become the most appropriate—if not the most favored—instrument for providing the flexibility implied by selective and controlled nuclear response strategy.

Fourth, it must be admitted that the U.S. approach to continental defense is an objective reality from which Canada cannot really escape. During the coming quarter of a century, the United States will probably ascribe the same high priority to matters of continental defense as has been given since 1945. Of course, this emphasis has fluctuated because of technological change over time, and technology will continue to play an important role.

Three major considerations will likely be uppermost in the minds of American leaders between now and the end of the century. First, Canada will continue to be perceived as a first line of defense for the North American continent. Second, with or without Canada's concurrence, the United States must protect its strategic centers of communications, command, and control. Third, even if Canada suddenly decided no longer to participate in North American continental defense, Washington could not accept the strategic loss of the vast expanse to its north. The United States would rapidly equip itself with suitable means for air defense, which, in addition to those deployed in Alaska, would eventually extend to Greenland and exoatmospheric space overlying Canada. Instead of being bordered to the south by a neighboring friendly power, Canada then would be in an environment controlled by the United States in all four directions of the compass, as well as in a vertical dimension. Moreover, in such a situation it is unlikely that the United States would be inclined to make any concessions to its northern neighbor. It was in this context that Dr. Sutherland spoke of the "involuntary American guarantee," and implied not only that the United States undoubtedly would protect Canada from any external threat, whether or not Canada wished it, but also that Canada could not afford the luxury of becoming a "source of insecurity" for its southern neighbor.

Finally, it should be noted that Soviet perception of the North American defense system scarcely can be different from that shared by those Americans and Canadians viewing it as an integrated defense network. In the event of war it is obvious that, from the

Soviet standpoint, North America would not be "divided" or "partitioned" according to a pattern of diverse and varied geographical mosaics, some viewed as friendly or neutral and others as hostile. Instead, it would be considered as an integrated system of strategically valued targets. This conclusion derives not only from military considerations, but also from economic ones. Because of the complex economic interdependencies between Canada and the United States, the Soviet Union could not logically contemplate delivering a mortal blow to the United States without also attacking Canadian interests. Nor could the Soviet Union attack Canada without triggering a response from the United States.

The possibility exists that the USSR, in response to a selective U.S. strike against one of her allies, might seek to "punish" the United States through a limited attack against Canada. However, the fact that Canada is integrated closely with the North American defense system makes such a scenario unlikely. Under these circumstances the U.S. deterrent plays more strongly in Canada's favor than for any other allied nation. The advantages of the U.S. "involuntary guarantee" probably are to be found at this level. According to some, this situation always carries the risk that, notwithstanding her possible reluctance, Canada would be involved in a conflict between the major powers or would bear the brunt of the consequences. In this context, Canada's argument always has been that the greatest military threat facing her is the prospect of nuclear war between the major powers; consequently, she continues to strive for its avoidance through participation in the integrated Western military structure founded on the principles of nuclear deterrence.

The probability of avoidance of nuclear war is related to the success of deterrence, just as the probability of unparalleled devastation is linked to the failure of deterrence. Therefore, the outstanding question for the long term is whether or not the probability of success of deterrence is greater than the probability of its failure. Thirty-five years without nuclear war does not prove a posteriori that nuclear war is impossible a priori. Reality is just the reverse. Precisely because nuclear war is possible, deterrence is important. Perhaps there is no absolute way to resolve this dilemma. About all that can be said is that if deterrence fails, it would be preferable for Canada to have the means available for protection and for limiting damage than to run the graver risk of unpreparedness. Equally, cooperation with the United States would be better than risking a situation so difficult for the United States that the stability of deterrence would be threatened. In this event the prospect of nuclear war would become even more difficult for Canada to endure.

Canada's strategic importance, therefore, derives essentially from her geographic situation. Her participation in continental North American defense clearly follows from a political decision based on the principle "no incineration without representation." This approach is predicated on the rationale that, from the standpoint of Canadian interest, it is better to try to mold the system from within than to stand opposed to it from without. The "benevolent participation" of Canada in the integrated North American defense system is in some way linked to the American "involuntary guarantee." Thus, the chances of avoiding nuclear war are tied to the calculated risk that should deterrence fail, the security of Canada would be better ensured within an integrated system than if she stood alone. This situation derives not only from military considerations, but also stems from the fact that Canada has enormous economic potential attractive to the United States.

The Strategic Importance of Canada's Air Space

Situated at the northern juncture of Eurasia and North America, Canada forms a direct corridor of communication between the USSR and the United States. All Soviet long-range surface-to-surface missiles targeted on the United States must necessarily pass over Canada to reach their objectives. The one exception is the Fractional Orbit Bombardment System (FOBS), conceived to approach the United States via a fractional planetary orbit over the South Pole. Also, the most direct air route from Soviet territory to strategic objectives on American soil passes through Canadian air space. Long-range ballistic missiles launched from Soviet submarines strategically located in the Sea of Okhotsk or the Norwegian Sea must traverse for at least part of their trajectories the exoatmospheric space over Canadian territory to reach U.S. targets in the Midwest or on the Northeast or Northwest seaboards.

What then are the main military advantages that Canada derives from her geographic position relative to ballistic missile and bomber threats? In the event of attack, one of the most vital requirements is to maximize the warning time to military command systems. It is critical that military commands have enough time to assess the magnitude of the attack, place their own forces on a state of alert, and protect their mobile retaliatory strike forces by ensuring that strategic aircraft become airborne and maritime strike forces reach the open sea. If necessary, the weight of the second strike to be executed in response to the expected threat also could be assigned. For each threat, advance detection systems either already are or will be deployed to ensure the longest possible warning time in all expected circumstances.

Distant warning can provide only a general indication of the extent, nature, and origin of an attack. Other systems must perform the tasks of computing the attack trajectories of missiles or the flight paths of hostile bombers. These functional tasks comprise the second phase of aerospace defense operations. They entail the precise specification of hostile movements, missiles or bombers en route to North American territory.

The third phase essentially concerns the operations of identification and discrimination. In case of missile attack, the defense must be able to identify or calculate the number of assailant warheads carried by each missile and, eventually, to distinguish warheads from decoys or chaff that accompany them in their trajectories. These requirements are especially important for the U.S. antiballistic missile (ABM) systems that may be deployed in the future. The task of identification and discrimination is just as important in the case of a potential airborne threat. This is particularly true in peacetime, because the "threat" may be posed by an aircraft that is simply lost, a friendly aircraft, or one that failed to file a flight plan with the air traffic control authorities. The requirement for "visual" identification would be less stringent in wartime since an unidentified aircraft probably would be considered an intruder and, consequently, an attack target.

Finally, the task of destruction is assigned to the active defense units integral to ballistic missile or air defense systems. The Soviet Union has at its disposal a very limited ABM system using Galosh interceptor missiles, while the United States has elected not to deploy an ABM system. However, the Salt I Treaty would permit each side to deploy a maximum of 100 ABM interceptors.

THE BALLISTIC MISSILE THREAT

Warning—Distant warning of a ballistic missile threat is virtually instantaneous. The boost phase of a ballistic missile lasts from two to five minutes. (The boost phase may be considerably shortened in the near future with the new generation of missiles.) During this phase the missile wake exhibits strong traces of ionized gas detectable by over-the-horizon (OTH) radar. In addition, the missile wake is hot and can be detected by means of infrared techniques, particularly once the missile has traversed the most dense layers of the atmosphere. Radar techniques were used largely in the 1970s for monitoring ballistic missile firings from the USSR. The transmitters employed were powerful over-the-horizon forward scatter (OTH-F) radar located in Japan, the Philippines, and Taiwan, and the receiving stations were located in Italy and West Germany. By these means, Soviet launches were almost instantaneously recorded on the radar screens of the receiving stations. Over-the-horizon back scatter (OTH-B) radar could also provide a similar capability. It appears that OTH radars are used today only for observing test launches of new Soviet ballistic missiles and that distant warning systems depend only on satellites.

With a network of three satellites placed in synchronous orbit to provide coverage of the entire planet, any missile fired from either a fixed or mobile platform, such as a submarine, can be detected almost instantaneously by using infrared techniques. In this method, the "transmitter" is the source of thermal energy produced by the missile during its boost phase, and the "receiver" is the satellite itself. Ground stations are instrumented to receive the radio signals from the satellites, and information is then transmitted in real time to Colorado Springs.

Distant warning systems, however, lose sight of the ballistic missile trajectory once the boost phase necessary to elevate the missile above the atmosphere ends. Several seconds later the ballistic missile trajectory is acquired by the powerful radars of the Ballistic Missile Early Warning System (BMEWS) that cover the northern approaches to the North American continent. BMEWS stations are located at Clear in Alaska, Thule in Greenland, and Fylingdale in England. An auxiliary station is situated at Shemya in the Aleutian Islands.

As seen in Figure 1, BMEWS is an advance detection system

Fig. 1. Ballistic Missile Detection Systems (Excluding Satellites).

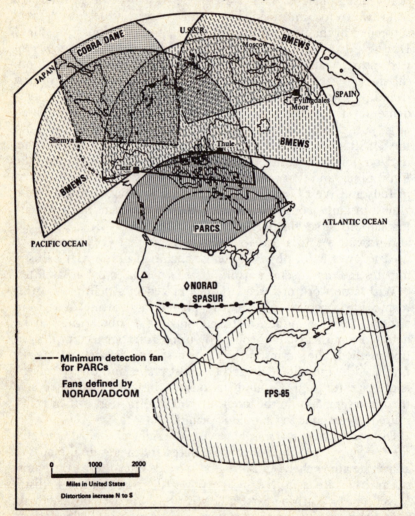

Source: John M. Collins, *U.S.–Soviet Military Balance,* New York: McGraw-Hill Publications Company, 1980, p. 160 (Plate 6). © 1980 by McGraw-Hill Publications Company.

able to provide multiply-redundant coverage since the detection fans largely overlap each other. Because each station can transmit more than one "pattern" of electromagnetic waves at differing altitudes, determination of the missile trajectory is extremely precise and rapid. The range of the BMEWS radar is estimated at 3,000 miles.

Most of the time, however, separation of the nuclear warheads from the missile nose cone occurs beyond the BMEWS line. Under these circumstances, a powerful phased-array radar of 1,800-mile range, operating over a circular arc of 130 degree Perimeter Acquisition Radar Characterization System (PARCS) can be used to make precise determination of the Multiple Independently Targeted Reentry Vehicle (MIRV) trajectories and to permit discrimination between decoys and attacking nuclear warheads. The PARCS, located at Grand Forks, North Dakota, is the sole surviving element of the former Safeguard system designed for ballistic missile defense (BMD).

Other types of electronic scanning radar are able to perform the functions of identification and discrimination also. The FPS-85, situated at Eglin in Florida, is oriented toward the South to provide warning of a FOBS threat originating in the Caribbean or South Pacific. To guard against the ballistic missile threat from submarines deployed in the Eastern Atlantic or Western Pacific, two powerful phased-array radar of 3,000-mile range, known as PAVE PAWS, will provide maximum possible warning time in case of attack. Although the coverage by these radars is not shown on Figure 1, they are located at the points designated by triangles, at Otis in Massachusetts and at Beale in California. Thus, besides the capability to destroy incoming warheads, all other capabilities required for BMD already exist. None of the systems involved is dependent on the use of Canadian territory.

Interception—It is a matter of speculation whether the situation would be any different in the future should the United States decide to equip itself with an ABM system. Assuming that a Low-Altitude Defense (LoAD) system were developed, there would be a definite advantage to deploy ABM interceptors on Canadian territory to defend U.S. land-based missile launchers. Interception could be effected much further north, perhaps prior to the separation of nuclear warheads from the missiles, although this would not be a prerequisite to the system's effective operation.

If the United States decided to complement the LoAD system with a space-based exoatmospheric interception system, Canada would not be involved in its development or deployment. Therefore, even though the exoatmospheric space above Canadian territory would be of vital interest to the United States, Canada would exercise no control over its use in detection, tracking, or discrimination in the final phases of the trajectories of attacking missiles. Hence, Canada's role is negligible. Technological evolution by the year 2000 may cause Canada to reassess her role in ABM matters should U.S. interest in such matters intensify. Even so, Canada's role would not be essential to U.S. security. The situation would be quite different if the United States opted for a widespread BMD system. Besides its extreme, if not prohibitive, expense, such a scenario appears the least plausible. Thus, a major change in Canada's marginal role in BMD is not anticipated.

THE BOMBER THREAT

Warning—Canada's strategic importance in defense against the bomber, as opposed to the missile, is quite different. Because detection capability of conventional radar is limited to direct line of sight, it is unable to acquire images of hostile aircraft approaching North American territory from below the local tangent to the horizon.

The developing technology of OTH-B radar probably would be able to resolve this problem were it not for the particular conditions at the North Pole. This region frequently experiences magnetic storms, characterized by the famous aurora borealis which extends over several hundred miles and whose intensity varies according to the season and time of day. If this phenomenon did not exist, two stations, located in Alaska or in Greenland, could provide the United States with distant warning far superior to that afforded by the advance warning systems that now form part of the Distant Early Warning (DEW) line, which more accurately could be called "Advanced Early Warning." It would seem for the moment that these problems have not been resolved, and indeed, many assert that it is simply impossible to operate OTH-B radar in the far North.

The United States is, therefore, looking more toward space and increased use of suitably instrumented satellites to provide effective distant warning of potential bomber threats. Even this goal has yet to be achieved, since problems posed by the concept of aerial detection from satellites are considerable also. The use of infrared technology as a means of detection requires the development of extremely discriminating sensors. For example, since a significant quantity of infrared radiation can be reflected when solar energy impinges on clouds or the ground, it becomes necessary to discriminate among various infrared emission sources. In addition, military aircraft designers go to considerable lengths to reduce to an absolute minimum the infrared signatures of the engine exhausts. When operating at very high altitude where air resistance is minimal, a bomber possibly could adopt a flight mode akin to a glider's except for short, intermittent periods of acceleration at maximum engine thrust. In overcast conditions, a bomber could fly under or through clouds so that detection from space would be much more problematic. The United States plans to conduct experiments to establish the absolute limits of these space-based techniques for distant aerial detection.

A second technique for distant aircraft detection from space eventually will involve the use of powerful radar located in Earth orbit. Unlike the passive infrared technique that depends on detection of the infrared radiation produced by the bomber itself, the active radar technique demands detection of the echo of a radar signal reflected from the aircraft. Thus, a very powerful satellite-borne radar source is needed to produce the primary signal, which may necessitate a space-based nuclear reactor.

Such systems as these may become operational during the 1990s. For the moment they are still in the drawing board stage, although several devices intrinsic to each system already have been tested in various experiments. Whatever the future of satellite-based distant detection systems, Canada's geographic location clearly will be of no advantage to the United States. Moreover, the implementation of such systems would diminish the relative importance of the DEW line, and, hence, further reduce U.S. reliance on Canada's geography.

Interception—The effectiveness of air defense systems depends not only on the means of detection employed but also on the associated capabilities for interception and destruction. As detection systems improve, the means for interception and destruction must also improve. Consequently, the U.S. perspective of Canada's strategic importance in matters of air defense could experience a shift in emphasis, and Canada could be faced with a paradox. As detection systems rely less on Canada's geographical advantages, her territory may assume decisive importance in the interception role. Evidently, technology has more than one trick in its bag.

In some respects, the United States is not dependent on Canada's geography. In others, Canadian territory could be important unless the United States decided to develop space-based systems designed to destroy hostile bombers. Although this possibility cannot be discounted, implementation of space-based destruction systems appears further distant than tracking systems designed to detect hostile bombers' movements after takeoff.

At present, tracking is provided by a network of advance warning systems whose main locations are shown in Figure 2. The DEW line consists of thirty-one radar stations scanning the Arctic region from the northwest Alaskan peninsula to eastern Greenland. Two other stations in Ireland and a third in Scotland complete the advance warning system, although they do not form part of the North American Aerospace Defense network. A second line of twenty-four elements is deployed further south and forms the Pinetree Line located entirely within Canada. These two early warning lines are obsolescent, unable to detect bombers flying at low altitude. Secretary of Defense Caspar Weinberger told the Senate Armed Services Committee in 1981 that the United States plans to modernize "in cooperation with Canada . . . present radar systems, while efforts will be made to introduce more resistant detection devices." The new radars would have fixed antennas and be transistorized to make them less vulnerable in wartime and less demanding of maintenance.

To offset the drawbacks of existing systems, NORAD deployed the E-3A Sentry aircraft in 1979. These airborne warning and control system (AWACS) aircraft are well known for their fully airborne detection, command, and control capabilities. The U.S. tactical aircraft commander has at least three dozen of these aircraft at his disposal, and seven are assigned to NORAD in peacetime. Evidently this system has the triple advantage of being mobile, able to detect hostile aircraft flying at low altitude, and capable of providing an airborne operational command post less vulnerable in wartime than regional ground-based command centers.

Fig. 2.   The Detection Systems of NORAD.

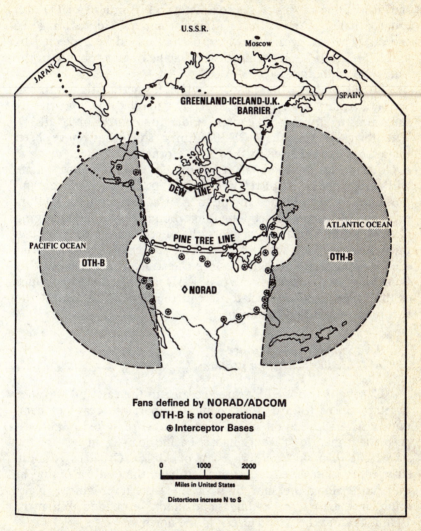

Source: John M. Collins, *U.S.–Soviet Military Balance,* New York: McGraw-Hill Publications Company, 1980, p. 165 (Plate 8). © 1980 by McGraw-Hill Publications Company.

To complement these systems and provide advance warning for the eastern and western flanks of the North American continent, the United States plans to deploy two powerful OTH-B radar stations having ranges of approximately 2,000 miles. An OTH-B radar situated near Cutler in Maine would provide coverage of the eastern flank, while the western flank would be protected by an OTH-B station on the northwest Pacific coast, probably in the state of Washington.

The task of destroying hostile aircraft, formerly assigned to batteries of surface-to-air missiles, is today entrusted to about twenty squadrons of interceptor fighters under the control of NORAD. The thirty-six Canadian CF-101 (three squadrons) have been phased out and replaced by the CF-18 Hornet.

Other things being equal, it is unlikely that technology alone will reverse the trend of relative decline in Canada's strategic importance, except perhaps in the area of active defense. The appearance of a new Soviet long-range bomber and the emerging Cruise missile threat are factors that necessarily will ensure a favored place for Canada on the U.S. strategic chessboard. But these developments will not restore the strategic importance that Canada formerly enjoyed when NORAD made its first appearance as the infant prodigy born to defend the free world against the threat of nuclear bombardment.

The Strategic Importance of Canada's Maritime Waters

Canada is bounded by three oceans: to the east and west her territory opens toward the two most important oceans of communication, while to the north her frontiers are locked in a quasi-permanent mantle of ice. Canada's Pacific coast is, in fact, of lesser extent than the southern coast of Alaska. Canada's Atlantic coast is her most extensive, stretching from the Gulf of Maine in the south, along the shorelines of the eastern provinces, Newfoundland, Labrador, Baffin Island, and Devon and Ellesmere Islands as far as the Arctic Ocean in the north.

The two greatest maritime threats that affect the security of NATO are posed by the potential of the nuclear ballistic missile submarine and the ability of Soviet forces to sever the sea lines of communication between Europe and North America. What then is the strategic importance of Canada relative to each of these threats?

THE NUCLEAR BALLISTIC MISSILE SUBMARINE THREAT

The United States would find itself in a very bad position if the vast geographic expanse to its north were an ocean. The United States would have to increase significantly its line of maritime defense and the warning time available for reacting to submarine defense; the warning time available for reacting to a submarine launch of a ballistic missile would be considerably foreshortened. If one were to exclude Mexico, the United States would then be no more than an island continent open to attack on four maritime fronts. To take an opposite view, the United States might then become the greatest maritime power in the world. However, Canada's geographic presence provides the United States with a natural "barrier" against any hostile maritime threat to the north.

Canada's strategic importance on the eastern flank is, moreover, far from negligible. The irregular coastline, which extends from the state of Maine to St. John's, Newfoundland, is over 800 miles long and effectively restricts access to American shores, particularly for Soviet submarines approaching from the North Atlantic. Further north, Canada and Greenland control the access lanes to the Davis Strait, which, in turn, controls access to Hudson Bay and the Arctic Ocean.

Although Canada's west coast is strategically less important, it is nonetheless significant because it forms the curve of a bay linking the United States–controlled Alaskan coastline to the north with the continental U.S. coastline to the south. The distance separating Victoria from the Dixon Entrance to the north is in fact less than that on the east coast which separates the border of Maine from St. John's, Newfoundland.

What is the nature of the threat posed by Soviet strategic submarines against the NATO nations? In some ways it is almost as global in extent as that posed by Soviet intercontinental ballistic missiles (ICBMs). Although viewed for the most part as a preeminent second-strike weapon system, the nuclear ballistic missile submarine has now acquired, through technological progress, the capability of participating in a first-strike operation. In the mid–

1980s the Soviets had about 3,000 available nuclear warheads deployed on board their submarines. Whereas the possibility of defending against incoming ballistic missiles does not exist, at least in the United States, the possibility of sinking a submarine always exists. Therefore, in a general war it is quite likely that both superpowers will exploit every means to destroy the adversary's strategic submarines.

It is a matter of conjecture whether or not relatively safe maritime sanctuaries where nuclear strategic submarines can operate in total serenity will exist. This is the hope of some arms control specialists. To the extent that such sanctuaries would exist, it would be possible in some degree to ensure the survival of these instruments of retaliation. Thus, neither side could strike first with impunity, which is equivalent to saying that the laws of deterrence would prevail. It is clear that the paths of technology do not lead in this direction, for it can no longer be guaranteed that these weapon systems will not be used in a first-strike operation. Such a scenario is nevertheless extreme and probably the least likely that the West will encounter. What is important for the West is to remain cognizant of adversarial activities and monitor at all times the deployment of strategic maritime forces.

Any unusual or irregular grouping of an adversary's strategic submarines revealed by advance warning or early detection systems could be a good indication that forces have been placed on a state of alert. Alternatively, if an adversary took no special measures indicative of a posture of general alert in the event of crisis, it might mean that there was no intention of matching word to deed. Other types of movement might signal a brewing crisis or indicate unusual and special surveillance on a particular region.

The operational functions of detection, tracking, identification, and destruction that have been discussed relating to the bomber and ballistic missile threats are equally applicable to the threat posed by the nuclear ballistic missile submarine.

The USSR is a continental land mass with limited access to warm water seas. To monitor Soviet submarine movements a Sound Surveillance System (SOSUS) is deployed around the world. The global extent of these fixed detection systems is comparable with the global spread of the ICBM detection systems. Each of the SOSUS ground stations is linked to a string of hydrophones anchored to the ocean floor, and the information gathered by each station is transmitted in real time via a satellite communications link to a processing center in California.

By means of the SOSUS distant warning system, Soviet nuclear ballistic missile submarines can be detected as soon as they enter the North Atlantic or the Pacific. This does not necessarily mean that they cannot be detected should they choose to operate within waters close to their own maritime shores or within inland seas. Obviously this depends upon the quantity and quality of other means of detection employed to achieve this objective. In this connection it may be noted that satellites, under certain conditions, can detect the presence of submarines. In point of fact, an attack submarine can serve equally well as a submarine detection platform, although its use in regions controlled by the enemy is hazardous. It is known that the Soviets have deployed their own acoustic network for submarine detection, particularly in those regions leading to the main approaches to their bases.

As far as the Atlantic is concerned, three underwater detection chains are worth noting. The devices situated in the Norwegian Sea to the north of the Arctic Circle comprise the first distant warning chain. Further south, in the Greenland–Iceland–United Kingdom (GIUK) maritime corridor, is a second chain that can be considered as the advance warning chain. The third chain extends along the length of the North American continental shelf and may be thought of as the near warning chain.

The SOSUS array is nevertheless only a kind of warning barrier. It can indicate the presence of a submarine in some perimeter arc, but the precise location of the target must be determined by other means. Techniques largely employed include active sonar, passive sonar, and those involving magnetic field measurement.

The main antisubmarine warfare (ASW) platforms include attack submarines, fixed-wing aircraft, helicopters, helicopter carriers, and other principal surface ships (corvettes, frigates, destroyers, and cruisers). Among the most recent systems developed to compensate for SOSUS system deficiencies are the Surveillance Towed Array Sensor System (SURTASS) and the Rapidly Deployable Surveillance System (RDSS). The first employs a towed array comprising a large honeycomb network of detectors sensitive to the low-frequency range of the acoustic spectrum. Data from this system are transmitted by satellite to ground stations for analysis. The second system depends on passive sonobuoys that either can be deployed from aircraft or surreptitiously released from a submarine's torpedo tube. They settle automatically on the ocean floor and can be activated remotely. In times of crisis, they are clearly of interest for monitoring of compulsory channels or lanes that provide access to an adversary's bases.

The achievement of ever closer integration among the various ASW platforms has improved considerably chances of fixing and tracking a detected submarine. Accomplished primarily by means of the Fleet Satellite Communications System (FLTSATCOM), this network facilitates comparison of information obtained from sea-based ASW platforms with that obtained from ground stations. Once a submarine is located, it must be identified as either neutral, allied, or hostile. "Visual" identification is obviously difficult underwater, but acoustic identification is possible since every submarine has its own "signature." After the prey has been identified, the question arises as to whether or not ASW forces should communicate this fact to the submarine. Practiced in peacetime, this cat-and-mouse game is a valuable way to reveal chinks in an adversary's armor.

The fourth operational mission of ASW is the destruction of the target itself. Only when the first three operations have been completed successfully can the fourth be possible. Obviously, this fourth objective of ASW is not practiced by the great powers. However, because the high seas are free and accessible to all, the first three operations are practiced on both sides with impunity, without any intent of following through to the limit. The available weapons of destruction include mines, depth charges, torpedoes, mortars, self-propelled missiles, and Cruise missiles. These considerations inevitably lead to a number of questions. Is Canada's participation in ASW strategically important for the United States? If so, to what extent does this relative importance depend on Canada's geography? In the worst situation, could the United States dispense with the Canadian contribution? Will progress in ASW technology bring into sharper focus the advantages derived from Canada's geography or, on the other hand, will it diminish her importance?

The last question is perhaps the simplest to answer. There is no doubt that the detection systems the United States uses today are infinitely more effective than those used twenty years ago. Important progress has been made in SOSUS equipment; satellite detection techniques; and new systems deployed from air, sea, or underwater platforms. In addition, improvements in OTH-B radar may allow detection of the hydrodynamic wakes of submarines in motion. These factors can render the sea much more transparent or "interpretable" than in the past.

Detection at whatever range, distant, advanced, or near, is still only one of the mission requirements of ASW. Although detection is vital, there is no doubt that tracking and identification are just as essential. Clearly the United States intends to ensure that it remains aware of all the activities of each and every strategic submarine that navigates the high seas. The areas to be covered measure an immense number of square miles. At the same time it must be recognized that Canada's maritime patrol aircraft and her surface fleet cover operational areas that are far from negligible. Given the distances involved, U.S. naval aircraft and surface vessels could cover these same regions only at a much higher operational cost. In this sense, important advantages again derive from Canada's geography.

In sum then, could the United States do without the Canadian contribution, and, if so, at what cost? In addition, would it be in Canada's interest if the waters off the Atlantic and Pacific coasts were to become essentially U.S. maritime regions? While Canada today exercises the protection of sovereignty over the maritime zone adjacent to her shores, she may one day become more interested in knowing what happens beyond them, either on her continental shelf or even the ocean floor.

As far as ASW matters are concerned, Canada is in a privileged position by virtue of her geographic situation and surrounding maritime regions. These regions are, of course, limited in relation to the total areas of the Atlantic and Pacific oceans. Thus, although Canada is only a link or a portion of the whole, her contribution forms part of an extensive, globally integrated system. Canada has elected to assume a role within this overall endeavor. Whether her participation is too much, too little, or just enough is quite another matter.

There is one final consideration of a technological nature that many observers have indicated. Will Canada's importance in ASW progressively decline as the range of the submarine-launched ballistic missile increases? In other words, will progress in ASW technology be neutralized by improvements in the offensive capability

tion

of the nuclear-powered ballistic missile submarine (SSBN) that will enable it to operate further from the defensive ASW installations now located near the North American shores?

There are two equally valid ways of approaching this issue. First, in the context of the globally integrated detection network, it is not so much a matter of determining a submarine's general area of operation, whether close to the U.S. coast, in the open ocean, or near its naval base. Rather, the essential problem is that of determining a submarine's precise location. Evidently, in periods of crisis, it would be to the Soviets' advantage to operate from distant bases, close to their own shores, where they would have greater naval air power and ASW capability. However, this does not preclude the possibility that submarines might venture close to the U.S. coast, so that the North American ASW systems would be just as important as those in the Norwegian Sea or in the North Atlantic.

A second way of answering the question stems from the observation that the ASW systems employed to detect SSBNs are the same as those that ensure the security of the lines of communication between Europe and the North American continent. Therefore, to provide a more detailed answer to this question, it is first necessary to examine the strategic importance of Canada relative to the security of sea lines of communication (SLOC).

The Security of Sea Lines of Communication

The scenario of a prolonged conventional conflict in Europe is generally not regarded as the most plausible because sooner or later it likely would degenerate into nuclear war. Nevertheless, NATO nations continue to plan their defenses on the basis of the ability to conduct a conventional war over at least a three-month period. But experts disagree whether or not supplies and reserves would be sufficient for supporting a conventional war lasting even one month—or even two weeks. Irrespective of the estimate's accuracy, the fact remains that substantial reinforcements would have to be dispatched to Europe to prolong in any way a conventional conflict.

The forces earmarked for dispatch to the front line of defense undoubtedly would be transported by air, but a substantial fraction of the remainder, as well as supplies, would be dispatched by sea, including a major part of required equipment. Maintenance of the security of the sea lines of communication is essential in order to support the allied countries and deter an enemy from waging a conventional war in Europe. It is only by maintaining adequate conventional forces, together with the capability to reinforce them rapidly and effectively when the need arises, that an adversary can be convinced that it would not be advantageous to initiate conventional conflict.

Canada really owes her maritime security to the defensive barrier set up in the North Atlantic by the allied nations. Even though largely sheltered within a well-protected zone, Canada is not spared the need to maintain her own maritime ASW capability. This capability must essentially meet two main requirements: to guard against nuclear strategic submarines and to maintain the security of the sea lines of communication. In wartime Canada would respond to a third requirement: to provide surveillance of her own ports and maritime waterways, especially those in the Gulf of St. Lawrence and other lanes of access to the Atlantic. In view of Canada's geography, surveillance of submarines needs to be particularly vigilant since submarines provide the Soviets with the best means of mining access lanes to Canadian territory.

In general the advantages for maintenance of the security of the SLOC that Canada derives from geography are the same as those related to Canada's participation in ASW activities against the SSBN, not surprising since common means counter both threats. Because Canada is an important trading nation, it would be even more advantageous to develop an independent ASW capability to accommodate the eventuality of a crisis. Canada's exports are valued at about 30 percent of her GNP, and over 30 percent of exported goods are sent by ship. In 1979, international Canadian shipments totalled 148 million short tons—35 percent bound for Europe. Canada is a major exporter of wheat and raw materials, and in wartime the demand for these products likely would rise rather than fall. In addition, Canada would have to ensure the security of her imports.

Canada contributes to ASW only to the extent that her modest means allow since she does not possess any aircraft carriers, amphibious assault ships, or nuclear attack submarines. Canada's main contributions are long-range maritime patrol aircraft, capable of scanning the vast expanses of her immense geography, and several ASW destroyers, which are ill-protected against aerial or antiship missile threats. Therefore, in wartime, Canada would have to count on allies or steer her civil or military convoys close to regions with guaranteed air cover if she assumes sole responsibility for escorting them.

Perceptions in Washington and Ottawa may differ concerning the strategic importance of Canada's maritime waters. In the ASW context, the United States would probably place greater importance on the ability of Canada to provide instantaneous information on Soviet strategic submarine activities than on her contributions to the security of the sea lines of communication. For the United States this order of priorities likely would remain unchanged in wartime; for Canada it would be more important to give a higher priority to maintaining the security of the sea lines of communication. ASW capabilities contribute to both strategic and tactical objectives, but those that contribute to one are scarcely distinguishable from those that contribute to the other, particularly since these capabilities derive from an integrated allied system. It is difficult to determine which can best serve Canada's strategic interests. For the time being, however, Canadian equipment is utilized in support of both objectives.

The Strategic Importance of the Arctic Ocean

Unlike the Antarctic, a veritable floating ice pack encircled by the sea, the Arctic Ocean is largely confined by land masses on all sides. The Arctic Ocean has an area of 5.1 million square miles and an average depth of 4,363 feet. The Arctic cannot be compared with other maritime regions such as the Mediterranean, which has been at the crossroads of many civilizations on the main communications routes linking several continents. There is little likelihood that the Arctic will develop as a similar focal point of maritime communication.

Surface navigation is impossible over most of the Arctic Ocean because of the permanence of the polar icecap. Only maritime traffic from the USSR navigates the rim of this ocean, usually during the summer season, and then only at the expense of immense effort involving powerful icebreakers. However, circumpolar navigation from Murmansk to the Bering Straits affords a sea route

1,200 miles shorter than the overland distance between this seaport and the extreme eastern seaboard of the USSR. Moreover, this "northern maritime route" eventually could provide the USSR with a maritime transit lane for ships between the Northern and Pacific fleets.

It is almost as difficult for coastal traffic to navigate the western rim of the Arctic coastline. As demonstrated by the voyage of the USS *Manhattan*, the Northwest Passage is the only practical one. This passage has attracted increased interest because of oil and natural gas fields in the Beaufort Sea and the islands of the Canadian archipelago. Intensive exploitation of the presently known fields, and those to be discovered, may lead, in the long term, to charting and development of sea lines of communication less hazardous and more secure than the Northwest Passage. For instance, immense underwater cargo vessels or submersible barges towed by submarines could transport combustible products extracted from the Arctic. These technological applications must withstand comparison with other transportation techniques, such as transport by air, pipeline, giant icebreaker, or a staging method involving temporary storage and subsequent recovery when climatic conditions permit.

In comparing the respective interests of the East and the West in Arctic navigation, it must be recognized that there are differences. The significance of maritime traffic along the respective southern shores of the Arctic cannot be viewed equally on both continents. In the East, the Arctic port of Murmansk serves Leningrad, one of the largest industrial centers in the USSR; in the West no Arctic port serves such an industrial center. In the northwest, of course, Alaska possesses rich subterranean resources, but no significant processing industries. In the northeast lies the Arctic desert of Greenland. In either area, only embarkation terminals are found, while the USSR has a disembarkation terminal in the region of Murmansk.

Arctic regions are "New Frontier" areas—areas whose potential can only be exploited through massive effort and investment. On both sides, these areas will be developed in accordance with the respective energy and mineral requirements of the two continents, and not for the purpose of promoting trade between them. Thus, for reasons of purely economic interest, the Arctic Ocean may one day become a zone of major strategic importance. Until then, the Arctic will continue to represent, at least for Western nations, regions that "lead nowhere." They conceal perhaps, as the Soviets are inclined to believe, over 500 billion barrels of oil, a quantity comparable with the world's proven reserves of petroleum. They probably also contain immense mineral resources, especially in the region of the polar basin itself. However, as far as oil reserves are concerned, the region is far from a supply zone comparable to the Persian Gulf in importance. As for mineral reserves, the Arctic cannot compare with other traditional sources of the Western countries.

It should be noted, however, that the Arctic could become a region of vital importance for the economies of middle-power nations. For instance, the possible discovery of important oil fields in the Norwegian Sea could well change Norway's international image. However, it is not because a country like Norway, Greenland, or Canada possesses, or could possess, important oil reserves that its strategic significance would change from day to day. For these countries, megaprojects in the Arctic could be even more of a strategic liability than a strategic asset. This would be less true for a major nation like the USSR or the United States whose supplies could be diversified in times of crisis. Other important discoveries of oil and natural gas might be made during the 1980s and 1990s in much more accessible regions with climates more hospitable. The exploitation of off-shore minerals could also retard or even postpone the development of advanced techniques and infrastructures appropriate to the needs of the Arctic.

This does not imply that the Arctic region neither has a long-term future as a zone of high economic potential nor that measures should not be taken to ensure the respect of national sovereignty in that area. On the contrary, it simply means that the pivotal axis of the East-West confrontation is not to be found in this region.

There is, however, one exception to the above observations that concerns use of the Arctic Ocean for underwater navigation. The Arctic Ocean is, in effect, bounded by vast land masses. The only access to the Pacific Ocean is afforded by the Bering Straits. On the western side of Greenland, only the Davis Strait opens on the Atlantic, while on its eastern side access to the North Atlantic is afforded by the Barents, Norwegian, and Greenland Seas.

The peculiarities inherent to the region itself should be noted.

In the first place, the Arctic is nearly covered by a continually moving polar icecap that averages between six and twelve feet thick. The movement of these masses causes ice protrusions to form, further increasing the thickness. There are, nevertheless, "skylights" across the polar icecap, and, according to some, a submarine would have no difficulty in taking advantage of them or even surfacing through six feet of ice.

The maximum extent of ice formation occurs toward the end of winter. Favorable areas for surface navigation are considerably contracted during this season. For a good part of the year, Baffin Bay, all of the eastern parts of the Greenland Sea up to the extreme north of Svaalbard, and the major parts of the Barents and Bering Seas are covered with ice. Between these extreme limits and the contour of the polar icecap, intermediate conditions vary according to the season. Toward the end of summer and into the early fall, the limits of surface navigation in some places approach the contour delineating the icecap.

Very little is known about submarine movements in the Arctic Ocean. It seems likely though that satellites equipped with ultra-sensitive infrared detection systems would be capable of discerning the passage of a submarine, especially against a cold background. This implies that a submarine might be detected and tracked up to the time that it could seek cover under ice packs floating on the surface. The obvious question that arises is whether or not satellites can "see" through the ice; a question that cannot be answered with available information. As noted earlier, attack submarines could install acoustic devices secretly (the best underwater listening platforms available to the major powers for possible future use in Arctic operation).

Control of the channels in wartime will be vitally important to prevent any submarine operating in the Arctic from reaching either the Atlantic or the Pacific. Access to the Pacific is controlled by the bottleneck of the Bering Straits and by a series of compulsory channels that exist in between the Aleutian Islands. Here the United States has important acoustic systems at its disposal.

NATO's main ASW network that controls access to the North Atlantic has already been described. The third and final zone of access is the Canadian Arctic, but, here again, its particular geographic features are of little advantage to the USSR. Although numerous straits staggered along the Northwest Passage probably provide the easiest points of access, they are also the most distant. They could be entered from the Beaufort Sea or the Parry Channel, which is accessible from the Prince Gustav Adolf Sea. The shortest route, however, would be through the Nares Strait, a series of successive channels situated between Ellesmere Island and Greenland that is narrowest at its Arctic extremity. If Soviet submarines could traverse these compulsory channels successfully, some might enter the Atlantic through the Davis Strait, while the more adventurous might negotiate the strait separating the Gulf of Boothia and the Foxe Basin in order to reach Hudson Bay, even though it is shallow and covered with ice most of the year.

Even in peacetime, it is important to control these straits if only to be cognizant of submarine activity. In wartime no eventuality could be discounted. In these circumstances, the prime objective probably would be to mine all of the strategic straits. As in the case of the GIUK line, Canada would probably count on the United States to assume this responsibility. In the interim, if needed, ASW maritime patrol aircraft can be assigned to the Far North, and acoustic systems are surely in place on the ocean floor, at least in the main points of compulsory channels.

Thus, the strategic importance of the Arctic Ocean is far from negligible. There is even a conviction among some observers that its strategic importance will increase as the North Atlantic ASW systems become more effective, because the USSR might then divert a part of its North Atlantic SSBN fleet toward the shelter of a certainly less hospitable, but probably more secure, region.

It surely is not in Canada's interests to see the Arctic Ocean become a United States–Soviet ocean. But, like other countries (with the possible exception of Norway), Canada does not possess the operational capability to act effectively in the Arctic, and the only effective ASW vehicle in these regions is the nuclear-propelled attack submarine. Because of its geographic location, the Canadian Arctic constitutes an important barrier to hostile submarines seeking access to the Atlantic. Although Canada's role is presently limited, it is likely to increase should the Far North witness any significant economic development in the future. At the moment, Canada's role is confined mainly to controlling the straits and performing tasks related to the protection of her sovereignty in the region.

Technological progress in the field of transportation, particularly in support of maritime navigation and icebreaking, could enhance Canada's presence in the region, but it is unlikely that such developments would influence Canadian defense priorities. However, to counter the influence of increasing efforts of the major powers in the Arctic Ocean, it is possible that some form of greater cooperative endeavor could be established between the northern countries. The example most frequently discussed is cooperation between Canada and Norway. Nordic multilateralism would develop perhaps in parallel with Canada's policy of multilateralism in international affairs. As far as possible, it would aim to counterbalance the influence of Canada's powerful southern neighbor whose omnipresence now extends as far north as the Arctic Ocean.

The Major Policy Issues

The German poet Novalis once wrote: "The eyes of chaos shine behind the veil of order." The management of East-West relations strangely resembles this veil of order behind which multifarious occasions for chaos miraculously have been avoided in the past.

THE MANAGEMENT OF EAST-WEST RELATIONS

Since 1945, Washington's efforts to contain Moscow and Moscow's determination, in turn, to loosen Washington's stranglehold have remained essentially invariant in an otherwise changing USSR–U.S. relationship. For the most part, the United States has pursued containment efforts in concert with allies, although on rare occasions, as in Cuba in 1962 or in the Middle East in 1973, Washington has intervened directly.

Moscow's systematic opposition in the 1950s was followed by virulent Soviet messianism ("We will bury you!"), toward the end of the 1960s by a dialogue culminating in the SALT agreements, and several years later by growing Soviet activism in the Third World. Soviet intervention in Afghanistan sounded the death knell for detente, in which, for lack of better policy, many still believed.

Among the most important transformations current in the United States is a strong resurgence of economic neoconservatism that is reinforced by a fierce desire, supported by the "silent majority," to rebuild a militarily strong America. Western Europe and Japan are not indifferent to this American will for regeneration, but they are awed at the magnitude of military expenditures and upset by the measures taken by the United States to restore its economy.

America's second wind comes on the heels of successive denunciations of the Soviet Union's behavior and in the wake of the policies of detente espoused by previous administrations. But beyond the words and anti-Soviet rhetoric hides a renewed will for power in the most classic tradition of interstate relations. It is not so much a matter of "containment" or anti-Sovietism, two ideological ingredients that inevitably become less palatable with time, but rather relates to America's place in the world: its role, power, and influence.

The two dimensions are not incompatible; for the most part they have been concomitants during the history of the cold war and, at most, present different perspectives since they are opposite sides of the same coin. Containment is sensible policy when exercised against expansion. As many have observed, the USSR recorded its greatest success during the two major periods of detente that occurred during the history of the cold war—the first immediately following World War II and the second during the 1970s. The United States, for its part, was most successful in the early 1950s and during the 1960s when it was powerful and, above all, respected.

The political consequences of this situation are scarcely difficult to discern. The eternal ambiguity of conflict and cooperation characterizing the nature of relations between the superpowers will continue. Periods of conflict will be followed by periods of detente, where detente is simply defined as a set of circumstances in which the opportunities for cooperation essentially outnumber the opportunities for conflict.

In 1982 in *Adelphi Papers No. 174,* French political scientist Pierre Hassner wrote:

> Nothing is more necessary for American policy than a struggle on two fronts, avoiding both the illusions of liberals bent on minimizing the Soviet danger and hence the role of military force and on exaggerating the hopes of detente, and the illusions of conservatives bent on exaggerating the former and on minimizing the latter and, more generally, on neglecting the autonomous

process of change in the Third World and the opportunities offered by favourable evolutions within the Communist world itself.

From that point of view, the right-wing conservative approach of the Reagan administration clashed directly with the tenets of the center left-wing approach of the Liberal administration in Canada. In a speech delivered in Quebec City in March 1981, the Honorable Gilles Lamontagne, the former Canadian Minister of National Defence, declared:

> It is obvious . . . that the deep gap dividing the rich countries and the poor countries, underdevelopment and social injustice all engender revolution, which threatens the security of peoples and nations and, in consequence, the stability of international order. . . . Therefore, the security of people and nations is to be found where the two great axes, North-South and East-West, intersect.

The dominant theme of the Liberal administration in Canada was that the USSR cannot be seen as the sole source of evil, that it has a right to exist, and that sources of instability in the Third World are more often indigenous than external. Most of these views are shared also by the Conservative party, and they cut across a large segment of interest groups in Canada, constituting a widespread opinion within the Canadian public at large. Though Canada recognizes the underlying nature of the superpowers' rivalry, she in no way is prepared to adhere to a strict policy of containment through force, but rather to the basic tenets of the 1947 Truman Doctrine, which saw in injustice and poverty the roots of revolution. This difference of perceptions is unlikely to disappear. Canada's foreign policy has taken a definite *tiers-mondiste* approach similar to that taken by many European countries, notably France. She will side with the United States in time of crisis, but does not intend to relinquish the right to differ with the conduct of American foreign policy in the Third World. In a sense, Canada's foreign policy typically reflects middle-power status. She wishes to deemphasize the power aspect of international relations in favor of the view of world order based on justice and human values.

THE GLOBAL NUCLEAR ISSUE

There is a widespread feeling within the public at large that the risk of nuclear war appears greater today than in the past.

Many reasons underlie the intense passions that fire the nuclear protest movements, particularly those in Europe. It goes beyond the ideological outbursts that set right against left, "hawks" against "doves," "liberals" against "conservatives": beyond the general economic malaise afflicting Western societies, and perhaps beyond the role of the increasingly challenged state. For the Europeans, undoubtedly, the reason is their refusal to become "victims of the play."

This determination not to pay the price for a limited nuclear war between the superpowers has, in part, been fueled by ill-considered statements from outside. It is, however, more deeply linked to the hope maintained by many Europeans that a new military order may be established in Europe, one that is oriented more toward Europe and less toward NATO than the current and, consequently, less susceptible to the whims of superpower politics. Although this idea is not new to European politics, it seems to be gaining more support than in the past as indicated, for example, by the revival by the French of the Western European Union (WEU) idea.

For many Canadians, the country has no enemy. Canada remains conscious of the dilemma into which the superpowers have locked themselves—the necessity to compete against the technological clock in an ever enduring attempt at stabilizing the nuclear balance. Canada has accepted responsibilities within NATO. The general premise of the 1971 Canadian white paper on defense still holds true for a majority of the population: Canada must do her utmost in order to avoid the catastrophic effects of a nuclear war.

In the course of the years, Canada has turned away from any nuclear role in NATO. In the summer of 1984, the last 1.5 KT Genie air-to-air missile (AAM) was deactivated in favor of the new conventional AAM carried by the CF-18. Pressure within the Canadian community is mounting also in favor of a more active role toward arms control and disarmament. The establishment by the Canadian government in 1984 of the Canadian Institute for International Peace and Security is a tribute to this new sensitivity. The institute doubtlessly will carry with it the voices of those who argue for greater restraint and control over arms procurement and defense budgets in favor of a more active arms control policy.

The two-track decision within NATO was adopted by the

NATO council in 1979. Its main purpose was to allow for the modernization of Long-Range Theater Nuclear Forces (LRTNF), while at the same time providing a coherent policy toward arms control policy on those particular systems. The Scowcroft commission in the United States achieved similar results at the overall strategic level. It is doubtful that the institute could pretend to such achievements, but it may bring together views hitherto far apart, or unheard of, in the traditional bureaucratic circles.

THE NATO ISSUES

Canada faces considerable problems meeting NATO commitments in Europe. The basic issue revolves around the deep gap currently existing between Canadian forces commitments and the resources available to meet them. As is well known, these commitments are numerous. Canada's Fourth Mechanized Brigade Group (MBG), comprising 3,268 military personnel, is presently deployed in Central Europe. In wartime, these forces would be complemented with a second brigade group, bringing the total strength to 5,608 personnel. In addition, the First Canadian Air Group (CAG) is stationed in Central Europe and comprises three squadrons of CF-104 aircraft, earmarked for replacement by the CF-18. Lastly, Canada is committed to maintaining a Canadian Air/Sea Transportable (CAST) combat group comprising 5,000 personnel, which would be dispatched to NATO's northern flank in Europe in wartime. Of this CAST group, one battalion is maintained in full readiness to join NATO's Allied Mobile Force (Land), which could be deployed to Norway, Denmark, or both, depending on the circumstances. In the air, Canada is committed to maintaining two squadrons of aircraft in operational readiness, which would be deployed to Europe in wartime.

In view of these commitments and other roles assigned to the Canadian forces within the framework of North American defense, the Subcommittee on Defence of the Senate Committee on Foreign Affairs in 1982 recommended bringing the regular force strength to 85,000 by 1985 and to 91,800 by 1987. The subcommittee estimated that in the long term, optimum strength of the Canadian forces should total about 108,000 personnel. For his part, the Canadian minister of national defence, pointing out that the subcommittee report was written prior to his briefing on the results of parallel studies conducted within his own department, acknowledged that "the conclusions of the (senatorial) report conformed in general to the results of these (in-house) studies." He added, however, that despite the anticipated 3 percent increase in the annual defense budget, "it will not be possible for some time to meet the capital needs required to ensure the acquisition of equipment authorized for the Canadian Forces or to reach the forecast levels in personnel." He concluded that an increase in strength at this stage only would make it more difficult to find a solution to the problem. In a confidential federal cabinet document obtained by the *Calgary Herald* (April 14, 1984), it was indicated that the Defence Department would need $55 billion by the year 2000 for defense equipment projects. It further reported that the government was then ready to provide only $28 billion.

These conclusions only reinforce those stated by the deputy minister of national defence in March 1981:

> Although the funds allocated by the Government since 1975 have actually allowed a gradual improvement in military capability, billions more would be needed to make a more rapid readjustment. The capabilities of the Canadian Forces will continue to feel the effects of these lean years throughout the 1980s and even beyond.

The working group charged with studying the effects of unification on the Canadian armed forces did not fail to note these lean years in its final report. Between 1963 and 1973, the share of the defense budget assigned to the acquisition of equipment fell from 14.8 percent to 5.9 percent. In 1979–80, this share stabilized at about 12.3 percent.

Only a substantial increase in the budget of the Department of National Defence would eliminate the deficit in personnel and equipment that accrued within the Canadian armed forces during a decade that the Canadian government judged too peaceful to justify heavy defense investments.

The options available to Canada in Central Europe are numerous. Nothing obliges Canada to maintain forces in Central Europe or to commit combat groups as important as the CAST group to the northern flank. Although Canada could equally well choose to confine herself to a single role, it would probably annoy one or both of her favored partners, Norway or West Germany. Furthermore, if defense of the North Atlantic Ocean were to become a matter of priority, Canada might choose to base CF-18 aircraft on

Newfoundland, her most easterly deployed terrestrial "aircraft carrier." Whether or not such a reorientation would be considered by NATO allies as an ally contribution is open to question. But the fact is that there are many options that may be open to future consideration.

Canada is not obliged to accept responsibilities both on the ground and in the air as far as commitments to the northern flank are concerned. The same could be said of commitments in Central Europe. Canada could, in fact, maintain the fourth MBG in Europe or, indeed, reinforce it, even if it meant withdrawing the first CAG. Conversely, intensifying air contribution and relinquishing the ground role is also a possibility. To go even further, Canada could convert her heavy brigade in Europe to a light brigade, which would permit greater "interoperability" between the various Canadian forces units and allow more compatibility to the Canadian forces that might be deployed on the northern front. The reverse would be more difficult to achieve, since the conversion of a light brigade to a heavy brigade necessitates the purchase of additional tanks and complicates logistics operations involving transport and general support.

Canada is, of course, free to modify the form of support to NATO in Europe at any time. Any rationalization would have to pass the test set by five critical factors. The first concerns the trade-off between technology and human resources. From Canada's standpoint, there is a fundamental difference between losing 100 tanks, 42 aircraft, or 5,000 personnel. Neither prophecy nor access to secret studies invoking the mysteries of military power is needed to realize that a war in Central Europe would be particularly disastrous. Human and material losses would be experienced at rates and on scales unprecedented in the history of conflict. Given the scenarios that likely would pertain to a war in Europe, a combat group of 5,000 probably would not hold up for more than ten days without replacement by an equivalent number. This situation would apply at least to the first few weeks of combat following the outbreak of hostilities. In one month Canada could lose between 15,000 and 20,000 troops, depending on the applicable scenarios and types of combat commitment previously accepted. As a result, Canada could be left without any combat troops on her own soil and find herself with an empty infrastructure.

If, on the other hand, Canada chose to limit herself to a single role in Europe, and it was an aerial one, then her commitment would have been fulfilled once the fifty or so aircraft based in Europe were replaced by those held in reserve in Canada. At $40 million each, and in view of the long production times involved, Canada's weaponry would be quickly exhausted. The purpose of this argument is not to compare the operational effectiveness of three squadrons of aircraft with 5,000 troops—obviously their functions are very different—but rather to stress the point that the nature of Canada's contribution within NATO has not been yet fully analyzed.

The second important factor is the relative commonality of equipment sought within the Canadian armed forces. This factor was vividly highlighted by General Charles Foulkes when he testified before a House of Commons committee in 1969 and 1970, the time when Canada's role in Europe was reexamined.

> We should be operating on the flanks where it requires a great deal more leadership, where it requires handling of communications . . . which is the same kind of task as we do in North America, and that requires the same kind of forces that we use in peacekeeping and so forth. In other words, it is getting away from heavy equipment and getting on to a more mobile base. . . .

An illustration is the CF-18, which will replace three types of aircraft, the CF-101, CF-104 and CF-5. It is relatively easy to appreciate its multipurpose application and the high degree of commonality that results from deployment of similar types of equipment in Europe and Canada. On the other hand, it is more difficult to imagine how the acquisition of the latest "Leopard" tanks could benefit Canada if they were deployed on her soil. Apart from the fact that they are fully effective only in the offensive role of frontal attack, they likely will be rendered completely obsolete before they end their useful lifetime due to developments and improvements in antitank weapons. In general, if Canada intends to rationalize her European commitments, thought should be given today to the likely situation fifteen years from now.

The third important factor is the obvious economic aspect. The Canadian aeronautical industry is one of the strongholds of Canadian technology (a euphemism, if ever there was one, for the Canadian defense industry). Next in importance is the electronics sector, especially its telecommunications component, followed by the shipbuilding sector. At the present time, there is little to indicate that Canadian-built equipment deployed in Europe eventually will find its way into the European market. Admittedly, competition is fierce in this area, and, in addition, most European countries favor their own defense industries. But, above all, it should be recognized that no Canadian military system is produced entirely in Canada. Since Canadian equipment does not filter naturally into the European weapons inventory, any decision relating to military equipment must take into account the industrial trade-off that may accrue to the Canadian economy.

The fourth fundamental factor is sociological in nature. Canadian forces comprise the three traditional military components— land, sea, and air. Any form of rationalization, if pushed to the extreme, might, for instance, result in the gradual elimination of one or other of the three services. Such an outcome would be totally absurd. Irrespective of actual proportions adopted, it is only by maintaining a certain balance and ensuring the development of the three services that security of a nation can be best served.

The fifth and last fundamental factor is the political consideration. The circumstances surrounding Canada's April 1969 decision to reduce the strength of troops in Europe from 10,000 to 5,000 are too well known to warrant repetition. The pressures exerted at the time by European allies on the Canadian government were considerable. It is unlikely, however, that Canada would be exposed to such strident recriminations if she decided one day to rationalize the presence of her military forces in Europe. At the time, the change proposals came only at the very last minute after it was evident that the prime minister's office had no intention of allowing the bureaucracy to prevail over its decision to change the nature of commitments in Europe. It must nevertheless be admitted that the bureaucracy itself could offer neither a clear proposal nor means of approaching the issue. Presently, everything points to the fact that one day Canada will have to reexamine this thorny issue; inevitably it will require extensive study. One can only hope that clear proposals will be developed and presented, first to the Canadian government and then to Canada's allies.

It is unlikely that any Canadian government will want to reorder a major reorganization of its forces within NATO. The

1969–70 decision has served Canada a lesson. At this stage the nation does not want to go through another "agonizing reappraisal." Canada has been strongly encouraged by a former secretary of defense in Washington "to put her forces where the enemy is." In a sense, Canada needs NATO more than NATO needs Canada. It provides the Canadian armed forces with a uniquely integrated military structure in the West.

Though a new white paper on defense is badly needed, no one seriously expects a major policy shift on Canada's contribution to NATO. The major reequipment programs militate against such a restructuring. Moreover, it seems more than likely that an increase in defense expenditures will be not only welcomed but also warranted.

Though the future is uncertain, the major potential source for disruption within the alliance does not come from Ottawa but from Washington. The recent debates on American strategy have all too often been used to camouflage the real problems in Europe—the need to strengthen the conventional shield of the alliance. The United States, with troops numbering about 350,000 in Europe, is becoming weary of being the second largest army in Europe. If Canada understands the relentless American drive to obtain from the NATO allies a greater articulation in terms of ground troops, Washington has done little so far to understand their allies' schizophrenic attitudes toward a war in Europe. The European allies do not want to fight a conventional war in Europe similar to World War II. Nor do they want to be confronted with the choice of a limited nuclear war.

In this strange debate, Canada so far has been loyal both to Washington and to her European partners. Any major shift of policy, be it in Europe or in Washington, could mark the beginning of a new era in terms of transatlantic relations. For the time being, Canada is caught between. But, presumably, any retreat toward a greater American continentalism would also be felt in Canada.

THE NORAD SPACE ISSUES

On March 11, 1981, the NORAD agreement was renewed for a further period of five years. The news was greeted dispassionately by the press and the general public. Yet this agreement was different from preceding ones. The new agreement replaced the one previously known under the name of North American Air Defense Agreement and bears the same acronym but reads differently: North American Aerospace Defense Agreement.

Of all the factors considered, technology changes most rapidly. NORAD has lost much of its importance insofar as the main threat is no longer presented by the bomber but by the intercontinental ballistic missile. The increased vulnerability of fixed missile silos and even nuclear ballistic missile submarines, with concomitant progress in Cruise missile technology, renewed the interest of the superpowers in the manned strategic aircraft. It is unlikely, however, that the bomber will rediscover the glory of the 1950s when it reigned supreme, because it would not be to the advantage of the superpowers to depend on only one system. Moreover, the record of disarmament shows that older systems are rarely dismantled once new systems have been developed.

Canada plays an indispensable role in air defense, one that likely will continue until the end of the century. This seems all the more probable in light of technological progress on two fronts: the appearance of the Cruise missile on one hand, and the ever-increasing sophistication of detection systems on the other. With the advent of space-based detection systems for air defense, Canada may find herself in a paradox. Canada's geographical advantages then will become progressively less relevant to the mission of detection but increasingly relevant to the mission of interception itself. As better control and detection systems are developed, with or without Canada's agreement or collaboration, they will impose more stringent requirements on the exercise of interception since the United States always will be interested in ensuring that interception takes place as far north as possible.

As far as BMD is concerned, Canadian territory is not involved in any way, whether it is distant warning, tracking, discrimination, or destruction. Therefore, the strategic importance of Canada vis-à-vis the ballistic missile threat is negligible. In this strategy, Canada is only of interest to the United States from the standpoint of increased warning time. Any incoming Soviet ballistic missile must traverse the exoatmospheric space located above Canadian territory. Thus, geography provides Canada with an "involuntary response," but not with a negotiable strategic asset. The extreme scenario obviously would be that Canada would one day install ABM interceptors on her soil should the United States follow that route between now and the year 2000. Such a possibility cannot be discounted; but if the United States pursued that path, enthusiastically or otherwise, it would be to develop a limited system. Furthermore, the United States has not yet decided which of the two potential BMD components (endoatmospheric or exoatmospheric) ultimately will be developed. It is conceivable to develop both. The use of Canadian territory would be of no value to the United States with the exoatmospheric defense option. Assuming that the LoAD system were developed, the installation of ABM interceptors on Canadian soil could have a certain value for the United States, but it would not represent a contribution essential to the system's effectiveness. In any event, Canada's importance in BMD is destined to remain peripheral.

Two major tests conducted by the U.S. in 1984 have, however, brought closer the possibility of a further militarization of space. The first one, conducted in January, demonstrated that it would be possible to establish an antisatellite (ASAT) capacity through the use of the F-15 interceptor. The ASAT missile fired by the F-15 did, in fact, reach a predetermined target that coincided with the potential orbital point of a satellite. In the second test, conducted that June, an ICBM was intercepted over the Pacific, for the first time in history. The direct hit used a parabolic steel net of about fifteen feet in diameter, and the guidance system of the ABM missile was based on a sophisticated infrared device that allowed interception on a purely conventional basis.

Canada's participation in NORAD has never given rise to violent protests as to the result of a Soviet bomber being shot down in her air space; that potential risk is being perceived as an integral part of the obligation involved through her participation in NORAD. But how would Canada react if a Soviet ICBM were intercepted on its low descending orbit over Canada's air space? This is, admittedly, a hypothetical question, but may cease to be hypothetical sooner than anticipated. The NORAD space issue, in fact, is likely to raise a whole series of intricate future problems.

First, there are basic American security functions that Washington may want to accomplish alone. Any ASAT capacity on limited ABM capability in the future could be undertaken by the United States, with or without the help of Canada. Second, the Canadian position on issues of the militarization of outer space in general and on ASAT in particular has been much tighter and tougher than Washington would have liked. The Pentagon plans in the future to establish an integrated space command. Whether Canada will be associated or not with these new important and vital activities may depend much more on Canada's stance regarding arms control issues in outer space than on the particular merits she may normally enjoy because of her geographic location. Those two elements point to the need for both sides to seek a closer and better integration of the interface between issues of arms control and defense, and to negotiate well in advance the conflicting positions that may emerge between the two countries. The secret Joint United States Canadian Air Defense (JUSCAD) study, undertaken at a cost of $1 million, was precisely designed to meet part of the requirements. Discussions of the problems, however, have been far too technical in scope. A larger study seems warranted as a matter of urgent priority.

The space environment is not totally unknown to Canada, which designed, built, and operated her own communications satellites. For several years now, within the framework of defense production agreements, Canada has been invited to compete for contracts from the U.S. Air Force Space Systems Division. Canada, moreover, has a world-class capability in several areas of aerospace.

Military communication satellites, for instance, mark a particular area into which Canada may orient herself. In fact, the possibility of improving military communications in the Canadian North is now being seriously studied in Ottawa.

Future interface between air space and outer space will become increasingly complex. For instance, new U.S. systems for aerial threat detection probably will be based in space. Canada must weigh the pros and cons of participating in the development of these systems, for sooner or later she will be faced with the prospect and associated costs of modernizing her own detection systems. Canada must face three fundamental questions. (1) To what extent will increased investment in high-technology industries contribute to economic growth? (2) What will be the domestic spinoff? (3) How will Canada's trade posture improve? Space certainly will assume increasing importance for communications, navigation, search and rescue operations, as well as for monitoring activities in one's own air space and, incidentally, that of others.

As previously noted the Pacific coast cannot be compared with the east coast because of its extent and strategic importance. Nevertheless, if she chose to do so, Canada could enlarge her Pacific operational zone. But how would this serve Canada's interests better? There is only a political answer. Asia accounts for 25 percent of U.S. trade, and the United States retains mastery of the Pacific at least as far as Hawaii. Japan imports mostly raw materials from Canada, materials probably indispensable in the event of war in Asia. While it is true that Canada's trade with Japan would also be affected in that event, Japan's trade with Europe or the United States undoubtedly would be affected more. Canada has never entered into a military agreement with an Asian country and, given the fluid nature of the regional system in Asia, it is unlikely that this will change during the next ten years. Therefore, at first sight, it would appear difficult to rationalize an increased Canadian naval presence in the Pacific.

It would seem fairly evident that the strategic importance of the oceans is linked more to the necessity of resupply than to trade, and this implies freedom of navigation and access to the seas. In this regard, while nature has made Canada's east coast a convergence node for North Atlantic traffic, this is not the case on her west coast. But the problem is more complicated since the means required to ensure freedom of the seas are substantially those needed to defend against submarines. Viewed this way, antisubmarine warfare capability is vital for both surface and subsurface navigation and just as important on the west as on the east coast. There is, nevertheless, the difference that the west coast essentially forms a bay enclosed between U.S. defense forces in the Gulf of Alaska and those situated on the northwest coast of the U.S. The zone of coverage in the Pacific is, therefore, much less extensive than the eastern operational zone.

Strictly speaking, Canada has no antimine capability; she possesses neither minesweepers nor helicopters that are used for this purpose. But whatever her actual or desired capability may be, the breadth of Canada's requirement must be weighed against the improved effectiveness accrued from the frigate program or from possible use of the CF-18 in a dedicated antiship or antiaircraft role. The greater Canada's capability for intercepting and destroying adversarial surface ships and naval aircraft, the lower are the adversaries' probability of successful mining of Canada's main maritime approaches. There remains the possibility, however, that an adversary could lay some mines on the ocean floor in peacetime and activate them remotely at a more opportune time. This potential threat warrants serious examination, and its possibility implies that a new function should be added in the future to the traditional tasks assigned to maritime command. The equipment needed to accomplish such surveillance activity would be useful in exercising Canadian sovereignty, either over the continental shelf or between the shelf itself and the water's surface. A myriad of underwater verification activities will be necessary in connection with the exploration and exploitation of the seabed likely to occur in the near future.

Conclusion

No observer of the Canadian scene expects a major shift of Canada's foreign policy in the 1980s. Some minor adjustments may be necessary here and there, but, on the whole, the thrust of Canadian efforts will remain the same. No white paper has been published on foreign policy since 1970, and the same holds true on matters of defense since 1971. There were some timid attempts in 1979 to undertake a major review of Canada's foreign policy. Those plans, however, were quickly shelved as soon as the Liberals came back into power shortly after the nine-month Clark interlude. Some ad hoc changes were noted in major speeches, such as greater emphasis on the Caribbean countries, the necessity for Canada to privilege her bilateral relations with some two dozen countries, as well as her relations with the Pacific Basin countries.

Apart from some elements within the New Democratic party, no serious political commentator advocates that Canada withdraw from military alliances abroad or disentangle herself from the broader North American defense complex. Within Canada, however, there exists a mounting number of activist groups—some anti-American, some antinuclear, some overtly nationalist, and others purely and simply branded as pacifists.

The Liberal policy over the years of disentanglement of any nuclear role within the alliance has had a marked effect on the Canadian population. The Gallup Polls indicate that a majority of the population favors NATO, but they also indicate that a majority has been against any testing of the Cruise missile in

Canada. The decision to test it in Canada originally was proposed by Germany as a token gesture by which Canada could support the 1979 NATO decision to deploy the Ground Launched Cruise (GLC) and the Pershing II missiles in Europe. Canada has stuck to that decision even though the cabinet took a long time to give the green light to the experiment.

The June 1984 ABM test over the Pacific may dampen the Canadian reaction against any potential development of an ABM system in North America. Until then it was feared that an ABM interceptor must be equipped with a nuclear warhead. The fact that this interception was conducted on a purely conventional basis and that destruction was realized by physical impact of a direct hit may resolve many of the reservations that were felt about the subject, particularly within the bureaucracy. This does not mean that the general public would welcome the establishment of an ABM system in North America. It merely indicates that defense based on conventional, rather than nuclear, means definitely has a different status, at least as such defense is perceived by the Canadian public.

From a military viewpoint, Canada was most important to the U.S. when the bomber threat was the single-weapons system with the ability to reach the American continent from the Soviet Union. The ubiquity of the threat that ICBMs and SLBMs have now introduced and that airborne Cruise carriers may intensify in the future has made Canada strategically less important to the U.S. Future technology may force the United States to reconsider the strategic importance of Canada, especially if it intends to strengthen active defense against bombers or to proceed with a limited ABM deployment in the 1990s. Whatever decision is taken, the overall relationship of the United States toward the rest of the world will not change. Canada can only be but one part of a closely knit defense effort. Everything will always be relative in one direction or another. But considering the totality of economic and military factors from an overall standpoint, it can only be concluded that today Canada is strategically less important than twenty years ago. In the meantime, a fundamental question must be answered. As her strategic image continues to fade, how can Canada find ways to strengthen both her own security and that of her allies?

Lynton K. Caldwell

6

Binational Responsibilities
for a Shared Environment

Canada and the United States occupy the greater part of the
North American continent and share a 5,000-mile boundary traversed by currents of air and water, migratory wildlife (including
microorganisms), goods, services, ideas, and people. Thus, they
share a continental environment energized by dynamically interrelated elements. Both nations are affected by transboundary in-
teractions involving ecosystems, resource flows, and complex
economic interdependencies. Both nations have a mutual stake in
sustaining their economies and shared environment, with responsibility for its custody and maintenance that neither can fulfill
without the other. Beyond its mutual advantages and practical

LYNTON K. CALDWELL *is the Arthur F. Bentley Professor of Political Science
and professor of Public and Environmental Affairs, as well as director of Advanced Studies in Science, Technology, and Public Policy, at Indiana University. He has served on the faculty of five distinguished universities and has been
a consultant to the U.S. Senate; the Congressional Research Service; the Departments of State, Commerce, and Interior; the National Institutes of Health;
and the Office of Technology Assessment. Dr. Caldwell is also a member of
numerous scientific, governmental, and advisory bodies and associations. He
has been a guest lecturer at more than 60 colleges and universities, has written
over 200 articles and monographs, and has published 7 books.*

necessities, this cooperation provides a constructive example for the rest of the world.

The state of world order is precarious—ecologically, socially, economically, and politically—and indicates a significance for Canadian-American relationships that transcends continental limits. The importance of binational cooperation in joint responsibilities for a shared environment cannot be comprehended fully unless placed in a global context. Neither the economic nor environmental policies of Canada and the United States are wholly determined by North American circumstances—the policies of both countries have been influenced significantly by conditions far beyond their borders. Policies regarding agriculture, energy, minerals, and defense, for example, are shaped significantly by other nations whose actions sometimes affect Canada and the United States in dissimilar ways.

Whatever success Canadians and Americans have achieved in resolving differences over environmental and natural resources issues, changing circumstances in science, technology, and economics bring into question the adequacy of existing arrangements to deal with binational responsibilities. These changes are apparent not only in Canada and the United States; they occur in various ways throughout the world and have caused environmental conflict among states. The record of Canadian-American conflict over environment-related policies is mixed. Resolving differences has often been time-consuming and expensive; ad hoc settlements are common but provide little help in avoiding other conflicts.

One need not assume the failure of present binational arrangements for responsible custody of a shared continental environment to argue convincingly that more effective arrangements are needed. At least two developments are necessary to obtain more responsible custody of the North American environment. The first is to shift values toward a continental-ecological perspective on public policies. The second is to restructure or supplement institutional arrangements to cope with real or perceived differences of interest within and across national boundaries. Institutional arrangements do not necessarily imply new governmental units—formal agreements and coordinated procedures among existing agencies "institutionalize" binational cooperation. New agencies, if needed, are most acceptable when they evolve out of experience and widely perceived necessity.

Neither value changes nor institutional innovation alone can ensure more responsible actions by Canada and the United States toward their shared environment. These developments may help; they may influence agenda setting and allocations of priority by the two governments and their political subdivisions. But there is no way wholly to eliminate differences of outlook and interest that may be greater within than between countries. The growth of environmental concern throughout the world led to the establishment of a large number of international arrangements for mutual advantage and protection of cooperating nations. The United Nations Regional Seas Programme and the environmental directives of the European Economic Community (EEC) indicate that concern for transnational environmental problems is not unique to North America.

Broader Dimensions of Binational Responsibilities

While there are important similarities in the political assumptions and values of North Americans, there is also cultural heterogeneity and diversity. What the peoples of Canada and the United States conspicuously share is joint occupancy of a large continent. One does not have to argue theories of geopolitics or physiocracy to demonstrate that it is from the North American continent and its environment that the lives of the people living upon it are largely sustained.

North America, from the Polar Sea to the Gulf of Mexico and from the Atlantic to the Pacific, is an ecological, biogeophysical continuity. It is well known that major interpositions in any fundamental aspect of an ecological system may affect large areas beyond its immediate environment. The forms taken by these repercussions may vary considerably. Thus, what begins as mining of high–sulfur-bearing coal in southern Indiana may ultimately result in ruined resort businesses in Ontario or Maine. High-technology agribusiness in the semiarid Great Plains may lower ground water reserves to a level that generates political demand for water diverted from other parts of the United States and, possibly, Canada. The fate of transboundary rivers and lakes in North America affects the lives and politics of people in both Canada and the United States.

Whatever ways that Canadians and Americans can be said to

"share" a common continental environment, they unavoidably share responsibility for the impact of their respective activities upon that environment. If North Americans cannot find ecologically sound ways to manage the "goods" of the continent, they must endure more of its "bads." Dust bowls, acid rains, and polluted waters that affect both Canadians and Americans are consequences of mismanagement of the continental environment and its resources. Regardless of where the mismanagement occurs, its occurrence is a matter of legitimate concern to the people affected by it, wherever they may be.

A widely recognized principle of international law (exemplified in the 1909 Boundary Waters Treaty between Canada and the United States) obliges nations to prevent the use of their territories in ways injurious to the welfare of their neighbors. The principle was accepted by both nations in the Trail Smelter arbitration (1935–41), which addressed injuries to American farmers from air pollution that originated in Canada. Since the 1960s, there has been growing acceptance of the principle. International consensus has been reflected in the resolutions of the 1972 United Nations Conference on the Human Environment and the 1982 United Nations Charter for Nature.

By now it should have become clear that binational responsibility for the North American environment alone cannot protect its people from the adverse effects of atmospheric contamination occurring in other parts of the Northern Hemisphere. Nor can good environmental management alone prevent the growth of pressures from abroad that result from depletion of the natural resource base in other countries—especially those experiencing unrestrained population growth. Thus, a mere continental North American perspective on joint responsibility for resources and the environment implies an unrealistically narrow view of circumstances affecting policy choices and their consequences.

Perspectives on the Environment

Among the various ways of looking at environmental and natural resources issues (and with due regard for inevitable variations in individual attitudes and values), two contrasting perspectives may be identified: political-economic and ecological. The terms alone do not convey adequately the substance of the attitudes they encompass. They are variable, not absolute, concepts and are not the only ways that perspectives on the environment may be categorized. For example, there is a technocratic point of view that rejects both of these restraints but may adopt political-economic rationale in support of enterprises, especially public works of dubious economic merit.

From an ecological perspective political boundaries and political programs are characteristically seen as artificial, often unwisely obstructing or disrupting natural relationships. Positions taken by the governments of Canada and the United States imply that their dominant perspectives are political and economic. People who officially deal with transboundary affairs must consider demarcations of legal jurisdiction and administrative authority. They will almost invariably consider the influence and objectives of political parties and national, regional, and local economic interest groups. Elected political leaders largely focus on constituency interests whatever they are—economic, ethnic, technological, military, and, in recent years, environmental. Political-economic perspectives are often more specifically human-centered than is the ecological-environmental viewpoint. The latter, placing humankind in nature, has a broader perspective in which human interests are qualified by the larger systems-constraints of the natural world. While ecological interest has a place in the political-economic perspective, many see it as a set of special interests and not as an alternative to the widely accepted political-economic view of the world.

Opinion surveys undertaken in both North America and Western Europe indicate a growing disposition, especially among the well informed and educated, increasingly to accept elements of the ecological perspective. Growth in scientific understanding of damage inflicted upon the environment and, subsequently, upon people has been the critical factor in arousing public demand for political response to threats posed, for example, by acid rain, toxic contamination, and destructive land use. Unprecedented increase in environmental legislation at the national level and in treaties and other agreements at the international level suggests a new world order for the environment is emerging that carries with it the potential for changing national perspectives on relationships involving natural resources, the economy, and the environment. Ecological awareness and environmental concern appear to be growing faster than is the capacity of political institutions to respond. A social lag retards rethinking political assumptions and characteristically narrows the political focus to immediate and short-term considerations by special-interest client demands and inflexible limited time horizons of electoral, legislative, and fiscal procedures.

Traditionally, political perspectives toward the environment have been largely economic and shaped by perceived private economic interests that seldom project beyond the lifetime of the current generation of policy makers. Ecological perspectives in relation to Canada and the United States tend to be continental within the larger global context. They project long-range foresight regarding the future of North America beyond the current preoccupations of Canadians or Americans on the assumption that it is the continent within the global biosphere that ought to be the focus of environmental policy priorities. It is the jurisdictionally limited political and economic divisions of the continent—including their natural resources attributes—that are the foci of political-economic perspectives, even when ecological and global considerations are recognized.

To the extent that conventional political-economic and the more recent ecological perspectives are mutually exclusive, conflicts almost certainly arise and may appear intractable. Conflict resolution is difficult where there is insufficient consensus upon which compromises or redefinition of issues can be undertaken. But Canadian-American transboundary conflicts have sometimes found solutions acceptable to both parties. Nevertheless, cases do exist that have thus far resisted solution. There is danger that their number may increase in the future unless better ways to cope with environmental conflict are developed.

A Taxonomy of Conflicts

Conflicts over shared environmental resources are particularly intractable when they arise over geographically fixed or nonsubstitutable aspects of the environment (particular lakes, rivers, coastal areas, fishing banks, or the indispensable atmosphere) because they cannot be moved or greatly modified without changing their relationships to the parties involved. Where affected parties see these environmental changes as unacceptably burdensome or exacting uncompensated or uncompensatable costs, redress is likely to be sought through political means.

Intractability lies not only in the inflexibility of the environment, but also frequently in the particular character of economic interests. In environmental and natural resources policy it is a rare conflict in which optimal solutions—everyone gains and no one loses—are possible. Governments are expected to defend the perceived interests of their constituents or particular groups of their constituents, but this responsibility becomes difficult to fulfill, or even define, as these interests diverge and conflict. The intermediary role of government amidst conflicting interests becomes even more difficult when conflicts assume international character. The concept of sovereignty and exclusive jurisdiction inherent in conventional political thought works against compromise and against giving equal weight to sometimes diffuse ecological considerations as opposed to specific economic interests of a government's political constituents.

A function common to governments is allocation of benefits and burdens throughout their societies. Every democratic government, acting unilaterally, is accountable to its own electorate for burdens imposed by policies for natural resources and the environment. But no government is accountable to the electorate of another country, even if its actions impose burdens upon that nation. Governments find this allocation difficult among their own constituents when dealing with common sustaining elements, such as air and water, that, while not privately owned, can be used by some people to the disadvantage of others. Not generally amenable to management through market forces, these basic environmental properties become the responsibilities of government. Difficulties of equitable allocation of benefits and burdens are compounded when binational implementation of environmental policies for air, water, and associated resources is undertaken. Expansion of modern technology multiplied both national and transnational environmental problems throughout the world; but neither science nor political philosophy has provided as yet a generally acceptable way to allocate the costs and benefits of environmental and natural resources policy. Thus, conflict resolution remains largely ad hoc.

If a government limits its official view of the international impact of its policies to a political-economic perspective, it may be hard put to justify modifying its own policies to accommodate other perspectives—including the interests of other countries. If a government unilaterally applies a greatest-good-for-the-greatest-number cost-benefit analysis to a project that imposes transboundary burdens, it may conclude that aggregate benefits accruing to its people outweigh relatively lesser burdens imposed upon fewer people in another country. Under this rationale there is no reason to redesign or abandon a project merely because of secondary disbenefits—the greater the benefits to one country the more excusable the disbenefits to the other. Such political-economic rationale is implicit in the history of the Garrison Diversion controversy between Canada and the United States, although the state of North Dakota and the U.S. Bureau of Reclamation have been unwilling to concede that significant disbenefits would be imposed upon anyone—including the province of Manitoba.

Garrison-type conflicts are especially intractable because views of adversaries are divided between political-economic and ecological perspectives. They are not merely differences between two separate sets of political-economic interests that money could help solve. Among competing political-economic interests, compromises are achieved less easily when one of the parties is also committed in some measure to a continental-ecological perspective. Where this happens, the conflict becomes more than economic in character. From an ecological perspective certain "rights" claimed under conventional interpretations of law and free economic enterprise may not be regarded as legitimate. A transboundary imposition of environmental burdens of whatever character upon one country by another may be regarded as ecological taxation without representation for the other country's benefit.

Few, if any, societies have condoned, explicitly or tacitly, the contamination of air and water or the destruction and loss of productive soil. But few governments have been explicit about what constitutes compensable injury that results from damage to these elements. In its consideration of the Poplar River controversy between Saskatchewan and Montana, the International Joint Commission (IJC), reflecting the Boundary Waters Treaty's emphasis on avoidance of injury, distinguished between pollution of a transboundary stream and injury to the "overall interests" of the downstream jurisdiction. It was injury in this latter—but undefined—sense that the IJC held to be prohibited (and, hence, presumably compensable under the Boundary Waters Treaty of 1909)—not the mere fact of water pollution. A similar position was taken with respect to the Garrison Diversion.

In fact, Canada has taken the position that the potential availability of compensation in no way offsets absolute prohibition of injurious pollution as set forth unequivocally in the Boundary Waters Treaty. If one nation could purchase the right of use of another nation's environment, the only issue would be price. It is at least questionable whether a nation can sell its responsibility to its citizens for the custody of their environment; sale of "rights" may not divest concomitantly a government of its associated responsibilities. Compensating trade-offs of environmental sacrifice in one area against environmental protection or restoration in another have not been acceptable in either Canada or the United States and obviously are not feasible across international boundaries. Promises by government or corporate enterprise to refrain from environmental degradation elsewhere contain no compensation to those affected by environmental pollution.

The Boundary Waters Treaty of 1909 does not define injury, and judgment as to what constitutes injury is left to the respective parties to the treaty in each case. Because objectivity and consensus may be difficult for each government, the IJC may be asked to develop a report to assist an agreed judgment (as in the Poplar River and Garrison Diversion cases). Findings and recommendations by the IJC do not constitute judgment; that is a responsibility legally vested in the governments of the two countries. In controversies over pollution it is the nature of the impact determined or estimated by scientific methods that affords the firmest basis for agreement on injury. Injury to community pride or cultural values is far more difficult to establish, although in the United States consideration of aesthetic and nonquantified values is required of federal agencies that are subject to provisions of the National Environmental Policy Act. The presence of nontangible values in transboundary environmental disputes makes them more, rather than less, intractable to resolution.

Moral issues also complicate disputes. From some ecological viewpoints it may be wrong to contaminate the environment to even a small degree, whereas from a political-economic perspective, it is often regarded as unfair or impractical to burden the economy with "excessive" antipollution strictures. While almost no one asserts that injurious pollution is good, many are prepared to argue that a little pollution is not necessarily harmful. In a particular conflict between the ecological and political-economic perspectives, no common basis of criteria may exist to move debate into rational discourse. Scientific evidence regarding actual causes and effects, however, may afford a potential basis for agreement or narrow the gap between polarized positions. Ecological and political-economic perspectives tend to divide on assumptions regarding impacts and implications of a given activity and on the values gained or lost by that activity. Actual evidence may not support fully the extremes of either perspective, but often may reveal alternative courses of action and clarify misconceptions.

The most intractable environmental conflict yet encountered by Canadians and Americans must surely be over the causes and abatement of acid rain. Hardly less stubborn, but with better prospects for resolution, has been the Garrison Diversion project in North Dakota. As of mid–1984 the conflict remained unresolved, but with some prospect for a compromise that could provide for project completion without an impact on the Canadian watershed. A commission of twelve was appointed in June 1984 by the U.S. secretary of the interior to review the project and make recommendations regarding its future.

These cases differ significantly. Acid rain is less localized than is the Garrison dispute. It is more intergovernmentally complex because a large number of American states share Canadian concerns. Moreover, the acid rain issue is also a major environmental concern in Europe; action taken there is certain to have some influence upon North American developments. No political jurisdiction has a vested interest in promoting acid rain comparable to the stakes of North Dakota and the Garrison Conservancy District in the diversion project. High–sulfur-bearing coal interests have opposed abatement regulations, which they regard as unreasonably burdensome. But there has been no public and official commitment to burn high–sulfur-bearing coal comparable to the intent of North Dakota and the United States Bureau of Reclamation to complete the Garrison project as authorized.

The Garrison Diversion project remained an unresolved controversy in the mid–1980s. Like most transboundary environmental disputes involving water, the alleged benefits of Garrison fell almost wholly on one side of the border, and environmental costs unaccompanied by benefits fell on the other. This asymmetrical distribution of benefits and burdens has been characteristic of transboundary environmental controversies, which largely explains why such controversies arise and why many appear intractable. For example, the Skagit-Ross High Dam as proposed would have flooded a valley in British Columbia to benefit users of electricity in Washington State; the Poplar River power plant in Saskatchewan would impair water quality in Montana for the benefit of Canadian power users; the Richelieu-Champlain proposal would raise the level of Lake Champlain, thereby impairing shorelines and wetlands to protect, primarily, second-home owners in the Richelieu valley from occasional flooding.

The difficulty in reaching equitable resolution in these cases is that acceptable trade-offs were rarely available. At stake were conflicting upstream and downstream interests that could not be resolved easily even within a single political jurisdiction. The Garrison Diversion project, for example, arose from an attempted resolution of upstream-downstream conflicts in the Missouri River valley. Here there were shared political-economic perspectives, but basic differences in how those perspectives should be realized as between downstream flood control–navigation interests and upstream irrigation and stream flow augmentation interests. Compromises in conflicts that might be available to one particular government may not be feasible when two or more represent their constituents' perceived interests. Dividing the Missouri River between upstream and downstream interests largely resolved the political problem in the United States since there was enough water to satisfy the respective claimants and no asymmetry of benefits and burdens. However, this solution was inapplicable to upstream-downstream interests in the transboundary disputes previously cited; given their asymmetrical effects, the "Missouri Compromise" would not have succeeded.

ANTICIPATING CONFLICTS

Neither Canada nor the United States is in a position to prescribe alternatives to contested projects that would have to be realized on the other's territory. Americans cannot prevent Canadians from building houses along the banks of the Richelieu River, and Canadians cannot require the Bureau of Reclamation to redesign the Garrison project to keep Missouri River water from Canada. Although not all conflicts can be foreseen nor their magnitude forecast, many environmental disputes described by John E. Carroll in *Environmental Diplomacy* (1983) and others might have been avoided if the full range of probable consequences had been anticipated. Shared values do not always override unshared and incompatible interests, but, nonetheless, a timely recognition of conflict probabilities might have reduced the level of acrimony and the frustrating delays of arriving at agreeable solutions.

To avoid intractable disagreements, attention must be given to conflicts in the making. In matters of binational interest, the field of inquiry cannot be substantially restricted to either country but must encompass both. To accomplish this ecological perspective, a binational arrangement to legitimize transboundary inquiry into prospective problems before they reach political controversy is necessary. This early warning system for discovering trouble on the horizon implies a continuing facility to monitor and evaluate.

To clarify the practical difficulties of binational implementation of shared environmental responsibilities, identifying at least three types of situations where environmental conflicts occur is helpful. As with most typologies relating to human behavior, these are neither absolute nor static. The type and nature of a conflict may pass through stages. Increasingly, scientific information moves an issue from one stage to another—as in the Garrison Diversion controversy, which began over downstream flooding, moved to lowered water quality, and culminated over biota transfer.

Inadvertent—Conflicts caused by inadvertent transboundary effects arise in the normal course of human events and are not deliberate human efforts to manipulate the environment. Examples of such inadvertent effects are air pollution—the subject of international controversy and arbitration in the well-known Trail Smelter case and, more recently, in airborne acidic precipitation—and water pollution and flooding, attributable to poor forestry or agricultural practices, careless industrial and municipal waste disposal, or migration of unwanted biota (alewives and sea lampreys) into the Great Lakes. Effects that are not the consequence of deliberate government planning or action are easier to resolve than are those that occur when governments have undertaken major development plans that turn out to be harmful to their neighbors. When the two national governments share responsibility and suffer mutual consequences, as in the case of sea lampreys in the Great Lakes, opportunities for remedial cooperation are obviously enhanced.

Developmental—This category of environment-resource conflict relates to unilateral planned development, including such obvious examples as the Garrison Diversion irrigation project in North Dakota and the proposed regulation of the waters of the Lake Champlain–Richelieu River basin. Also, frequently included are energy-related issues involved in such projects as the Atikokan power plant in Ontario, the Skagit-High Ross Dam in Washington, the Poplar River power plant in Saskatchewan, and energy development in the Beaufort Sea. Conflicts between Canada and the United States over the Georges Bank and the Strait of Juan de Fuca are energy-related and, to some degree, follow from planned development. In the Georges Bank case the interest of American oil firms in prospecting for petroleum has been a factor in a boundary dispute, and in the Pacific Northwest shipment by tanker of Alaska crude oil to the lower forty-eight states is classified as intended development.

In each of these cases conflicts that might have been foreseen are from projects that were unilaterally undertaken and blessed with official support. Although the sovereign rights issue occurs frequently in inadvertent transboundary cases, it is more strongly marked in those where official federal, state, or provincial action has aroused conflict. In such cases governments risk the appearance of acceding to external pressures—a stance that public officeholders everywhere prefer to avoid.

Latent—The third category involves latent or potential occasions for conflict. A major interbasin transfer conflict was latent in the Garrison Diversion case before it became an inadvertent cause of Canadian-American controversy. Latent conflict is already present in proposals to divert large amounts of water from the Great Lakes for various purposes, notably to recharge the Ogalalla aquifer that underlies a vast area of the Great Plains in the United States. In the early 1960s the North American Water and Power Alliance (NAWAPA) proposed the diversion of water from the Canadian Northwest to the American intermountain and desert Southwest, including west Texas. Canadian reaction to NAWAPA was as cool as the glaciers of the Columbian ice fields. But water users of the U.S. West and Southwest have not changed their ways of water usage. Thus, NAWAPA may not be dead but merely dormant, to be revived in some form in the future when, in the considered opinion of the community of U.S. civil engineers, agriculturalists, journalists, and politicians, Canada, rich in water resources, has a moral obligation to share its watery wealth with improvident, politically powerful, and economically subsidized U.S. agriculture.

Across North America—including its submerged continental shelf—energy moves over electric powerlines, through pipelines, and in the hulls of tankers at sea. There are latent environmental risks in mishandling energy resources. Moreover, international political-economic repercussions are likely to occur in the event of the failure of expected amounts of energy-related materials— oil, gas, and uranium—to cross from Canada into the United States and effectively generate power. Both ecological and political-economic repercussions may follow from oil spills on either side of the border or from environmental impacts of transboundary powerlines or pipelines.

Values versus Interests

Obviously, these three categories of conflict—inadvertent, developmental, and latent—are not watertight and are not the only types of conflict situations. But to understand distinctions that characterize them, with a view to finding ways to prevent their occurrence, they are useful. Because they relate to the time sequences of conflict development, they have some bearing on efforts to foresee, avoid, or ameliorate those circumstances that tend to confuse or obstruct binational approaches to issues that neither nation can satisfactorily confront without cooperation from the other. If conflict is regarded as harmful to international relations, its avoidance is preferable to its resolution. Impact analysis is needed to avoid or resolve conflict and, to be effective, must reveal a broad spectrum of the probable consequences of proposed or anticipated developments. In designing a system to promote socioecological integrity and stability and prevent destabilizing conflict, account needs to be taken of the causes, courses, and consequences of unwanted events. There is at present no binational arrangement between Canada and the United States that is charged or equipped to deal in an anticipatory manner with environmental or natural resources problems having potential for conflict.

Given an identical set of facts and values, people may understand and interpret them in different ways. Yet it can never be easy to obtain a rational, mutually agreed solution to shared environmental problems as long as the problems are approached with unshared viewpoints and values. Agreed-upon criteria to interpret and evaluate facts are a requisite for cooperative action, even if they offer no guarantee of agreed-upon solutions.

To rely upon the premise of shared values as a basis for agreement is futile when political interests are not shared and, in fact, may be incompatible. It would be unrealistic to suppose that societies as large and heterogeneous as those of Canada and the United States would ever arrive at a substantial uniformity in attitudes, values, or interests. A requisite for cooperative action is a sufficient degree of common consent on facts and values so that political action can proceed on a basis of long-term binational sustainability that allows real differences of interest to be reconciled, reduced, or accommodated.

Resource management technologies used by governments in pursuit of internationally incompatible objectives can damage prospects for joint policies of shared environments and possibly create persistent political problems even after the physical problems have been somehow resolved. Unless Canadians and Americans establish a common basis to interpret and evaluate their common environmental concerns, little hope exists for significant improvement in the prospects of bringing about joint responsibility for a shared environment. Indeed, under possibly straitened conditions in the future there is risk that transborder relationships relating to environment and resources could worsen.

Political "realists" may argue that this assessment is unduly pessimistic and that as long as trade-offs and bargaining are possible, conventional politics, however short-range and parochial, will continue to obtain a resolution of issues. This view assumes that conventional politics will continue to "work" even though the issues confronted may have scope and impact that transcend continental limits and threaten environmental changes unaccept-able to large populations on both sides of the Canadian-American border. The acid rain issue could be one of these.

Political values, like human nature, can change, and they must, if the human species is to continue to live in the kind of world it now has shaped. The prospects for conventional politics "work-ing" are diminished by the growth of what some students of pub-lic opinion describe as the rise of a new environmental para-digm—an *ecological perspective*. Studies by Riley Dunlap, Lester W. Milbrath, and William Cameron Mitchell indicate that this ecological perspective has become widely shared among better in-formed, better educated, and more affluent Canadians and Ameri-cans. Transborder collaboration has occurred among like-minded Canadians and Americans upon a number of different environ-mental issues arising between their countries.

In its purest form the ecological perspective clashes with con-ventional political and economic values across a broad range of specifics involving attitudes toward economic growth, legal rights (particularly in the ownership and use of property), national sov-ereignty, and the necessities of national security. The ecological perspective on life and the world for North Americans tends to be continental in a global context. Primary consideration is given to the physical-ecological properties and dynamics of the conti-nent. This is not to be confused with a continental perspective from a political-economic viewpoint, which, depending on which side of the border the viewer is situated, can lead to very different conclusions. Canadians may be understandably apprehensive about continental viewpoints situated south of the international border regardless of perspectives. For example, the ecological per-spective implicit in the Great Lakes Water Quality Agreement prohibiting reductions in water quality aroused apprehensions among development interests in Canada. The effect of these re-strictions on relatively unpolluted Lake Huron and Lake Superior would preclude the type of economic growth already attained on the American south shores. In another circumstance the state of Minnesota objected to emissions from the Atikokan coal-fired power plant in Ontario not as much for environmental reasons (although acid deposition could impair the Boundary Waters Wilderness Area) as for industrial reasons, since the ambient air quality lowered by emissions from Atikokan could compromise future industrial development in northeastern Minnesota.

From an ecological perspective, political boundaries more often are deplored than viewed defensively. They are not regarded as sacrosanct by persons concerned with restoration and preservation of water quality in the Great Lakes, elimination of acidic waste from the atmosphere, protection of the fragile Arctic environment from destructive resource development, preservation of wetlands, and opposition of the homogenization of river ecosystems through hydropower and water diversion schemes. Obviously, an ecological perspective does not and may never offer a panacea for Canadian-American controversy. Indeed, it might exacerbate conflicts between those holding this more inclusive view and those with more strictly "national" perspectives. However, fundamental improvements in Canadian-American relationships would occur when this viewpoint and its underlying values became sufficiently widespread in both countries to affect decisively perceptions of public interest and thereby influence political thinking and decision making.

Can Ecology Redefine Interest?

Were a truly continental perspective to prevail in North America, what would be its implications? Some ramifications would surely arouse surprise, and perhaps dismay, on both sides of the border. A continental perspective in a global context giving priority to sustaining the natural environment and its resources, over the reshaping of the continent for economic development, would be ecological in character. Were either country to gain from this perspective (not a certainty), in the long run it could well be Canada, because its natural environment and resources have experienced the impact of human activities less severely, and its future could be designed for sustainability. The United States would face a much greater task of ecologically sensitive restoration and redevelopment.

The application of an ecological perspective to the interests of Canada and the United States in their shared environment obviously implies that greater attention would be given to the benefits of binational cooperation and costs of insufficiently examined unilateral initiatives. From an ecological viewpoint, wholly unilateral planning affecting a shared environment would be generally unacceptable to both Canadians and Americans. Before authorizing or undertaking any large development project in either country, a binational impact analysis would be expected, including not only an assessment in the narrower sense but also consideration of economic impacts and candid use of risk assessment and binational cost-benefit analysis. Objectors to the hypothetical costs and delays associated with these procedures should consider first the costs and delays associated with the controversies over projects such as the Skagit-High Ross Dam, the Poplar River power project, and the Garrison Diversion. Projects found to be wasteful, destructive, or inequitable in the long run might be stopped before they gained the political momentum that makes reversal difficult. For example, political "foot-dragging," not analytic procedure, has delayed action to abate acid rain.

An ecological perspective on binational interests also implies that a binational consensus is needed to define those issues regarded as "continental." Basis for such consensus already exists in the natural sciences and is being continually enlarged. For example, atmospheric science has, in effect, made burning of high-sulfur coal in the Ohio River basin an ecological issue with major economic dimensions. Less obviously, prognosis of the depletion of the Ogalalla aquifer by center-pivot irrigation in the western high plains of the United States may become a continental issue. The consequences of depletion in the United States are certain to be felt in Canada—particularly if the demand for supplementary water leads to political pressure on Canada to get transfers from the Great Lakes or the Canadian Rockies to try to salvage an improvident regional economy.

With a continental-ecological perspective, equities would be determined on a more inclusive and complex basis than with conventional political assumptions. Quality factors would be included; quantitative considerations alone, either of people, economic demand, or resource supply from a particular area, would not be decisive. Translated into political terms, an ecological perspective, continental or global, has institutional implications. For example, planning in transboundary affairs would require coordinated interagency and interdisciplinary participation, such as studies sponsored by the International Joint Commission. Collaboration among Canadian and American researchers in universities and government and private sector agencies would need to be reinforced and extended.

This, in turn, implies some redeployment of financial resources and suggests the development of binational provisions for continental surveillance and review of planning, perhaps attained through the enlarged competence of existing organizations devoted to these purposes. To argue that it is politically unrealistic to expect such development is, in effect, to argue that a continental-ecological perspective with sufficient power to influence national politics in the respective countries is also unrealistic. This objection can only be proved by history yet to be made. There are, nonetheless, more reasons for believing that a continental perspective will gain influence and political relevance than that it will not. Time will tell.

Binational Strategies

How would an ecological perspective be given practical application in political decision making? When nations collaborate, formal agreements regarding principles and procedures are necessary. In developing a Canadian-American ecological perspective on the North American continent and beyond, agreement might be embodied in a new treaty or in an extension of the Boundary Waters Treaty of 1909. Whatever its form, it should include four provisions.

PROVISIONS OF AGREEMENT

First would be an agreement in principle—a consensus on binational responsibilities on issues that cross the boundary and affect the continent. Second, agreement would be required on the means for determining what would constitute a binational, continental issue. This would, of course, include agreement on the nature of the factual basis and criteria for defining such an issue. Third, there would need to be agreement on the methodologies of inquiry, involving both procedural and jurisdictional considerations. The investigations conducted by the IJC on possible impacts of the Garrison Diversion project illustrate the kinds of arrangements to be considered and agreed upon if a general policy for binational investigations is to be accepted. Fourth, there would need to be arrangements to make sure that such findings receive appropriate consideration. Commitment short of unequivocal acceptance of the findings, but more than merely acknowledging them, would be necessary if the strategy were to be taken seriously. While it could be argued that an obligation to respond to a recommended binational course of action would be tantamount to relinquishing national sovereignty, it could be argued equally well that it merely clarifies the modification of sovereign freedom of unilateral action already agreed to in the Boundary Waters Treaty. These provisions would represent no more than further development of principles and mechanisms to implement more effectively the expressed intent of both nations, in effect since 1909. Need for these elaborations is explained by greatly increased understanding of the implications of ecological relationships for the health of the continent and its inhabitants, and by the equally great increase in capabilities for environmental alteration.

These agreements should not be expected to be implemented with perfect understanding and accord. No international agreement is susceptible to precise and unequivocal interpretation, and none can anticipate and provide for all future circumstances. Nevertheless, if they are serious about alleviating present strains between themselves over policies regarding shared resources and environment and, more especially, warding off future confrontations, it would seem reasonable for the United States and Canada to work toward some such agreement. Merely making a case for such an agreement is not sufficient to obtain its realization. Strategies of explanation and persuasion are also necessary and may need to be continued over a number of years before a comprehensive binational arrangement becomes politically feasible.

SHARED DATA

A fundamental strategy upon which to build an informed consensus is a reliable and mutually agreed-upon data base for North American ecological and natural resources information. Science has been a major influence in changing attitudes toward the environment; it has already been an influence in the initiation of multinational environmental protection programs. A system based on science to obtain and maintain mutually shared factual information is necessary not only to enable people to see where they agree but also where they differ. Such a data system must be based upon mutually accepted methods of data handling and be accessible in ways that would facilitate political decisions on both sides of the border to reduce the influence of self-serving public or private interests that generate conflict. The building of such a system or data base is time-consuming and may appear expensive. Yet, compared to the costs of uninformed controversy, disputes over facts, and confusion over real differences, the cost of the data base may become a rewarding investment.

It would hardly be feasible to contemplate an information system or data base that fully describes all aspects of environment and natural resources on the North American continent. Such a comprehensive information system might be feasible before the end of the twenty-first century, but it is not a likely possibility during the twentieth. The strategy, therefore, is to develop a binational information base adequate to deal with those issues now pressing—or those likely to become so in the future. Although not all continental issues are amenable to ecological analysis at any given time, recognition of the scope and ramifications of particular issues is desirable, even if a political consensus regarding those issues may not be obtained immediately. In this way, latent conflict may be identified before it grows to divisive proportions.

Binational Optimality—Beyond the data or information base, a strategy for obtaining informed consensus must examine the extent of shared assumptions and values. Consideration of interests and equities—both contemporary and prospective—is a part of this strategy. To the extent that the parties to controversy can agree upon what values are to be honored, how priorities are to be set among economic interests, and how equities are to be defined, actual differences that separate the parties can be narrowed and clarified. Binational strategies for consensus building are unlikely to accept transboundary zero-sum outcomes or heavily one-sided benefits or costs. Where benefits can be allocated evenly, agreements may be facilitated to the extent that they approach what economists sometimes call the *Pareto optimality,* solutions in which everyone gains something and there are no net losers. This type of optimality might improve the prospect that a larger number of Americans as compared to Canadians would not be an automatic factor in determining the allocation of benefits between the two countries. If binational agreement is sought, proposals incapable of Pareto optimal formulations should bear the burden of proof that inequities were justified.

One great advantage of a continental-ecological frame of reference in contrast to the present ad hoc and localized definition of issues is the possibility for trade-offs and rational compromises on a continental scale. As previously noted, many Canadian-American conflicts over transboundary environmental and natural resources issues remain intractable because choices for finding optimal resolution of differences are limited geographically. However, broadening the field of possibilities may enlarge the number of possible ways of satisfying some, if not all, of the parties concerned. Precluded from this strategy would be such options as binational acceptance of degradation of a prairie river to offset protection of a salt marsh on the Atlantic coast. An acceptable compromise might be abandonment of an ecologically damaging project by one country in return for joint efforts elsewhere in which environmental damage was lessened or eliminated. If a broader continental information system for assisting environment-shaping decisions already had been in place, the rationale for allocating tens of millions of dollars to the parochial Garrison Diversion project might have been less persuasive to the U.S. Congress. Skeptics who doubt that institutional arrangements have much influence on policy results might consider the relationship between the committee structure and procedures of the U.S. Congress and the leverage enjoyed by localized interests in the allocation of the nation's financial resources. An institutionalized counterleverage might assist broader based binational efforts.

Not all environmental controversies can be resolved through compromise, and in these cases the advantage of binational pre-planning review of projects becomes evident. Although it may be possible to plan environment-affecting or natural resource development projects upon a binational optimal basis, this politically desirable outcome may be obstructed by unilateral planning that leads to commitments beneficial to one nation and harmful to another.

Finally, institutional arrangements for binational continental surveillance should draw upon past experience and utilize existing effective means, modifying or extending them as necessary to obtain a truly integrated approach to problem analysis and proposed solutions. Existing institutional arrangements for transboundary environmental and resource inquiries are almost wholly national and may be expected to continue to be so. It would be politically impossible to act as though Canada and the United States did not exist as independent nations accustomed to making and implementing unilateral decisions. Nevertheless, there is evidence that a continental approach is possible within a binational context. The evidence may be drawn chiefly from the experience of the IJC in its consideration of issues referred to it by these governments and, more especially, in certain of its study committees. This commission very often has taken what might be regarded as a continental-ecological perspective instead of two separate political-economic viewpoints.

Extending the Binational System

A continental-ecological basis for policy regarding the shared environment of Canada and the United States is most feasible where the need for it is clear and present, helpful precedents are available, and adversarial positions have not solidified. As previously suggested, there is no approach to an environmental or natural resource problem that can guarantee binational agreement or ensure that problems can be resolved to the satisfaction of both parties. Where adversarial positions appear to have solidified, as in the Garrison Diversion and, at least to some extent, with respect to acid rain, a continental-ecological approach ultimately may have to be taken to settle the issue.

With respect to acid rain, official positions on assumed national interests have been taken both in Canada and the United States. However, in the United States public opinion is divided, and there is no binding official agreement on the issue's seriousness or the extent of obligation for remedial action. There is substantial agreement among environmental scientists in the northeastern United States and eastern Canada that if necessary, drastic action should be taken to prevent continuation of the harm now being done. The acid rain problem remains to be solved and, in all probability, will be solved in some way, but perhaps not one based upon a continental-ecological perspective, which, nonetheless, has been an underlying influence on policy in both countries. Weight of political influence, rather than agreement upon facts and values, seems likely to obtain a binational solution to this problem.

Binational strategies that mobilize support on both sides of the international border show greater prospects for consensus of implementation of water quality agreements regarding the Great Lakes. These policy positions have neither crystallized nor solidified, but remain advantageously fluid and may be channeled toward some form of integrated binational decision making. Binational perspectives and interests appear to coincide on the restoration and protection of Great Lake fisheries. The incipient bioregional movement, if it develops, may reinforce in some measure binational collaboration among private ecology-minded groups in both countries. A similar movement toward transnational cooperation is reported by observers of the Green parties in Europe.

Today more than ever before potential conflicts may be recognized in advance of their occurrence. Prevention of political conflict or ecological error is almost always less costly than coping with unwanted events. But politicians and the public generally prefer to "let sleeping issues lie." Politicians often try to avoid overt recognition of trends and circumstances that might press them to take action that they would find personally disadvantageous. Therefore, means outside of the conventional political structure are needed to scan environmental horizons for sources of possible trouble. There is need for a surveillance and monitoring arrangement protected from political manipulation, but structured so that neither the public nor its political leadership can ignore its findings. Characteristics of such a system and ways that it might be effected are outlined as follows.

DEVELOPING A SYSTEM

The assemblage and integration of such a system would require a high order of organizational skill, information, and imaginative exercise of political strategy. Given prevailing circumstances, only two types of organizational arrangements appear to be suitable. Unsuitable would be a unified continental system, wholly separate from either national government. At this point in history it would be politically unacceptable and, in any case, would duplicate existing national services that might otherwise be employed.

A possible arrangement, however, would be a negotiated, mutually coordinated system for concurrent collaboration of Canadian and American institutions, each developing its own data and assessments, but with identical criteria and format. This arrangement would provide for joint publication of accumulated data. Funding could be provided by respective governments, supplemented, perhaps, from private sources. There are precedents for such an arrangement. For example, the World Weather Watch, established by the World Meteorological Society (WMO), provides for concurrent monitoring and reporting by the weather services of many independent nations. The success of this system, however, depends upon WMO acting as a central point for coordination and oversight, as well as for the establishment of standards of performance and information.

An Alternative—Actually an extension of the first possibility would be concurrent national responsibility for program operations coordinated by a central autonomous agency or office with the capability to supervise and assist coordination of the system. This central body would be created by the two national governments but would not be subject directly to their detailed political control. To be effective and economical, the system should have outreach relationships with scientific and research academies and councils in both countries. Some type of arrangement for periodic formal review of its performance would be a condition of political acceptability. Within limits necessary to its orderly functioning, the system should be open to not only the dissemination of information to the people of both countries but also to the input of ideas, suggestions, criticisms, and inquiries from the general public, as well as from various groups with particular concern with the findings produced through its operations.

Exploratory planning of the system should probably take place informally on the basis of a memorandum of intent negotiated between the two countries. Although diplomats and international lawyers are needed in the preparation of an international agreement, provision should be made for the scientific and technical judgments even more needed in planning a binational monitoring system. Thus, an early step toward agreement would be the establishment of a binational advisory committee, multidisciplinary in character, that could be subdivided into two major divisions, one that addresses the scientific and technical aspects of the system and another that examines the institutional arrangements among governmental units and agencies necessary for the system's success. The former group surely would be the larger and almost necessarily would be subdivided into specialized sections to deal with particular aspects of the environment and natural resources. But there should be continuing liaison between the two major divisions of the committee, and final action by the committee should be taken in plenary sesssion when both drafters of the international agreement and developers of the system would adopt recommendations addressed to a central steering committee or senior negotiating group that reports to the governments of the respective countries (or perhaps to the IJC).

Were a system to be established, what would it do? Its first task would be the assemblage and development of data bases for current or anticipated issues. Although the overall task would be formidable, it would not be as great as if all aspects were to be investigated *de novo*. An important part of the task would be to collect, critique, and integrate previous work done on selected problems. The system, as suggested here, does not contemplate the establishment of a large bureaucracy separate from existing governmental agencies. A considerable part of its personnel and monetary cost is already provided in the course of governmental support for existing environmental and natural resources activities. Some of the staff engaged in the construction and maintenance of the data base might be engaged also in the normal activities of these agencies or institutions. A redundant bureacracy is precisely what is *not* being recommended; it would not be an effective or efficient way to obtain desired results. Advances in computer technologies greatly enhance prospects that such a system ultimately could be more accurate, more informative, and perhaps less costly than present data sources; updating and maintenance would also be greatly facilitated.

The data bases are only instruments of forecasting, evaluating, and decision making; they do not make decisions. Policy-relevant findings would be the end result of the system. Its role in factfinding, analysis, and recommendation is to provide a reliable, verifiable basis for binational policy and decision making. Here the precedents set by the IJC in implementing the Boundary Waters Treaty of 1909 have obvious value. The system could build upon and extend the functions of the IJC and could benefit from an examination of the IJC's experience. At the very least, the system should have an autonomous investigatory power and not be wholly dependent upon referrals from the two governments.

The relationship of this proposed system to the IJC is, of course, a major political and organizational question. Would it replace the IJC? Would it be an extension and elaboration of the IJC? Would it be a complementary binational agency functioning with respect to matters of environment and natural resources beyond the present competence of the IJC? One possibility would be to reconstitute the IJC, with the present six-member commission charged to be the binational representative oversight body for the entire system and perform a "board of directors" role. Developing the system under the executive authority of a strengthened IJC could be a conservative and practical way to launch this enlarged binational effort.

The technical feasibility of such a system is more easily demonstrated than is its political acceptability. An initial reaction of Canadians might be that the "continentalizing" of their natural environment (including its natural resources) would be almost wholly advantageous to the United States. But the system, if properly constructed, need not lead to this conclusion. Under a continental-ecological system, Canadians would have a voice in the environmental and natural resource policies of the United States that they now lack. Canadian interpositions in developments such as the Garrison Diversion project, the Skagit-High Ross Dam, or the U.S. position on abatement of acid rain have been regarded by some Americans as interference in U.S. internal affairs.

Were Canadians disposed to favor a sustainable and environmentally conserving utilization of their natural resources, they might have more to gain than would the United States from implementation of such a system of information development and fact-finding. For the first time Canadians would have a regularized method of inquiry into U.S. resource and environmental policies that might have long-term adverse repercussions on Canada. This is notably true with respect to water-related policies in the western part of the United States and matters affecting fisheries in the Great Lakes, and on the Atlantic, Pacific, and Arctic coasts of the continent. The proposed system would not be designed for sharing consequences of short-sighted and improvident natural resources policies on either side of the international border. In such a system, Americans might find a means to reexamine ecologically harmful and economically inequitable water projects of the western states, which, when their course is ultimately run, will lead almost certainly to pressures for compensatory water resources from Canada. The system should be constructed, staffed, and directed so that it would serve equitably the interests of the people of both countries.

The Larger Dimension
of Binational Responsibilities

There are two reasons that a continental-ecological perspective on the environment and resources of North America must have a global dimension. First, many aspects of the North American environment, most obviously its atmosphere and maritime coasts, are affected by occurrences outside continental limits. Both Canada and the United States, moreover, are affected by the policies and practices of other countries in relation to natural resources. The Canadian economy and important segments of the U.S. economy are heavily dependent upon trade; but the extraction or harvesting of a resource has environmental implications that are usually multidimensional and often multinational. Exports of food alone tie both countries to the world political economy. Therefore, environmental conflicts over water that affect food production may have international implications.

Second, it is important in today's world to maintain ecological and political stability where it exists. It is significant not only to North Americans but also to others in the world (whether or not they know it) that the continental island of North America provide a reliable example of sustainable, progressive stability. Serious quarrels between the two largest political occupants of North America in some measure would jeopardize not only their ability to respond constructively to needs and opportunities at home and abroad but also would fail to provide a model for international cooperation badly needed in today's unstable world.

The world today is in a precarious state. Whatever can be done to contain or reduce global disorder surely would be in the interest of people everywhere. In the responsible custody of the shared environment that they largely occupy, Canada and the United States have an opportunity to advance not only their own long-term interests but also to make a positive contribution to the survival of a viable world.

John H. Sigler and Charles F. Doran

7

Twenty Years After:
Change and Continuity
in United States–Canada Relations

Introduction

In 1927, shortly after his arrival in Washington to join the staff of the new Canadian legation, the young Canadian diplomat Hume Wrong, later ambassador to the United States after World War II, drafted a general memorandum on relations between Canada and the United States. It is a document with a remarkably temporary ring, unlike most of the diplomatic documents of that more innocent age. It sets out many of the elements of continuity in the diplomatic agenda of the two countries. Of the factors promoting continuing friendly relations, Wrong listed a common continental feeling, general similarity of economic conditions, mutual economic interdependence, the large amounts of U.S. capital invested in Canada and the even larger complementary per capita Canadian investment in the United States, the enormous volume of transit traffic, and the declining significance of borders due to changes in technology. Among the factors likely to lead to friction he cited were Canada's different international commitments; tariff policies; U.S. exploitation of Canadian natural resources, and the danger of U.S. resentment which any Canadian program of conservation might engender; Canadian domestic legislation which could be represented as confiscatory of U.S. capital; the greater tolerance of Canadians for public enterprise which might lead to U.S. resentment of what U.S. conservatives would interpret as Canada's more "socialistic and radical" character; the impact of American broadcasting; and the differences in political system, particularly Canadian lack of understanding for the "cumbrous machinery for directing foreign affairs in the United States and the absence of executive responsibility in Congress."

The examples have changed over time, but the agenda is much the same. The previous chapters in this volume and its predecessor twenty years ago in the American Assembly series chronicle the specific items of friction and continuing cooperation which are implicit in the history, culture, and geography of the two North American countries.

In writing on Canadian-American relations, there is an inevitable tendency to borrow the usual nation-state system shorthand which speaks of Canadians and Americans as entirely separate national actors with unified views within each country. While the actor designations "Ottawa" and "Washington" are expected to convey the idea of unified government policy in each country, the many studies on bureaucratic politics over the past quarter century have shown how many differences on policy matters remain even within governments. If ever a pluralist approach was justified in trying to understand political process, it is true in Canadian-American relations where the degree of cross-boundary activity, in business corporations, in labor unions, in voluntary organizations, and even in bureaucracies, is perhaps the most intense anywhere on the planet. National sovereignties do remain distinct and are likely to be so for the foreseeable future, but in using the shorthand of "Canadians think" or "Americans think" we should keep well in mind the overgeneralization. What we are really saying is that some Canadians agree or disagree with some Americans some of the time on some issues, and the process of coalition building within and between the two countries is likely to intensify in the coming years even as governments may try to contain and control the process to serve their own ends as articulators of state policy.

The pluralist perspective carries with it the idea of considerable untidiness in trying to understand shifting agenda and the shifting coalitions of actors who are salient on a given issue. This pluralist approach plays down alternative approaches which seek to identify the key actors and the key issues and reduce explanations of behavior to a small set of principal propositions, whether these be psychological, economic, geographic, or political in nature.

Interpretation of Canada–U.S. relations often tends to favor a single theme or factor as explanation of the enduring features or as the source of crisis or tension. Usually a good case can be made for the importance of each particular source of explanation, but not as a sole or even predominant explanation. Leading examples of predominant factors include personalities of the key leaders, institutions, and foreign policy style, all of which will continue to exercise considerable influence on Canada–U.S. relations.

PERSONALITY, INSTITUTIONS, AND FOREIGN POLICY STYLE

In explaining the conduct of the relationship, the personality of the prime minister, or the president of the United States, or the principal cabinet officials on either side, will often receive considerable emphasis. In a relationship as interwoven and familiar as that of Canada and the United States, compatibility of leadership outlook is important because it sets the tone for discussions at every level of the bureaucratic hierarchy. It warns bureaucrats and public servants lower on the ladder of responsibility that if they fail to cooperate or give an issue the proper attention, they will be monitored and they may be overruled. When the personal chemistry of the top leadership is good, even the rough spots of diplomatic conduct seem smoother and the commitment to proceed appears more definite.

But personality does not account for everything in Canada–U.S. relations. Canadians, in particular, are skeptical that compatibility of leadership personality can accomplish very much if other factors do not coincide. They are reminded of the good personal relations and mutual respect between President Carter and Prime Minister Trudeau, but the growing pressures of an international crisis agenda increasingly preoccupied the White House, and domestic political pressures in the U.S. Congress blocked progress on the East Coast Fisheries Treaty despite strong White House support. Canadians also worry that affability will be used as a substitute for substantive momentum, that "atmospherics" will supplant serious intent to move ahead on issues that for domestic political reasons are not often easy to resolve in terms of foreign affairs. The Canadian viewpoint often is that compatibility of personality is desirable if it is used to promote progress in bilateral negotiations and not to cover up the lack of progress.

A similar set of arguments can be addressed to the relative importance of institutions and institution building in Canada–U.S. relations. Americans tend to look at the bilateral institution as a bridge; Canadians often conceive of institution building as a buffer. But whether bridge or buffer, the bilateral institution surely has a place in preserving harmony and in achieving diplomatic results in the relationship.

A major question, however, is whether to lean more heavily on bilateral institutions or whether to steer tough policy questions away from such institutions into traditional diplomatic channels. The matter comes to a head in reflecting upon the role of the International Joint Commission (IJC), the venerable environmental institution that has established a reputation for objectivity and political neutrality matched by few other transborder entities. If the IJC takes on more responsibilities, it stands to make a greater impact on the relationship and to expedite the resolution of problems, especially in the sphere of air and water pollution abatement, and, possibly, resource management.

But at the same time the more responsibility the IJC assumes in policy, in contrast to fact-finding, the more autonomy it will need from the direct control of the two governments and the more visibility it will acquire. Even assuming that increased autonomy and increasing diplomatic visibility are not dangerously opposed, an enlarged and more powerful IJC would become a more conspicuous target for criticism in the Canadian cabinet and in the U.S. Congress. Whether the members of the IJC, known for their admirable political neutrality, could withstand this kind of pressure and still vote along objective and nonnational lines on issues, such as acid rain cleanup, that are highly charged politically is a question unanswered by historical IJC experience.

Institution building and reform is not an insignificant aspect of better Canada–U.S. relations. But bilateral institutions can bear only a fraction of the weight of highly politicized issues. Institutions serve other purposes such as the creation of a web of social and personal interaction that carries the relationship through difficult times when the governments on other counts seem to be out of phase with one another. Bilateral institutions can also serve as a useful training ground for a sensitive and competent elite of officials and staff committed to managing the relationship in a responsible way. But more ought not to be expected of bilateral institutions than those institutions are capable of providing.

Finally, style of foreign policy leadership is significant because it conveys obliquely what substance would reveal too nakedly about governmental priorities in foreign policy. By varying foreign policy style, a government is able to transmit signals regarding its satisfaction or dissatisfaction with current policy. The style of political leadership often has its roots as well in the domestic electoral imperatives within the country. Former Prime Minister Trudeau, for example, like John Diefenbaker, tended to thrive on political combat, whether with the provinces or with a foreign government. Prime Minister Mulroney, like Lester Pearson before him, tends to excel at harmonization and conciliation. The political style that each leader brought to his government was to some extent the political style that would color negotiations with foreign governments as well. Both Washington and Ottawa have often had a difficult time comprehending the origins of differing political styles, however, or the practical purposes to which those styles were being put. Analysis of political style involves the analysis of nuance; nuance is a critical element of Canada–U.S. relations since the limits within which the relationship is allowed to vacillate are so pronounced.

But important as personality, institutionalization, and political style are to the understanding of what drives Canada–U.S. relations, none of these factors in isolation explains very much in totality about the good times or the bad times facing the two countries. Discussion of these factors is indispensable analytically.

Bilateral Statecraft in a Multilateral Context

A constant in the relationship is the felt need of Canada to try to subordinate bilateral statecraft with the United States into a multilateral framework. Because of its size and global obligations, the United States displays the opposite tendency, namely, to treat North America as an isolated dyad within the international system. Unless the grounds for each of these opposed propensities are understood, it will create serious difficulty in the effort to generate harmony in Canada–U.S. relations.

Canada, for example, needs the North Atlantic Treaty Organization (NATO) not only for security purposes as a shield against possible Soviet aggression; Canada needs NATO as a multilateral counterweight to the overwhelming continental presence of the United States in political terms. If NATO were to fragment, Canada would be forced to define its security largely in continental terms. It would be left alone in North America to cope with the political dominance of the United States.

A similar example is the Trudeau policy of trade diversification. In Canadian domestic politics the Trudeau years may be best known for the effort to achieve biculturalism, the struggles over federal-provincial relations, and the patriation of the Constitution from Westminster to Canada. But in terms of foreign policy perhaps the most remembered initiative was the early 1970s proposal to diversify trade. Known as the Third Option, and announced by Mitchell Sharp, then secretary of state for external affairs, the trade diversification initiative attempted to reorient trade toward Europe and Japan in order to reduce possible vulnerability and dependence with respect to the United States. But since the United States, by far Canada's largest trading partner, also imported a higher percentage of manufactured goods from Canada than any other trading partner, trade diversification would also lead to some decline for Canada in the ratio of the export of manufactured goods to commodities.

By 1983 the sectoral trade initiative proposed by the Trudeau government overshadowed the former Third Option and gave to trade relations between the two countries even more of a North American focus than before. But problems of vulnerability in the highly interdependent relationship between Canada and the United States were not resolved by such bilateral initiatives and as far as Canada was concerned would continue to require attention.

The scale and disparities of production and consumption of energy in Canada and the United States make energy-related issues always matters of concern within each country and in relations between them. The oil shock of 1974 and following events intensified this concern and made energy, particularly oil and gas, a persistent theme and source of stress for much of the Trudeau years. In Canada issues of control over development and income from natural resources, above all energy resources, were a central point of tension in federal-provincial relations—between the producing provinces and Ottawa and between the former and the consuming regions of the country.

In chapter 1 Gordon Robertson discussed how federal-provincial differences affected the course of the constitutional debates of the 1970s. Energy was a source of irritation between the two federal governments as well, most recently and visibly in the case of the National Energy Program described by Richard Lipsey.

Another set of issues of a different sort than those relating to oil concerns the financing and building of gas pipelines. The delivery of gas in North America preoccupied governments and private sectors on both sides of the border. A new Canadian government approach to foreign investment (including investment in energy), recession in both economies, and a surplus deliverability of oil, all helped remove energy as an irritant in bilateral relations by the end of the Trudeau period. A longer range look at the North American and world economic and energy pictures suggests, however, that the lull is but temporary and that energy in all its forms can be expected to regain prominance on the U.S.–Canadian agenda.

Another important agenda item is agriculture. Over the last two decades world production of principal grains has increased from 900 million metric tons to 1600 million metric tons. Countries which for years had absorbed large export surpluses from Canada and the United States had become self-sufficient—particularly India and China. The EEC has become a major exporter in its own right, and new countries including even India and China are themselves beginning to export food and feed grains. Dramatic prospective improvements in genetic biological technology in agriculture promise to make this shift in trade and consumption patterns permanent, to bring more and more new countries to self-sufficiency, and to lead to new competition in diminishing markets. The Soviet Union and sub-Saharan Africa may be the slowest to benefit from these changes, but many agricultural scientists believe that in the next two decades seeds and growing techniques will be available which will significantly ease even the adverse crop conditions (if not distribution and social constraints) limiting production and consumption in these areas.

The implications of these marked changes for both U.S. and Canadian agriculture are enormous, both economically and politically. These changes could create major strains between the two countries as they compete for shares of a declining market through attempts at subsidies, market regulation, and government intervention. Wiser by far will be a new and franker effort toward consultation and collaboration in confronting the major domestic transitions to meet the changing situation—steps which neither country, nor other major grain producers, has begun to undertake.

It would not be surprising to discover that those who favor an inwardness of international political and economic viewpoint in the United States would also favor conversion of perceived multilateral weakness into growing bilateral association with Canada. The greater the disappointments in the multilateral trading and commercial environment, the more the American propensity to seek redress and achievement on the North American continent. Some Canadians would share this view and see recent trade and investment patterns as signs of the future.

Given the natural advantages of the North American trade setting, many economists are not prepared to see the North American market further assisted at the cost of the global trading system by measures of a sectoral or preferential sort that would cause trade distortions or trade diversion. For this reason both Canada and the United States are predisposed to multilateral trade initiatives as a first choice, and preferential, bilateral initiatives only as a second-best solution to the problem of economic stimulus through external trade.

Bilateral diplomacy in a multilateral context is a norm within large trading and alliance systems. Governments are always trying to convert less valuable currency into more negotiable foreign exchange. But Canada and the United States ought to understand that incentives for dealing with a bilateral/multilateral mix cut in opposite directions for the two polities in several areas and that these legitimate differences of priority must be acknowledged and effectively managed. Indeed, acknowledgment, at least implicitly, will go a long way toward proper and effective management of plausibly divergent attitudes toward statecraft.

DIFFERENCES ON CULTURAL ISSUES

The different ways Americans and Canadians perceive culture sometimes create problems for managers of the relationship. Canadian elites tend to disdain American mass culture and deplore the relative lack of emphasis on high culture. Because American culture is not more esteemed, the omnipresence of that culture is even more oppressive for many Canadians.

Americans have a hard time understanding why Canadians are so self-conscious and earnest about government intervention on behalf of cultural development. The attitude in Washington, for example, is one of deep suspicion. American policy makers are convinced that Canadian governmental support has little to do with an interest in Canadian culture per se and has much more to do with economic priorities. In this view cultural concerns are often seen as a mere veil for the desire to subsidize economic enterprise.

What Americans tend to forget is how regionalized Canadian society is, and how unique are the problems of sustaining biculturalism and binational unity. In part because of the casualness with which most Americans allow the marketplace to determine cultural values in the United States, cultural perspectives on opposite sides of the border are likely to clash.

A constant in the relationship, however, is the commitment of Ottawa, that is its determination, to use culturalism, regardless of the party in power, to further the objective of nation-state unity and political identity. That this task must occur under the shadow of the American cultural presence makes it that much tougher. American understanding regarding the differing cultural priorities in the two polities will make this aspect of bilateral relations run much more smoothly.

SHARED ENVIRONMENT AND RESOURCE DIVISION

One of the constants of the relationship is that when viewing the North American continent as a whole, Canadians and Americans perceive reality quite differently. It is not so much that Americans are all "continentalists" and Canadians are all "nationalists" because the labels simply do not fit the subtlety of actual behavior and perceptions. When assessing geopolitical reality, Americans tend to emphasize the advantages of resource sharing and the attractiveness of treating environmental matters as though they obeyed borders. Canadians, on the other hand, stress national solutions to resource matters and the quite evident continent-wide obligations of environmental protection. The United

States seeks to share resources but divide the environment; Canada attempts to preserve a division of resources, while stressing the shared social burden of protecting the environment.

The problem for the analyst is that in each case the perceptions are both right and wrong. Resources are not only owned on each side of the border, but in Canada they are owned by each province. Only in an international and interprovincial sense are they regulated and controlled by the federal government. In the United States, resources are owned by individuals, firms, and an array of governments including the federal government. They are also regulated at a variety of levels. But insofar as markets and capital are concerned, resources are to some degree shared as well (economists, for example, value demand as greatly as supply when determining price).

Similarly, environmental jurisdictions are both divided and shared. Enforcement of protection norms may be natural, but impact is surely mutual and continental in scope. While each government may in quasi isolation decide how to handle its own contributions to transborder pollution, the obligation to severely restrict transboundary spillover is certainly acknowledged in international law. If environmental degradation is shared, the obligation to enhance the environment is also shared.

Perhaps the single most troubling problem in Canada–U.S. relations for the last half of the 1980s is the problem of acid rain. No Canadian government can afford to take the political pressure off the United States on this question. The only unknown is how far Canada will push forward *unilaterally* to try to achieve more progress. Given the point-source character of emissions in Canada, new bilateral formulas are likely to look more attractive than further unilateral restrictions beyond those already contemplated for the INCO smelters and the Noranda facilities.

No U.S. government can afford to treat acid rain as unimportant. Regardless of who occupies the White House, the U.S. government will have to move beyond the step of recommending further research designed to determine the exact relationship between cause and effect. Enough research has already been done to demonstrate serious effects. At the very least, coal-fired utilities and other major sources of air pollution ought not to increase their level of emissions regardless of increase in economic production or output. Sorting out the exact mixture of the complex molecules associated with long-range air pollution is less important than reducing the overall levels of both the sulfur and nitrogen oxides in the air. Once the general carrying capacity of the air has been exceeded, as is the case today, fine-tuning local emissions levels will not get to the source of the acid rain problem.

In both Canada and the United States the impact of acid rain on forests is an increasingly valued and visible cost. As the forestry industry and related interests begin to see the cost of acid rain to themselves, the political process in Ottawa and Washington will move more swiftly. Since within the United States the acid rain problem is also a regional issue, and, since neither political party in the United States can accept all of the credit or all of the blame for activity involving acid rain restrictions, formulas that cross regional and party boundaries and enable the financial costs of cleanup to be distributed somewhat more broadly than is sometimes recommended will speed up the process of congressional action. But in the absence of such actions, acid precipitation will continue to be a major grievance in Canada–U.S. relations and a trouble spot for diplomacy regardless of who is elected in Ottawa or Washington.

On the resource side, demands in the United States for access to large amounts of clean water for a host of purposes including agricultural irrigation are likely to be heard with increasing urgency. On the high plains of Texas the rich farmland is about to suffer from the lack of irrigation waters as the aquifers dry up. Similar patterns are occurring in California and part of the American Midwest.

Canada has already indicated a distaste for negotiations involving water transfer. This distaste is magnified by the reality that although, for example, water is plentiful on the Canadian Shield, it is not water that is easily replenishable. Part of the negative reaction to water transfer in Canada is fear of negative environmental consequences in Canada from transfers, such as damage to the Arctic Ocean coastal areas. Part of the reaction is merely a deeply felt fear of large-scale resource transfer. But whatever the source of the Canadian reluctance to meet growing American water needs, the reluctance is likely to manifest itself unless the issue is handled with the greatest sensitivity in the United States.

A third future problem has to do with the efforts in both Canada and the United States to cope with the decline of the economic heartland in the Midwest. Much of this decline is associated with the decline of the smoke stack (resource) industries because of productivity problems, lack of investment, insufficient technological innovation, and foreign competition. The principal consequence is the loss of jobs and the corresponding political effort to bolster these jobs through protectionist activity and government intervention that, unless coordinated, will pit one region against another and one country against another.

Each country will be tempted to establish an "industrial policy" devoted to the creation of new industry and the reinvigoration of older industry. Competitive incentive creation, subsidiaries, and investment restrictions are likely to result, justified largely in domestic political terms. Such cross-border competitive policy making could lead to bitterness and retaliation. Firms and labor unions may find themselves caught in the middle of a struggle between governments to try to meet the demands of rival groups of constituents.

Industrial policy must at the very least be coordinated along North American lines if it is to avoid serious economic distortions and much intergovernmental tension. But the problems of structural unemployment and industrial decline, much of it related to the fate of resource industries, will demand attention from Washington and Ottawa as North America seeks to retain its share of world markets.

Economic versus Political Reality

A continuing item on the policy agenda is that the two countries ought to, are about to, or should not enter into some kind of free trade area. Neither the concept of the free trade area, however partial or encompassing, nor the detailed consequences of the formation of such an area are spelled out very clearly by defenders or proponents.

Former Canadian Minister of Trade Gerald Regan championed a section of the trade review undertaken in 1983 that advocated bilateral sectoral free trade with the United States in four areas: agricultural and farm machinery, steel, informatics, and surface transportation. Other areas such as petrochemicals and textiles were discussed in cursory fashion but were regarded as more problematic. Canada considered each of the proposed sectors as industries in which Canada could compete worldwide and in which nationalization along North American lines would yield substantial benefits in terms of the larger market size. While the United States felt it had less to gain in immediate economic terms from the sectoral initiative than Canada, the United States went along with the idea largely to use these discussions as a possible wedge to open multilateral free trade talks on a global scale.

The principal advantage of the sectoral approach is that it seems like half a loaf when a whole loaf would be more difficult to obtain in Canada for political reasons. It seems like a compromise on the way to total free trade. But the difficulty with the sectoral approach is several-fold as the discussion groups set up to evaluate the sectoral idea soon discovered. First, the sectors chosen were more attractive to Canada than to the United States. The United States held open the possibility that it would add other sectors as the dialogue proceeded. Second, a sector-by-sector approach is extremely difficult to negotiate because obvious specific, rather than generalized, trade-offs across industries will be required and the industries and labor groups involved will lobby hard to resist cuts. Inevitable distortions could also occur in intraindustry trade patterns. Third, in terms of actual economic benefit relative to the effort involved to negotiate the tariff reductions, the United States stands to gain very little. Hence it tends to see the discussions as a prelude to global multilateral trade negotiations while Canada tends to see the sectoral discussions as an end in themselves. A clash of objectives results.

For all these reasons, alternate trade initiatives sometimes are discussed. One such initiative would involve the elimination of government procurement legislation on both sides of the border, thus opening up large markets in areas like surface transportation. But nontariff barriers at state and provincial levels as well as at federal levels are becoming more and more of a problem and may already have offset many of the trade gains in the area of tariff reduction. Alternatively, Canada and the United States could opt for multilateral free trade negotiations, perhaps emphasizing, as the United States would prefer, reduction of constraints on services such as in telecommunications, insurance, and banking.

In fact, the Tokyo Round of the General Agreement on Tariffs and Trade (GATT) determined that, by 1987, 85 percent of Canadian exports would enter the United States duty free and that 60 percent of American exports would enter Canada duty free. Except for a few industries like petrochemicals where tariffs remain quite high, goods are already flowing back and forth across the borders unimpeded by the high tariffs that still mark trade with many other regions of the world. Thus, from an economic perspective, one can argue that for the most part free trade is already here, or, conversely, that efforts to obtain additional measures of free trade, at least in formal tariff terms, are likely to add only small increments to the wealth and gross national product of each country.

The tighter economic ties between Canada and the United States have led to increased irritants and friction in managing the relationship. The greater the scope and intensity of interaction on economic matters, the greater has become the burden on the already overloaded staffs of the Canadian Department of External Affairs and on the U.S. Department of State to try to cool tempers and to work out acceptable solutions on behalf of governments primarily responsible to domestic constituencies. Increased friction does not urge a reduction in the scale of economic interaction because that interaction yields benefits to each polity in terms of increased welfare and more jobs. Nor does the presence of increased friction necessitate the formalization of overarching and more encompassing political structures.

A very high degree of economic interdependence between Canada and the United States is a present fact and is likely to remain a future reality. Of course, firms and governments on both sides of the border will continue to try to expand economic opportunity outside North America as well. But trade and investment inside North America and outside it are not opposites; they are reinforcing, and will tend to follow market dictates. Multilateral trade liberalization will always remain key to the viability of North American economic enterprise whatever the proposals for restructuring the North American market per se.

The Changing International System: What It Means for Canada–U.S. Relations

Change originates not so much in how Canada and the United States look at each other, but in how world politics and economics impinge on each of them and, therefore, on their respective foreign policies toward each other. Change is not most pronounced in the bilateral relationship itself, as the citation from Hume Wrong in 1927 shows, but largely through the impact that the international system has had on North America and on each government individually.

In 1945 the fear remained that the United States might lapse back into the isolationism which had prevented such a powerful actor from playing a constructive role in international diplomacy and blocking the rise of aggressive Axis powers in the 1920s. Canada played a not inconsiderable role in the establishment of NATO in 1949, firmly committing North America to the development of an Atlantic community, a foundation for building broader international community organizations in the future. The institutions which were developed in that early period had by the mid–1970s come under considerable strain with the revival of the cold war between the United States and the Soviet Union in the last years of the Carter administration, the disarray in international financial and monetary institutions, the breakdown in international arms control negotiations, rising protectionism, economic dislocation, and attacks on the utility of the network multilateral global and regional international organizations that were established to try to cope with the problems of managing an age of complex interdependence.

The debate over how to deal with this increasingly turbulent international environment has been more intense in the United States than in Canada. This is hardly surprising as Canadians have always had a more modest view of their own responsibilities for leadership on the world stage, although many have forgotten that in 1945, with much of the rest of the industrial world in ruins, Canada stood as the world's fourth ranking military power and a partner with Britain and the United States in the development of the atomic bomb, which has had such a profound impact on altering our inherited wisdom about national security and military defense.

Although the American power base was much broader than the Canadian, and the ascendancy was long in the making, the dawn of the nuclear age catapulted the United States into a position of decisive international military superiority. It was also accompanied by striking international economic predominance. To cite some statistics that recur frequently in the ongoing U.S. debate on the relative decline of American power—in 1950 the United States had well over 50 percent of the world's expenditure on armed forces and 39 percent of the world's production of goods and services. By 1980 these figures had declined to 28 percent of the world's military expenditures and 21.5 percent of the world's economy. On the other hand, the Canadian decline in terms of absolute levels has been far more modest but, in terms of rank, more precipitous. In 1950 Canada ranked fifth in economic power, but by 1980 it had fallen to ninth rank and to fourteenth in military power. The important point here, however, is that while U.S. power declined *relative* to the international system as a whole, the United States and the Soviet Union retained their ranks as numbers one and two respectively by a wide margin. With the continuing role as the leading noncommunist state, the United States also retained most of its global responsibilities. What is significant in citing the comparisons is that Canadians have paid so little attention to these factors of relative international standing, partly, one could argue, because some of the dominance of North America in the early postwar period was an artifact of having been spared the destruction of World War II. But even though the interval of reconstruction was artificial, set against the backdrop of the twentieth century as a whole, the relative decline of U.S. power has been quite gradual while the decline of interests has been even more inertial. The problem of a possible disparity between interest and the power to pursue those interests results.

The economic and political recovery of Japan and Europe after World War II, the steady increase in Soviet military capability, the rise to major trading prominence of the newly industrializing countries, and the diffusion of population centers and power toward the Third World have transformed the systemic roles of Canada and the United States toward each other and the outside world.

U.S. diplomacy in the 1970s was devoted to the search for a formula to ensure stability in this period of increased diffusion of economic and military power. Detente with the Soviet Union was the principal formula of the Nixon administration, and these efforts received strong support in Western Europe and in Canada. The Carter administration's foreign policy was based at least initially on the logic of "trilateralism," namely the doctrine that the United States needed close cooperation among the industrialized democracies of North America, Europe, and Japan to work out common policies for managing both international economic problems with the Third World and for managing security questions vis-à-vis the Soviet Union. The trilateralist view built upon the "summit diplomacy" of the advanced industrial nations initiated at Rambouillet in France in 1975. Canada, thanks to American insistence, joined the summit meeting in Washington in 1976.

The Carter administration, in its first two years, also emphasized "world order politics" and the "global agenda," international protection of human rights, and curbs on the conventional arms trade and joined with Canada in trying to put further roadblocks on the horizontal proliferation of nuclear weapons. The crumbling of the Shah of Iran, the seizure of U.S. hostages in Teheran, the Soviet invasion of Afghanistan, all contributed to the unraveling of Carter's foreign policy and the search for more reassertive policies.

In contrast to previous administrations, both Democratic and Republican, who spoke of adjusting to the realities of reduced American power, the Reagan administration spoke boldly of reasserting American supremacy. The first element was to rebuild America's economic base, which would then sustain a dramatic build-up of America's military force. The large government deficits, high interest rates, and an overvalued American dollar brought sharp criticism from America's allies as huge capital inflows into the United States from abroad severely handicapped their own efforts to escape the ravages of world economic dislocation and to benefit from the American economic recovery. Faced with increasing criticism from its allies over its policies, the Reagan administration was divided between advocates of a greater measure of pragmatism and reduced rhetoric and those who argued for a more go-it-alone orientation or the reassertion of a greater measure of unilateralism in foreign policy. The ideology that appeared to work in restoring public confidence in a strong American leadership and a challenge to the Soviet Union did not have the same effects abroad.

As tensions mounted between the Soviet Union and the United States in an accelerating arms race, Prime Minister Trudeau in late 1984 mounted a peace initiative in an effort to generate pressure from other concerned states within and outside the NATO and Warsaw Pact countries for a reduction in rhetoric and renewed efforts to resume serious international arms control talks.

At the end of his career, Trudeau had returned to the broad internationalist intermediary role which he had deemphasized in taking the reins of power from Lester Pearson in 1968. In the intervening years, Canada had gained an increased role as interpreter of the interests of the developing countries, but it had lost influence on peace and security questions. Its contribution to NATO and NORAD had declined in quality and quantity over the years, and the lack of sustained attention to these foreign policy questions by Trudeau and the Liberal party had not provided the political weight that an active and competent Canadian diplomatic service requires if it is to sustain its influence on the international scene. With a broad mandate for change, the Mulroney government that took power in the fall of 1984 was committed to restoring better relations with the United States and improving Canada's defense posture while still maintaining the emphasis on arms control and an active Canadian role in multilateral organizations.

As the two advanced industrial democracies of North America enter the last years of the twentieth century, major issues of strategy and purpose await their statecraft, jointly and separately. They must, for example, decide what relative emphasis to give to North-South as well as East-West questions. The difference in outlook expressed by Prime Minister Trudeau and President Reagan at the Cancun summit is the classical debate over priorities in multilateral statecraft that occurs within and between countries and that can shape the entire direction of Western statecraft. Not only domestic party preference and ideological orientation are at issue here. Politics within the international system will determine to some extent what is possible diplomatically and what is not, just as was true at Cancun where the debt situation in the aftermath of the energy crisis, and the increased rivalry with the Soviet Union for military ascendancy, shaped the policy agenda.

Second, the governments of North America must decide the extent to which they will stress ties and commercial interaction with Western Europe or with Japan and the Pacific. Canada and the United States will continue to trade in both directions and to strengthen political ties in both directions. But the momentum of growth and development, just as the momentum of crisis events, can carry government interaction more in one direction than another. It is conceivable that Canada may favor a single orientation, and the United States another. But the priorities of specific governing political parties aside, the capacity of other trading partners and unforeseen political situations to shape North American foreign policy preferences in a similar direction is substantial.

Third, North America in the last decades of the twentieth century will have to decide whether the international system is receptive to new rounds of multilateral trade talks or whether the international system is becoming increasingly Balkanized into trade regions, thus forcing Canada and the United States to think along lines of preferential bilateral trade deals possibly of a sectoral variety. Certainly the preferences of Canada and the United States for their own individual reasons would stress the liberalized multilateral trade approach. Preferential bilateral trade deals are distinctly second-best. But apart from the difficulty of trying to negotiate in North America itself on trade liberalization, the international system at different times in history will be either more or less permissive. North America is not determining its priorities in a global vacuum. Thus the direction of future international trade talks is of critical importance to the welfare of Canada and the United States, yet the feasibility of progress in trade liberalization to offset the gains of nontariff barriers is only partially in North American hands.

Canada and the United States have learned not only from the challenges they face globally but from the dialogue that has gone on between them, especially since the age of high interdependence. Elements of continuity will continue to guide the formation of foreign policy in each polity vis-à-vis each other and the remainder of the system. But elements of change may predominate, not because of choice in either Ottawa or Washington, but because the structure of the international system will not permit extensions of the status quo. Success in bilateral relations will result not only in how Canada and the United States manage their own relationship but in how each polity responds to the slowly emerging transformation of the international system. More and more, North America is a part of the global system even in intervals when the two polities dream of retreating, in economic or security terms, from the vicissitudes of world politics.

Index

FINAL REPORT
of the
SIXTY-EIGHTH AMERICAN ASSEMBLY

At the close of their discussions, the participants in the Sixty-eighth American Assembly, on *Canada and the United States,* at Arden House, Harriman, New York, November 15-18, 1984, reviewed as a group the following statement. This statement represents general agreement; however, no one was asked to sign it. Furthermore, it should not be assumed that every participant subscribes to every recommendation.

INTRODUCTION

Canadian-U.S. relations are marked by a complexity and intimacy that are unique in international relations. Since World War II both countries have greatly increased their activities and interests outside North America, but the flow of goods, services, capital, information, and people along their more than 5,000-mile frontier has increased even more than their movements abroad. The inevitable frictions that accompany such intense relations generally have been handled with sensitivity and candor. Strains have frequently come from differences in policy over the proper response to a rapidly changing international environment. Given the increasing dependence of Canada on trade and investment with the United States over the past decade, the need for greater sensitivity, consultation, and more careful coordination of policy in both Washington and Ottawa has also increased. Regular quarterly consultations were instituted in 1982 between the American Secretary of State and the Canadian Secretary of State for External Affairs. Efforts at better consultative arrangements frequently have followed periods of strain in Canadian-U.S. relations. The new Progressive Conservative government elected in Canada in September 1984 expressed a commitment to refurbishing relations with the United States by a "multi-layered bilateral dialogue characterized by trust and confidence."

This meeting of Canadians and Americans explored the principal issues that are likely to appear on the agenda of this continuing dialogue in Canadian-U.S. relations: freer trade, environmental quality, investment, resource policies, cultural sensitivities, defense, and the broader international agenda. In scanning the future, no effort was made to try to achieve consensus on all the policy issues discussed; many will be defined within the political process of each of these independent countries. The frank exchange of views and opinions, often reflecting differences among nationals of each country, provided much insight into the problems of managing such a complex relationship in a period of increasing global uncertainty and challenge.

ECONOMIC RELATIONS IN AN ERA OF RISING PROTECTIONISM

The major trade relationships between Canada and the United States have developed and are conducted in an open system virtually unparalleled in the world. While the United States and Canada have long advocated freer global trade, neither will find it easy to move rapidly in the direction of further bilateral liberalization. Although both countries are committed to multilateral principles and the strengthening of the General Agreement on Tariffs and Trade (GATT), they face bilateral trade problems that cannot be neglected. In particular, Canadian producers are increasingly concerned over foreign competition at home and uncertainty of access to the U.S. market. In addition, there are practices involving trade in goods and services in both countries that impede and distort trade flows and are not adequately dealt with by existing arrangements. Failure to cope with these will multiply future disputes and exacerbate frictions between the two countries. Some of these are being explored in sectoral discussions, but opinions differ in both countries as to whether a more general approach would be preferable. The relatively greater significance of bilateral trade to Canada means that under most circumstances the benefits, as well as the relative costs, of any reductions of tariffs or loosening of other barriers tend to be far greater for Canada than the United States. The United States would be receptive to such proposals because they encourage trade liberalization generally and because Canadian markets in a healthy Canadian economy are in the U.S. interest. At the same time the United States might seek trade-offs outside the range of trading issues, such as in the treatment of U.S. investment in Canada. Whether the aggregate of any such negotiations on a bilateral basis could lead to an agreement so broadly based as to be politically acceptable to both sides is problematical. It must be borne in mind that Canadians are sensitive to the possible implications of social and cultural integration following any steps to lower the barriers to trade at their otherwise undefended border.

Liberalization of bilateral trade has moved up on the agenda of both countries, not only because of economic recovery in the United States in the 1983-84 period, but also because of the growing concern in both countries over heightened competition facing many industries from outside North America. Improved efficiency of capital and labor markets is essential to both Canada and the United States as they adjust to these external realities. Concern has been expressed in some policy circles that attempts to prop up declining industries in both countries are self-defeating in the long run. Instead, many argue that such problems should be met by adjustment in noncompetitive industries, and governmental policies should be designed to facilitate these adjustments. Increased public and private sector attention should be given to activities favored by comparative advantages.

The amount of Canadian and other foreign investment in the United States has increased markedly in recent years. Real or perceived uncertainties in the administration of the Foreign Investment Review Agency, as well as taxation policies, are believed to be factors in the decline in U.S. investment northward in the late 1970s and early 1980s. Although concern with respect to major take-overs remains, current attitudes to U.S. investment to create new jobs are positive. The Canadian economy is still in a stage of development where external capital, both equity and debt, plays as significant a role as does liberalized trade in assuring economic growth, improved living standards, and increased employment.

The flow of capital into the United States, combined with the high exchange value of the U.S. dollar, is creating major changes in U.S. current trade and financial accounts, with possible consequences for the Canadian economy that require continuing attention.

NATIONAL IDENTITY, CULTURAL DIVERSITY, AND INTERDEPENDENCE

Citizens of both countries have had a long-standing concern for the preservation of their cultural, political, and social values, however defined. Among English-speaking Canadians, this concern has been a natural consequence of Canada's proximity to the United States; among French-speaking Canadians, it has derived from the challenge of having to dwell within a continental sea of nearly 250 million Anglophones. In both cases the resulting fear of cultural—and even political—assimilation has led to the development of public policies explicitly designed to protect and nurture indigenous cultural activity. On occasion these initiatives have caused difficulties in Canada's bilateral relationship with the United States.

The problem has been complicated by the belief (especially in English Canada) that there may be linkages between the growth of economic interdependencies on the one hand and the loss of cultural distinctiveness on the other. Historically, for example, discussions within Canada of the possible advantages of concluding freer trading relationships with the United States have been profoundly influenced by concerns that the development of a Canadian-U.S. free-trade arrangement might have as one of its side effects the erosion of a cultural identity that some English Canadians have perceived to be fragile.

Whether there is actually a cause-and-effect linkage between economic activity on the one hand and cultural and social values on the other is a complex matter upon which solid evidence is hard to obtain. But there now seems to be considerable agreement that Canadians—Anglophones and Francophones alike—are more secure and confident in their cultural identities than ever before. There is substantial agreement in Canada, as in many other countries, that some indigenous cultural activities require state assistance if they are to survive against the overwhelming influence of cultural "imports." Indeed, this new cultural confidence is part of what is helping to make the possibility of initiating a freer trading relationship with the United States a more viable political option on the Canadian side of the border.

The political values of the two countries—how their citizens perceive the proper role of government in relation to individuals is a case in point—may be rooted firmly in their political institutions; thus they may be resistant to transformations resulting from economic or other factors. Popular entertainment cultures on the other hand are much more prone to homogenization under the pressure of American creativity in this field.

It has been commonly held that Canada is a "mosaic" and the United States is a "melting pot," and some observers still accept these descriptions as at least rough approximations of reality. But close examination reveals that American society has its own profound diversities—the regional and the ethnic not least among them—and these diversities have been accentuated in recent years, as in the past, by waves of immigration. The greater correspondence of language divisions with political boundaries creates complications in Canada that do not exist in the United States. While cultural diversity is a positive benefit to both countries, there is evidence to suggest that Americans are facing significant problems of adjustment in certain regions. This comes at a time when political conflicts rooted in linguistic differentiation within Canada appear in some measure to have subsided. U.S. problems probably will be resolved in the future as they have been in the past—painfully, perhaps, but successfully in the end—but the common tendency of many Canadians to perceive the United States as culturally homogeneous needs constantly to be modified in the light of the very real diversities of American society. Although it is unlikely that these American difficulties will intrude directly on the bilateral Canadian-U.S. relationship, Canadians need to respond with sympathy and understanding to American attempts to deal with the problems arising in their cities and elsewhere from the diversity of their population.

In Canada, some policies to support culture will continue to involve actions that Americans may find unfairly restrictive. Americans should be aware, however, of the wish of many Canadians to protect and encourage their artists, writers , and communications media. This may require greater understanding on the part of the United States since such policies have implications that may adversely affect American economic interests and run counter to practices normally associated with freer trade and may be interpreted as impeding the free flow of information and ideas.

ENVIRONMENTAL CONSCIOUSNESS AND RESOURCE DEVELOPMENT

Certain environmental and resource issues have appeared and reappeared over the years in the Canadian-U.S. relationship. The governments have developed solutions to many of these problems, some with the help of the International Joint Commission. A newer topic is now of paramount interest. Acid rain is in the forefront amongst issues of bilateral concern and a major source of friction between Canada and the United States. On the U.S. side there is a deep regional split, which presents a considerable barrier to achieving an agreed approach. There are as well enormous costs involved, particularly using present technology, and obvious disagreements as to how they should be borne, with a myriad of variants between "the polluter should pay" and "it's a national problem; all should share." There are also some unanswered scientific questions, particularly in regard to the effect of acid precipitation on forests. As a result of these considerations, the case for delaying costly control strategies has been advanced. The present U.S. position, which calls for further research prior to action, is not shared by the northeastern states or by Canadians.

Canada has agreed to cut its allowable levels of sulfur-dioxide emission by 50 percent by 1994 based on 1980 levels. There is a widely held view on both sides of the border that perfect knowledge in this as in other areas is not a prerequisite to public policy decisions. Canada and many Americans believe that enough is now known to proceed at once with an initial pollution reduction program even as further research continues.

Domestic and international problems affecting resource extraction industries remain high on the agenda of both countries. Mutual concerns include those caused by subsidization and other forms of governmental intervention, particularly in less developed countries; higher costs in North America; moderation of the cyclical nature of commodity prices; the grade of known deposits elsewhere in comparison to the diminishing grade of known resources in the continent; and numerous others, all exacerbated by the recent world-wide depression and reduced prospective rates of growth of demand on a free-world basis. Policy responses are diverse, but it is now generally recognized that they do not include artificial price supports over any long term, except where deemed national security imperatives require. There must be transitional assistance for those workers displaced by the swings of fortune that characterize resource extraction, and innovation must be supported that allows, to the maximum extent possible, the maintenance of these industries on the continent.

Energy policy questions seem to have faded somewhat, although the long-range problems are still there. The current global energy situation provides an important opportunity for the two countries to advance their longer term interests. Elements of the 1980 National Energy Program (NEP), which called, among other things, for incentives for increased Canadian ownership in the petroleum sector, have been a source of exasperation to the United States, while their positive benefits are still debated by Canadians. The new Canadian government has expressed its intention to address aspects of the NEP that have raised concerns on both sides of the border. Significant gains have been made over the past year to ensure long-term mutually beneficial markets for Canadian natural gas exports at competitive prices. Electricity trade between the two countries has now grown to major proportions, and is a positive match of a Canadian resource and U.S. market that should contribute to economic growth in both nations. It behooves each government to devise policies that will encourage conservation, domestic petroleum and natural gas exploration and development, and development as well of alternative energy resources without causing distortions in the allocation of capital that will be counterproductive in the end.

Fresh water, long considered inexhaustible and hence a "free good," now begins to appear as a—perhaps *the*—major long-range resource issue on the continent. Although the quality of both surface water and ground water is already of concern in some places, the issue of water quantity is further down the road in terms of impact and, for that reason, suggests a different kind of bilateral attention than acid rain now receives. If unaddressed, rising demand over the next decades, especially by Americans, can cause problems of unprecedented seriousness since water is clearly the most precious of all continental resources. Complex and expensive schemes for water diversion have been and will be proposed. Long-term planning is essential, taking into account such diverse factors as climate change, world population pressures, and food needs. It would be desirable for the two governments to initiate now a systematic and coordinated review of impending or future changes and problems so as to have early warning and the capacity for whatever joint or separate action may be appropriate or possible.

BILATERAL RELATIONS IN THE INTERNATIONAL CONTEXT

Canada and the United States each hold foreign policy views toward the global system. Their roles differ largely in terms of responsibility. Their structural positions are also different. Canadian ties with the Commonwealth and Francophone countries contribute to Canada's sensitivity to Third World concerns. The global security responsibilities of the United States lead it to focus particular attention on East-West matters. While both Canada and the United States are committed to the North Atlantic Treaty Organization, there are differences of emphasis between the two countries as to the nature of and response to the Soviet challenge. The United States tends to emphasize the global nature of the Soviet threat and the military strength required to meet it. Canada tends to emphasize the importance of managing the superpower relationship in such a way as to avoid confrontation and the importance of nonmilitary factors in dealing with instability in the Third World.

Emphasis in trade and commercial policy for both Canada and the United States may be shifting toward the Pacific Rim. But Europe remains a major area of strategic interest. While Canada and the United States interact closely with each other and maintain a strong North American orientation, neither country is isolationist. Indeed, the economy and society of each is extraordinarily open and international in foreign policy emphasis.

Canada's allies have urged it to place a higher priority on defense spending and preparedness. How these expenditures are to be allocated is a matter of some continuing debate in Canada. Whether a more specialized role (such as antisubmarine warfare) for Canada is desirable is open to discussion. Prior Canadian defense reviews indicate that the basic problems to be resolved remain the same. Changing weapons technology may reinforce the importance of Canadian air space in a continental context as cruise missiles and cruise carriers are developed in the future. Space and satellite technology may diminish the importance of the Canadian role as far as detection is concerned, but the problem of interception may remain. Procurement aspects of defense policy have considerable economic importance for Canada. There is a need for the closest coordination between continental and North Atlantic security, which are interrelated yet administratively and organizationally distinct. Both Canada and the United States continue to affirm their commitment to the defense of Europe.

Over the years the use of Canadian forces for peacekeeping activity, although sometimes burdensome and controversial, has served a very significant purpose. American efforts in Lebanon and elsewhere have demonstrated the difficulty the United States experiences in peacekeeping when conditions for a clear mandate are not met. But the prolonged duration of many of the Canadian peacekeeping operations, such as the one in Cyprus, has led to some frustration. Canada also has emphasized the importance of peacekeeping under the United Nations rather than under independent auspices. But Canada has distinguished itself in this capacity, and the interests of the United States and Canada's other allies are well served by Canadian peacekeeping activities.

In short, Canada and the United States maintain close and continuing consultations on their foreign policies in pursuit of their respective interests and their shared concerns for global peace and stability.

RECOMMENDATIONS

1. The two countries should accelerate the serious consideration of arrangements for freer trade between them, paying attention both to tariff and to nontariff barriers. Consideration should be given both to sectoral initiatives when choices involve what to include and to broader agreement when choices involve what to exclude. This assessment should take account of implications for trade with others and for the strengthening of the GATT, which is in the interest of both countries.

2. In the cultural field, Americans should recognize that Canadians have a legitimate interest in maintaining and providing government support for indigenous cultural activity. Canadians on the other hand should understand that public policies designed to accompiish these ends may

impinge on legitimate American economic interests. Both interests will need to be balanced carefully in order to minimize irritations in this sensitive area.

3. On the problem of acid rain, Canadians should recognize the regional, economic, and scientific concerns that the United States government must take into account in developing its policy on the problem. The United States should give priority attention to Canadian concerns about environmental damage and their proposals for reducing pollutant loadings. The governments should at once expand their discussions on this important matter and develop appropriate additional national and joint measures to address the problem in North America.

4. The two governments should initiate a coordinated and systematic review to assure that detailed study of long-term environmental changes, such as water quality and supply, world and continental climate, diminution in soil fertility, and other developments currently unforeseen is undertaken to provide early warning and the capacity for appropriate joint or separate action.

5. The current global energy situation provides the opportunity for Canada and the United States to move forward on longer term energy issues, to their shared advantage. We therefore recommend that both governments increase the level and scope of their bilateral energy consultations—addressing outstanding matters that affect energy supply and investment.

6. Widespread agreement exists that Canadian involvement in international peacekeeping operations and training has been a constructive contribution to the maintenance of international peace and security and, in appropriate circumstances, participation in such peacekeeping operations should continue to be a priority for the Canadian government.

7. Agreement also exists that, while the United States has the major power and responsibility for defense of the North Atlantic Treaty area, including North America, Canada has a significant contribution to make and that it is in the general interest that that contribution be as effective as possible. Both governments should continue to maintain consultations as to how they can best meet their security requirements within the alliance.

8. The United States has a lasting interest in an independent, strong, and prosperous Canada. Canada needs a strong and prosperous United States to give the enlightened leadership that it alone can provide in the international community. Individual problems have to be dealt with on their merits, but the policies of both countries should be shaped with a full recognition of these larger considerations.

PARTICIPANTS
THE SIXTY-EIGHTH AMERICAN ASSEMBLY

C. MICHAEL AHO
Legislative Assistant
Office of Senator Bill Bradley
Washington, D.C.

MICHAEL ALEXANDER
Executive Partner
Touche Ross International
New York, New York

WILLIS C. ARMSTRONG
Board Member
Atlantic Council of the U.S.
Washington, D.C.

CHARLES F. BARBER
Former Chairman
ASARCO Incorporated
New York, New York

LISE BISSONNETTE
Editor
Le Devoir
Montreal, Quebec

ALLAN BLAKENEY
Leader of the Opposition
Saskatchewan Legislature
Regina, Saskatchewan

WILLIAM BLOCK
Publisher
Pittsburgh Post Gazette
Pittsburgh, Pennsylvania

ROBERT M. BORDEN
Chairman
Bumper Development Corporation Ltd.
Calgary, Alberta

SUSAN PARIS BORDEN
President
Bumper Development, Inc. (U.S.A.)
Calgary, Alberta

† CARROLL BROWN
Director
Office of Canadian Affairs
U.S. Department of State
Washington, D.C.

SCOTT COOPER
Legislative Assistant
Office of Representative Al Swift
Washington, D.C.

JOHN CURTIS
Director
International Economics Program
Institute for Research on Public Policy
Ottawa, Ontario

CHRISTINE DAWSON
Legislative Assistant
Office of Senator Daniel Evans
Washington, D.C.

WILLIAM DIEBOLD
Nyack, New York

CHARLES F. DORAN
Director
Center of Canadian Studies
School of Advanced International
 Studies
The Johns Hopkins University
Washington, D.C.

STEPHEN C. EYRE
U.S. Cochairman
Canadian-American Committee
Washington, D.C.

ELLIOT J. FELDMAN
International Affairs Fellow
Council on Foreign Relations
Washington, D.C.

JERRY S. GRAFSTEIN, Q.C.
Member
Senate of Canada
Ottawa, Ontario

J. L. GRANATSTEIN
Professor
Department of History
York University
Downsview, Ontario

MARY JEAN GREEN
Professor
Department of French & Italian
Dartmouth College
Hanover, New Hampshire

JOHN G. H. HALSTEAD
Professor
School of Foreign Service
Georgetown University
Washington, D.C.

WILLIAM HEINE
Former Editor-in-Chief
London Free Press
London, Ontario

ALFRED O. HERO, JR.
Belle Chasse, Louisiana

† JOHN W. HOLMES
Canadian Institute of
 International Affairs
Toronto, Ontario

† Delivered Formal Address

** SUSAN C. SCHWAB
Legislative Assistant
Office of Senator John Danforth
Washington, D.C.

J. B. SEABORN
Chairman
Canadian Section
International Joint Commission
Ottawa, Ontario

GARY G. SICK
Program Officer
International Affairs Programs
The Ford Foundation
New York, New York

JOHN H. SIGLER
Professor
Department of Political Science
Carleton University
Ottawa, Ontario

** CLAIRE D. SJOLANDER
Harriman Scholar
Department of Political Science
Carleton University
Ottawa, Ontario

* DENIS STAIRS
Chairman
Department of Political Science
Dalhousie University
Halifax, Nova Scotia

† ROBERT STANFIELD
Former Leader
Conservative Party of Canada
Ottawa, Ontario

* ALEXANDER C. TOMLINSON
Director
First Boston, Inc.
New York, New York

SANDY VOGELGESANG
Economic Minister-Counselor
American Embassy
Ottawa, Ontario

SIDNEY WEINTRAUB
Dean Rusk Professor
Lyndon B. Johnson School of
    Public Affairs
University of Texas at Austin
Austin, Texas

DOV S. ZAKHEIM
Assistant Undersecretary for
    Policy & Resources
U.S. Department of Defense
Washington, D.C.

* Discussion Leader
** Rapporteur
† Delivered Formal Address

COUNCIL ON FOREIGN RELATIONS, INC.

ABOUT THE COUNCIL ON FOREIGN RELATIONS

The Council on Foreign Relations is an educational institution, a research institute, and a unique forum bringing together leaders from the academic, public, and private worlds.

The purposes of the Council are several and overlapping: to break new ground in the consideration of international issues; to help shape American foreign policy in a constructive, nonpartisan manner; to provide continuing leadership for the conduct of our foreign relations; and to inform and stimulate the Council's membership, as well as to reach a wider audience, through publications and other means. The Council is private and nonpartisan and takes no positions as an organization.

The Council conducts meetings that give its members an opportunity to talk with invited guests from the United States and abroad who have special experience and expertise in international affairs. Its study program explores foreign policy questions through research by the Council's professional staff, visiting Fellows, and others, and through study groups and conferences. The Council also publishes the journal, *Foreign Affairs,* in addition to books and monographs. It is affiliated with thirty-eight Committees on Foreign Relations located around the country and maintains a Corporation Service Program that provides meetings and other services for its approximately 200 corporate subscribers.

The Council's headquarters, staff, and library are located in New York City where most meetings are held. Some meetings are held in Washington and occasionally in other cities. The Council's basic constituency is its members, but it also reaches out to the broader public so as to contribute to the national dialogue on foreign policy.

ABOUT THE AMERICAN ASSEMBLY

The American Assembly was established by Dwight D. Eisenhower at Columbia University in 1950. It holds nonpartisan meetings and publishes authoritative books to illuminate issues of United States policy.

An affiliate of Columbia, with offices in the Sherman Fairchild Center, the Assembly is a national, educational institution incorporated in the State of New York.

The Assembly seeks to provide information, stimulate discussion, and evoke independent conclusions on matters of vital public interest.

American Assembly Sessions

At least two national programs are initiated each year. Authorities are retained to write background papers presenting essential data and defining the main issues of each subject.

A group of men and women representing a broad range of experience, competence, and American leadership meet for several days to discuss the Assembly topic and consider alternatives for national policy.

All Assemblies follow the same procedure. The background papers are sent to participants in advance of the Assembly. The Assembly meets in small groups for four or five lengthy periods. All groups use the same agenda. At the close of these informal sessions participants adopt in plenary session a final report of findings and recommendations.

Regional, state, and local Assemblies are held following the national session at Arden House. Assemblies have also been held in England, Switzerland, Malaysia, Canada, the Caribbean, South America, Central America, the Philippines, and Japan. Over one hundred forty institutions have cosponsored one or more Assemblies.

Arden House

Home of The American Assembly and scene of the national sessions is Arden House, which was given to Columbia University in 1950 by W. Averell Harriman. E. Roland Harriman joined his brother in contributing toward adaptation of the property for conference purposes. The buildings and surrounding land, known as the Harriman Campus of Columbia University, are fifty miles north of New York City.

Arden House is a distinguished conference center. It is self-supporting and operates throughout the year for use by organizations with educational objectives. The American Assembly is a tenant of this Columbia University facility only during Assembly sessions.